THE Other SIDE OF THE FENCE

Love
Loyalty
Respect
Betrayal

A WOMAN IN THE MOTORCYCLE CLUB WORLD

SADGIRL

Outskirts Press, Inc.
Denver, Colorado

The opinions expressed in this manuscript are solely the opinions of the author and do not represent the opinions or thoughts of the publisher. The author has represented and warranted full ownership and/or legal right to publish all the materials in this book.

The Other Side of the Fence
Love, Loyalty, Respect, Betrayal
All Rights Reserved.
Copyright © 2010 Sadgirl
v2.0

COVER DESIGN: JENNIFFER BIGHAM

This book may not be reproduced, transmitted, or stored in whole or in part by any means, including graphic, electronic, or mechanical without the express written consent of the publisher except in the case of brief quotations embodied in critical articles and reviews.

Outskirts Press, Inc.
http://www.outskirtspress.com

ISBN: 978-1-4327-5604-8

Outskirts Press and the "OP" logo are trademarks belonging to Outskirts Press, Inc.

PRINTED IN THE UNITED STATES OF AMERICA

This book is dedicated to
Sons of Silence Brakeline 1%
My mentor, friend, and family.
He taught me everything I know about the MC world.
Thank you for your faithful friendship in spite of it all!

Acknowledgements

Thank You
Jerry E. Bigham
Nov 17, 1958 – Sept 17, 2000
For the gift of riding.

*For Rodney Starling
You will ride again!*

I want to thank Bandido Murray 1%, President of Arkansas Bandidos who took me on board his ship and had a kind heart towards me. A special thank you to Bandido Jim 1%, President of Louisiana Bandidos, and to Bandido Nomad Stubbs 1% for the love, loyalty and respect given. I would like to thank Bryan Steele for letting me ride with his club, the Arkansas Road Barrons MC. Last but not least, I want to acknowledge Highway and Hedges Motorcycle Ministry for all the love and support given when I most needed it.

I must personally thank the following people for their support, contribution, friendship and faithful fortitude in me. James 'Bubba' Edens, Andy Whaley, Debbie Tedder, Stephanie Nazario, Amy "Sparkles" Reeves, Will "Wish" Honeycutt, Connie Davis, TomKat,

Bobbie Whaley, Tiffany Ferguson, Candice Ferguson, Cherice Hefner, Alan Anderson, Shawn Anderson, Anthony Stone, Richard Ratzburg, Tabitha Brakeline Tatum, Jerry "Punkin" Melton, Rhonda Melton, LeeAnn Estes, and Richard Estes.

Table of Contents

Introduction vii
1 The Beginning of the Highway Chicks 1
2 Brakeline 1% 15
3 The ARCOMc 35
4 Damn the Torpedoes, Full Speed Ahead! 51
5 The Highway Chicks First Heart Patch 61
6 The Highway Chicks Second Heart Patch 73
7 For Better… For Worse! 85
8 Mud on Our Boots 105
9 Playing the Political Arena of the MC World 121
10 The Shepherd on the Other Side of the Fence 133
11 Patch Holders are People Too 153
12 Out in Bad Standing? 171
13 Blood on the Barbwire 183
14 Saying Good Bye to my MC Family 207
15 Crash course on the MC Lifestyle 227
16 6 Steps to Starting an MC 261
17 Original Laws and Bylaws of Highway Chicks Biker Club 267
18 Highway Chicks Motorcycle Club Updated Laws,
    Bylaws and Guidelines 275
19 Highway Chicks Statistics 2002-2007 283
20 Glossary 1% and MC Terminology 289
Photos & Memories 305

Introduction

The *Other Side of the Fence* is a five-year journey of being a woman biker in a motorcycle club, and my association with the 1% clubs in Central Arkansas, predominantly the Bandidos and the Sons of Silence. I wrote this book so the reader can have an understanding of the general politics inside the motorcycle club world for most women.

It is the chronological account through my eyes, of the Highway Chicks Motorcycle Club, founded by Debbie T and me from 2002 until 2007; when I left the club after serving as President for almost two years. Our eccentric manner of conduct was so distinguished that we became the first, female Bandido Support Club in the nation. Bandido Murray 1% appointed me Secretary of the Arkansas Coalition of Motorcycle Clubs and with great pride, I served my brothers.

I had the privilege and honor to sit under the mentorship of Sons of Silence Brakeline 1%, a 36-year "old school biker" who taught me the conduct and politics of the MC world. I learned the correct protocol from the beginning and always made damn sure I applied it.

As you turn the pages of this expedition, you will look at the politics inside the MC world and the rigorous standards I lived by for many years. Through total commitment and absolute submission to my Colors, I endured personal forfeits as a woman in a male-dominated world. You will also see how the Louisiana Bandidos offered my club and me their friendship and brotherhood. I very much appreciated these virtues, given the prejudice many old school bikers had towards us.

We strived to be the first all female official MC club in Arkansas with a three-piece patch and an mc cube. We wanted to be the first female club that lived the lifestyle of outlaw bikers and rode just as men. We rode hard, miles after miles, interstates, highways, back roads, curves, in the rain, in the cold and in the blistering hot sun. We weren't afraid to become full fledged, bona fide bikers and definitely not in the least worried to prove it. That was our single-minded focus. I truly believe we would have totally achieved this, if my vice president hadn't incited an insubordination against me in an effort to acquire the capacity I held in the MC community. You will catch sight of a woman's betrayal to sisterhood and the domino effect of that treachery.

The *Other Side of the Fence* also tells the intriguing, passionate story of the illicit love affair between two 'Patches' from opposite club Colors. One an MC President; the other a 1%'er, and the plan they conceived to bring unity in the motorcycle community through Christian ministry. You will walk through the personal lives of these bikers from beginning to end as you feel the gravitational pull on this roller coaster ride.

I have included two special educational chapters at the end of the book, which is for understanding and interacting with the MC culture. Chapter 15 offers a basic crash course and overview of the MC lifestyle, and in Chapter 16, I present six steps on how to start an MC in your town. I highly recommend that you read the entire book before your formulate an opinion. I wrote it in the best accurate sequential format based on my notes, photographs, recordings and contributing witnesses.

Being a part of the MC world has been the best experience of my life and I do not regret it. The wonderful people I have met throughout the years have brought me everlasting memories of remarkable times. Looking back at all the parties, events, and riding stories, I can truly say it was the opportunity of a lifetime.

I observed in my period as a patch holder that there is a commonality in the MC family. It is the love of riding a motorcycle and the desire to associate with each other. A desire that delights in the *love, loyalty and respect* that is offered by a person and received by another.

As you read this book, you will laugh and perhaps cry as you journey all the way through these factual, adventure-filled pages. The wealth of information you will discover in each chapter reveals a clear understanding of the biker's way of life. For countless readers it will serve as a handbook for starting a motorcycle club, and for those of you who believe this book is about divulging club secrets, well… you will have to read and find out for yourself.

—Sadgirl
Author

We put a lot of work and sacrifice into the Club,
but it seemed like no matter how much we tried,
we were always on the other side of the fence.
We were a woman's club in a man's world and regardless of how
much we accomplished, how much we rode,
and how many great parties we put on,
we could never cross over to the side of the 1% world.
—*Sadgirl*

1
The Beginning of the Highway Chicks
Once Upon a Time ....

It all began on September 17, 2000 at 10:30 pm in Hot Springs, Arkansas, when a Garland County Sheriff Deputy knocked on my door to inform me that my husband, Jerry Bigham had been involved in an automobile accident. He crossed a double yellow line on a hillcrest to pass a slow moving vehicle in front of him and hit an oncoming car in a blind spot, killing him instantly. He was riding a friend's Harley Davidson™ Chopper.

I sat at the country kitchen table in the 2,100 square foot home we had purchased three years prior. As I heard the devastating news I bowed my head, put my left hand over my forehead and in deep sorrowful regret I said to the bearer of bad news, "I knew it! I knew you were going to tell me this."

I could not cry. I could not be angry. All emotions seemed to come to a standstill. I thought of how I should react, like how women do in the movies when they receive bad news. However, I could not bring myself to an emotional breakdown.

The Sheriff asked if there was anything he could do. I did not acknowledge his question but silently got up and left him standing in the kitchen as I went to my children's bedroom to inform them that their daddy would no longer be coming home.

Several days later, I gave Jerry a biker funeral. The entire ABATE District 13 and other bikers, honored my request to have as many bikers possible for his funeral. Jochebed, my oldest daughter, carried Jerry's ashes in a beautiful wooden box. She rode with my good friend John Houpt on his Heritage Soft Tail. I led the memorial ride, riding Jerry's Road King directly behind a police escort. It was the first ride I ever led. There were over 125 bikes for this sad but honorable final ride for a fallen biker.

I had bought the Harley Davison for my husband the previous year for Father's Day. I did not know how to ride a bike so my son Shalom and I rented a U Haul truck and drove to the Jonesboro Harley Davidson dealer to pick up the bike I had ordered and purchased over the telephone, sight unseen. After signing the paperwork and closing the deal, the shop guys loaded and securely fastened the striking two-tone burgundy-silver cruiser. My son and I headed back to Hot Springs with the Road King that was fully chromed and dressed out. She sat in the back of that rented truck in our possession ready for her new home.

We got home about 3 pm and loaded the rest of our kids in the truck. They had been anxiously waiting to deliver their dad's surprise Father's Day gift. We headed up the scenic county road to his part time job at the Hwy 7 Boat Repair Shop.

We owned and operated the Hwy 5 NAPA Auto Care Center in Fountain Lake, Arkansas. For several weeks, I had been telling Jerry that I was going to purchase a brake lathe for the shop. When I pulled up at his work with the kids in the U Haul truck, I informed him I had purchased the brake lathe and wanted him to inspect it and make sure it was suitable for our shop.

He wasn't expecting me. I remember he made a funny face and asked me, "Why did you bring all the kids?"

"Oh…, they have never ridden in a U Haul truck and just wanted to come along for the ride," I said to him as I smiled at the kids for they knew I was lying.

He slowly walked to the back of the truck as he wiped his hands on the grease rag he carried in his rear left pocket. After he wiped his face, he stuffed the rag back in his pocket, pushed his glasses up on his nose, and slowly walked to the U Haul. We were all watching him and waiting for the moment he set eyes on the Harley.

He unlatched the roll door and pushed it open as the kids and I anxiously watched him take a gander at what he thought was a brake lathe. When he saw a beautiful Harley Davidson Motorcycle, he froze! He covered his face and sobbed uncontrollably into his cupped hands.

For the seven years we had been married he always told me that all his life he had wanted a Harley Davidson, but he knew that he would never afford one. Every time a Harley would pass us by, he would always say, "One of these days …."

He had been such a good husband and father, that on Father's Day we gave him his dream come true, a Harley Davidson. A motorcycle was something that I much never cared for. In reality, I hated the idea of owning one let alone riding it. I hated motorcycles and the biker lifestyle. However, he had devoted seven years of his life to us, thus bringing unforgettable years of happiness and comfort to my children and me. Therefore, to give him the gift he had wanted all his life was a small token of our gratitude.

He turned around and hugged me as if he'd never hugged me before. He latched on and his energy completely encompassed my entire soul as he continued to cry hysterically. I remember telling him to calm down or he was going to have a heart attack and it would be my fault. He laughed as he went to hug the kids one by one.

He finally made it inside the truck to the bike where there were two Father's Day cards on the bike seat. He read them as he continuously glanced at the bike. He was still dumb stricken that there was a Harley Davidson at his reach and it was his. After he finished reading the cards, the kids and I helped him unload the bike. He kissed me and took off on the Harley as we watched our hero get his lifelong dream rolling on the road.

A year later, he took his last ride. His biker funeral honored my fallen husband who'd left me with the gift of riding and the best memoirs of my life. After he died, I was left with the Road King the kids and I had bought him that Father's Day of 1999. I had a choice. I could either sell the bike or learn to ride it. I chose the latter and decided to ride in his memory.

The Road Barrons MC

As the new owner of a Road King, I began to ride to places where I could meet other bikers and therefore make new riding buddies. On one of those casual riding trips, I met the Road Barrons MC out of North Little Rock in the late fall of 2001. At that time I had begun a riding association called "Top Riders" and we were having our first meeting at Pop-A-Top Bar in Hot Springs, Arkansas. After the meeting was over, the Road Barrons invited me to their clubhouse and I was eager to accept the invitation.

The first time I rolled into their clubhouse was on a Sunday afternoon. I had never been to a motorcycle club's meetinghouse and had no idea what to expect. To my surprise, it was a regular two-bedroom home in a lower class neighborhood. I was received with a warm welcome and refreshments. The inside of the clubhouse looked like a fortified private saloon. The walls were decorated with their club Colors and motorcycle memorabilia. The bar was well stocked with beer and whiskey and they even had a pool room where the members were shooting pool over casual conversation.

The Club President, Bryan, introduced me to all his members. I found it unusual that he is one of the few motorcycle club members that I have found to use his real name instead of a handle. He was a clean cut, large man with a touch of arrogance but at the same time, very secure in his role as a biker. He handled his men quite well and I was impressed with the list of rules and club events that were posted on the bulletin board. He invited me to ride with his club and attend their parties.

I sprouted an instant friendship with a member by the name of Baby Huey. He was the youngest member and a prospect. We had many fun times and long rides. Then there was Jim. He was different for he rode a pretty Gold Wing and was proud of it. He rode for Trudy, his deceased brother. Red (R.I.P) was the oldest member and had trouble remembering the rules of the road. He loved his Heaven Hill Whiskey. Pluto was the member no one wanted to ride behind for his bike leaked every type of fluid and it was a nightmare. Wild and Strange were the old school bikers who never said much. Doc always did the right thing but loved to party. Ben was a Nomad and an old timer. These are the ones I remember the most, and made an impression in my life and I enjoyed riding with.

I was instantly hooked on the MC lifestyle. The culture quickly appealed to me and I became fascinated with the protocols of motorcycle club and especially the riding formation. I began riding with the Road Barrons to all their rides, events, and parties. I met the other Road Barron Chapters in Louisiana and Tennessee. I also met their allied clubs, the Highwaymen MC, the Kinsmen MC, the Family MC, the Swamp Riders MC, the Confederates MC, and the Association MC. Their Road Captain put me on the tail of the pack beside their Prospects. After this day, I never rode with the Top Riders RA again.

I learned to ride in formation, at a steady speed on the Interstate. I learned the do's and don'ts of the MC world including when to speak, who to speak to and how to approach club officers. I learned that when you enter another man's clubhouse, you enter with respect. I learned to greet club officers first and show them the utmost respect. I learned that ol' ladies are kept out of club business but are very much a crucial part of their ol' men. They are the workforce for the great parties that the MC members put on.

Most of all I learned how to conduct myself as a patch holder. I was not a patch holder, an ol' lady or a hang around, but I observed the different ways people acted and who received and earned respect. The ol' ladies acted different then the MC members. They were giggly, loud and fun partying girls. The men on the other hand were more reserved and their interest was in talking with other club members over a cold beer or a game of pool. In observing these different behaviors after almost 9 months, I decided that I wanted to be like the patch holders. I did not want to be an ol' lady for although they have their place in the MC world, they were at a complete different level. I wanted the respect that these patch holders showed one another.

After riding with the Road Barrons MC for almost 9 months,

their Road Captain put me in the middle of the pack. I was nervous at first but then I realized that I had learned to ride like them and therefore other than not being a club member, I could keep up and wasn't a threat to the pack. It was an honor to ride beside these great men of the MC world. For the entire period that I rode with them, I became convinced that I wanted to be a patch holder and belong to an MC club. However, there was a problem, a huge problem. I was a woman and there were no women MC in Arkansas. I could continue to ride with the Road Barrons for as long as they would allow me to, but I would never be one of their patch holders.

I remember one of the last runs I participated in. It was a club stag (no lo' ladies allowed) run to Arcadia, Louisiana to the Confederates MC annual party. The ol' ladies were not allowed to go because it was a stag run, however, I was invited to ride with them for the reason that I rode my own bike and I wasn't an ol' lady. That did not go too well with them. They questioned their husbands as to why I got to go and they couldn't. They were told that I was a biker and not one of them.

After this day, the ol' ladies acted differently towards me and I realized that it was time for a change. I was grateful and forever in debt to the Road Barrons for teaching me the basic rules of the road and for allowing me to ride with them for two years, but it was time to graduate.

It was a warm, dry Monday night in July of 2002. We were on our way to a nightclub in Hot Springs, Arkansas for our weekly Friend's Night Out. A tradition I had started a couple years back.

The DJ hosting the karaoke played loud music and had a strong voice. We asked the waitress if she would ask that loudmouth DJ guy to turn it down.

"Well, actually, that's not a guy. It's a girl," she said with a tone of being used to hearing customers refer to the DJ as a 'him'.

"A girl! No way! He looks just like a guy," I said in utter surprise. All my friends agreed with me and chuckled as we walked closer to the dance floor to get a better view of the DJ. When we discovered she was indeed a girl, we all went back to our table to eat our $2.99 steak dinner and dismissed the notion as unimportant because it really didn't matter to us what the DJ was and what she looked like.

We did our usual food fight as the waitress watched chunks of steak fly across the room and hit several customers who happened to be in the line of fire. Airborne ice cubes, plastic glasses of water, Crown and Coke and anything else that we could get our hands on followed the food fight. We sometimes got a little rowdy but the wait staff allowed it since we were the main group and we spent good money every Monday night.

During the karaoke break the DJ came up to our table to thank us for faithfully coming every Monday night and supporting her.

"Hey, we come because it's our Friend's Night Out' and our tradition," I said to her as I tried to get a closer look and confirm she was indeed a she.

"Well thank you anyway and if there is any song you all want to hear, just let me know. I have eight thousand songs to choose from," said the DJ to me in an attempt to secure our business.

The following Monday we were back at the club for our usual Friends Night Out and cheap steak dinner. I walked to the bar to get myself a drink and the DJ happened to walk up at the same time and ask for a Coors Lite. She introduced herself to me again and asked me if I rode a bike.

"Yes. I ride a purple Road King," I said to her in an unfriendly tone. She held out her hand and I shook it.

"I'm Debbie T and I ride a bike also. I have a 1984 Virago that has been restored and I'm glad to see there are more women riding today." She had a big smile and seemed overly friendly with me. I was somewhat reserved since I was aware of her sexual orientation and I did not want her hitting on me.

"I'm thinking of starting a motorcycle club for women and I'd like for you to get involved with me in this thing I'm planning," she said to me as she never let her smile fade.

I had been waiting for this opportunity. Another woman interested in riding could be the perfect chance to start a motorcycle club for women.

"I am a graphic artist specializing in communications. I will be back here next Monday with a patch design, a name, and colors," I firmly said to her.

She made known her only concern. "All I want is to use the colors blue and gray. That is because I am a diehard fan of the Dallas Cowboys and I want those to be the colors for our club." I told her that I hated football but I would incorporate the Dallas Cowboy colors in the design for our patch. That night we formed a partnership that would last a lifetime. A joint venture brought together by a passion of riding motorcycles but that would later evolve into a true friendship based on heart and not just motorcycles.

I left the bar and joined my friends for a fun night of singing, laughing and dancing. My friends and I were very close and were included in my everyday life. We called ourselves "The Home Crew". First, and foremost there was Andy, my first best friend, known for being the funny one in the group. Then there was Bubba, my second best friend and the one who wanted to fight when he got drunk. Cowboy was my third best friend. He was the one who got drunk and stripped. Ratz was also in the Air Force and he was the one who always made sensible choices. Alan and Shawn were the brothers that got wasted, never remembering what happened on the following day. Robert was the hottie of the group and Will was the quiet one. William was the talker, while Kincannon seemed to be the weed master.

Bobbie was married to Andy. She was the Hip Hop queen and Cherice was known as the back scratcher. Kim was the happy-go-lucky party girl who happened to fall into our circle at Boogies, as well as James, the NA non-drinker who became one with us. Vinny joined us every other Monday and usually stayed until he managed to leave with some cute blonde on the back of his Harley. Sparkles and Rocky was the mother and daughter team that partied over abundantly and argued about which one of them would call themselves my best friend.

Crystal, Tabeel, Moochie, Nutty, the twins, Hector, and many others would occasionally join us, including the underage girls that I would sneak in to be with my group. The group would grow in numbers but the faithful Home Crew would always consist of the core of my most trusted friends whom to this day remain just that. They were a crazy bunch but they were my friends. We stood together against all storms and rode it out with fun and kindness. Ten years later our bonds of friendship have never been severed in any way. To this core of friendship was later added Wish, Micah and Stephanie.

The next week marked the beginning of July 2002 and summer was beaming high and hot. I got an email from Debbie T with some name suggestions for the club. Among them were "Women on Wheels," "Diamond Star Club," and "Women on Bikes." By the names she was suggesting, I was able to see that she had no clue about the protocol and operational guidelines of the MC world. I didn't know much either but I had two years of riding experience with the Road Barrons and knew how to conduct research and find the appropriate people who could teach me. That week I worked on a patch design and a name for the club.

The following Monday I arrived at Boogie's earlier than normal for Friend's Night Out. I brought the startup package for the new woman's motorcycle club idea we had conceived the previous week. Debbie T saw me come in and came to greet me. I handed her the package and said that it contained everything we needed to start the club. She opened it, looked at the center patch design and the color choice. She seemed to be pleased with it.

"I really like this! You did a great job. What about the name? Have you got any ideas?" she said to me with excitement and enthusiasm.

"Yes I do. I thought ROAD CHICKS would be appropriate because we will be on the road on our bikes a lot," I said to her as I thought of my home club the Road Barrons. She seemed to like the name so we chose it to be the official name of our new motorcycle club.

"OK then. I am going to go have a lady design our patches and we can put them on as soon as they are done. I also have two other girls who are interested," said Debbie T.

I jumped in as soon as she finished her statement, for I knew that we could not just put on patches and like magic begin an MC club. I knew there were certain procedures concerning motorcycle rules we needed to follow, so I said to her, "There is no way we can just have Colors designed and put on. We have to talk to Murray and ask permission before we do anything. We have to ask him to approve our patch design."

"Who the hell is Murray and why do we have to ask his permission?" she asked as her eyes opened wide with inquiry. I informed her that Murray was the President of the Bandidos Motorcycle Club in Arkansas and that he was in charge of the motorcycle procedures for Arkansas. She did not understand why we had to go through him if we only wanted to ride for fun but agreed to let me handle it.

Two months later in September of 2002, I called Bandido Murray at his work and arranged a meeting with him. I brought the patch design, color choice, laws and bylaws, and our intentions. He sparingly revised them and said, "The only problem I have is the name. You cannot use the name 'ROAD' because of the Road Barrons." I told him that was not a problem and that we would pick another name. Debbie T called her girlfriend from the bar and told her what happened. She suggested that we use the name HIGHWAY CHICKS instead. She consulted with me and I told her that it seemed like a good name.

"We better hurry up and inform Murray before he changes his mind," I said to her as I grabbed all the paperwork and went back to the bar. We told Murray of the new chosen name and he said it sounded OK to him.

"Come back in a year, if you have made it to then, we can talk about the MC," said Bandido Murray. We shook hands and left the building with our new venture.

The Bandidos are a 1% Motorcycle Club with a worldwide membership. The club was formed in 1966 by Don Chambers in Texas. Its slogan is "We Are the People our Parents Warned us About." They have many members in 14 different countries.

The Bandidos, also called the Bandido Nation, are the fastest growing outlaw motorcycle club in the world with over 90 chapters in the United States, 90 chapters in Europe, and another 15 in Australia, and Southeast Asia. In the United States, the club is concentrated in Texas, but extends into Louisiana, Mississippi, Alabama, Arkansas, New Mexico, Colorado, Nevada, Montana, Wyoming, South Dakota, Utah, Idaho, Nevada, Washington State, Oklahoma, Nebraska, and several other states. The Rock Machine Motorcycle Club in Canada patched over to Bandidos in 2000. It even has several Australian chapters in Adelaide Ballarat, Brisbane City, Cairns, Sydney Downtown, Geelong, Gold Coast, Hunter Valley, Ipswich City, Mid North Coast, Mid State, Nomads, Northside, Noosa, North Victoria, Sunshine Coast, Sydney, and Toowiimba, acquired with much blood.

In recent years the club has also expanded heavily into Germany, Denmark, Norway, Sweden, Finland, Belgium, Italy, Luxembourg, France, and the Channel Isles of Great Britain; and are looking into setting up shop in Russia and Eastern Europe and also in the tiny island of Singapore, as well as Malaysia, and Thailand.

The Bandidos are organized by local chapters, with state and regional officers, as well as a national chapter made up of four regional vice presidents and a national president.

Bandido Murray is the President of the Arkansas Bandidos. He approves all new forming MC's. He had allowed us to become The Highway Chicks and put us on a one-year probationary period. We had obtained his blessing for our new club.

We had our first meeting at the Pit Stop the following week. It was a neighborhood bar located in Benton, Arkansas. Rain was pouring like a broken faucet and it was very cold, nevertheless, we rode our bikes to our first meeting. We were a proud bunch that day. We had become overnight bikers and we wanted to start acting like such. We parked in front of the bar in the brown clay-like mud and sand. We shivered off the bikes into the warm, smoke filled bar. The owner was on premises and paid for two rounds of drinks for us women in the new motorcycle club. He reserved the only round table at the saloon, which we used for our first meeting. The President-elect was Debbie T. I was elected vice president and road captain, and a girl named Sherri was elected secretary. I turned down the vice president office for I only wanted to be Road Captain. I learned that office with the Road Barrons and I was good at it. There were two other girls present but I cannot remember their names at this time. They never came back to another meeting anyway.

The first original Highway Chick Charter members in September of 2002 were, Debbie T, Sadgirl, Vickie, Linda, Cheri C, and Rebecca.

By the sixth month, we had picked up two more girls, ABC and Felisha. Our first ride with just us girls was not a good one for Cheri C had an accident while riding her bike. ABC tells the story.

"When I first walked into Lucky's Bar & Grill, I thought they (the Highway Chicks) were a bunch of dykes on bikes and wasn't sure I wanted to be involved. I was told HC was formed for chicks to have something to do. They were a riding club and just hung out. From the first event (Road Barrons) on Sadgirl's land, I saw it was going to be a lot of work, but a good group to hang around with. Nothing beat that first ride with the pack when we went to meet Cheri C.

We were in Little Rock to have some chick social time on a Saturday afternoon. We all jumped on our bikes and headed to a comedy club. We rode down Cavanaugh Hill. We had these newcomers trying to ride side by side in heavy traffic (not the smartest idea). Cheri and I were both intimidated by the hill, the curves, the slope, the speed and the traffic. I backed off to ride behind her instead of side-by-side as we were instructed to. Cheri C was on the outside part of the lane and I on the inside nearer to traffic.

As we got to the bottom of the hill, I noticed that she took the curve at a wide angle and hit some loose gravel. I thought that if she didn't slow down and compensate quick, something bad was going to happen. She didn't compensate and her bike veered a little off course over a concrete triangle patch at an intersection. This must have scared her because she wobbled on her bike and hit the throttle. She went over the curb at that intersection and hit the throttle more. Her bike remained upright for this whole time. The front wheel hit the bottom of a Texaco sign and proceeded a few more inches into the bushes and concrete. She flipped off of her bike after her head went through her own windshield. She came down hard with one leg bent and the other extended. I got off my bike and quickly ran over to her. I shouted for the Texaco attendant to call 911. When I got to where she was lying I wouldn't let anyone move her or remove her helmet. She had a pulse, but her eyes were not open.

The ambulance arrived and took her to the hospital. We got her bike towed and all of us met at the hospital to wait and see what would happen. We were all stunned and shocked. I felt guilty for a while because I believed that perhaps I was crowding her and that is what caused the accident. We went to visit her often at the hospital. She had several broken bones and bruises, but the main problem was the head injury. She had a subdural hematoma. Doctors tried to relieve the swelling on the brain but it was too late to avoid the apparent permanent damage."

In spite of what happened, we began to attend as many MC functions that we could. We were trying to build a name for ourselves. We were determined to be the first women's motorcycle club in Arkansas. Many people still identified me as *the Road Barron chick* when I arrived at their functions. It took over two years for this image to rub off. It didn't bother me for I was proud to have been schooled by this great club, however, it did bother the rest of the girls in the Highway Chicks.

We began to meet many patch holders and attended almost every MC event hosted by the other clubs that participated in the Monday night pool tournaments. We made sure that Murray saw us and was aware of the extent of our participation. We were extra careful not to piss anyone off, at least not intentionally, and we were especially sure to have several of our club members at every Monday night pool tournament.

The Monday night pool tournaments were established by Bandido Murray a few years back in order to get all clubs talking and getting along. All patch holders and guests played in a pool tournament and had a great night of fun and fellowship.

It felt like a full time job and at times the weight and demands of this kind of lifestyle dampened the *fun* out of the club. However, I had to remind myself that achieving the club's singleness of purpose demanded hard labor and a great financial chunk out of our pockets as well. We were on Probation and we wanted to do the right thing.

We wanted to be the first all female official MC club in Arkansas with a three-piece patch and a MC cube. We wanted to be the first female club that lived the lifestyle of outlaw bikers and rode just as men. We rode hard, miles after miles, interstates, highways, back roads and curves, in the rain, in the cold and in the blistering hot sun. We were not afraid to become bona-fide bikers and definitely not in the least worried to prove it. That was our single-minded focus.

In the emotion of our dedication, some of us put the club before our families, leaving behind the memories we never embraced of missed graduations, football games, and other important events in the lives of our children. Some of us with small children would often leave them poorly attended in order to go to an event. The Highway Chicks and the Red and Gold world became our number one priority. It was almost like an obsession that mesmerized us into total assimilation, all because we wanted to be *the first ones....*

We so totally dedicated ourselves to the club that our entire life, attitude, incentives and ambitions created a transformation almost at a cellular level. It seemed like we had found the rationale for the void that lingered in our hearts for so long. The more we immersed into the club life, the further our lives morphed into a new breed of women bikers in the Southern Dixie States. In this year of probation, we were determined to learn and to be known.

2
Brakeline 1%

One year had passed by and we had managed to survive as a Probationary club without getting in trouble. I paid Bandido Murray a visit at the Long Branch Saloon where he worked as a bartender. Once again, I was the spokesperson for our club.

"Well Murray, a year has passed and hopefully our probation is over," I said to him with respect and hopefulness that he would grant us our permanent Colors.

"Do you have your bottom rockers made up yet?" he asked.

"Yes we do," I said to him as I turned around and showed him my vest.

"Oh no.... You cannot have that on your vest!" He said to me while nodding his head fervently from side to side.

"Well why not?" I asked.

"Because the ARKANSAS bottom rocker is only for 1%'ers and we will not allow you to wear it," he firmly said.

"OK. I did not know. I was under the impression that we could but that is my bad. I will take it off as soon as I get home."

Today I know that Murray had absolute power to enforce his authority and take my vest from me at that moment. Why he didn't, I do not know. Why he let me ride home with ARKANSAS on my back, I guess I will never know. Why he let a woman disrespect his state in such a matter will forever remain a mystery.

I asked him for a suggestion on what to put on our bottom rocker. He suggested HOT SPRINGS. I said that would be OK since we were out of Hot Springs anyway. He told me to come back on Monday for the pool tournament night and he would introduce the Highway Chicks to the rest of the clubs. I thanked him for all his help and told him I would see him Monday.

As I was walking towards the front door, I made a 180 degree turn, returned to the bar and innocently asked him, "Can we put an MC cube on our vest?"

He thought about it for a few seconds and responded, "Would you settle for a WMC for now?"

"Yes I will… but just for now." I said to Murray with a sweet smile as I waved good-bye and once again headed towards the front door. I got on my bike and quickly drove off before he could change his mind and take my vest. I got to a parking area down the road and stopped to call Debbie T.

"We got it!" I said to her with great excitement. "We were approved by Murray to put on a HOT SPRINGS bottom rocker and he said that on the next Monday night pool tournament at Long Branch, he would officially introduce us to the other clubs."

Debbie T was extremely happy to hear the news. "Now do you understand why it was so important for us to do the right thing and secure Bandido Murray's permission?" I said to her in a disciplinary tone.

"I had no idea who Murray was and did not know that he was in charge of everything," she replied. "Well I'm glad I did or we would have been in a shit load of trouble." I informed her concerning the incident with the ARKANSAS bottom rocker, and why we could not have it. I told her we were to take it off immediately.

The following Monday, September 18, 2003 approached with enthusiasm to all us girls. We walked into Long Branch Saloon proud as could be. Most people gave us a warm welcome but some of the old school bikers were not happy that women were allowed to ride a motorcycle. They stared us down the entire night but I did not let it dampen my spirits. When Murray got ready to make the announcements, I knew there was no turning back. All the patch holders and several citizens gathered in the center of the bar as Bandido Murray began his usual announcements.

"We have a new club. They are the Highway Chicks. They have done their one-year probation time and now they are an official MC club. If anyone has a problem with it, see me in my office in the back," he said as he chuckled. His short speech was followed by a loud applause.

The Road Barrons congratulated me and told me they were proud of how much I had accomplished. I reminded them that I was schooled under their Club and would forever be grateful. I hugged Road Barron Wild and told him I loved him. He was always very special to me. My respect and honor goes to the Road Barrons MC.

I took in a breath of relief in that smoke filled bar. It sure was a good thing that no one became violent with us or opposed Murray's decision. We were now sanctioned by the Arkansas Bandidos to ride as a motorcycle club. We had a three-piece patch that included a city bottom rocker and a WMC. It was a historical event for such a matter had never been sanctioned by a 1% club in Arkansas. Debbie T and I were proud to be the first and done it right.

The following Tuesday, I had the pleasure of meeting the Sons of Silence, Arkansas President, Brakeline in person. Brakeline is the founder of the Arkansas Sons of Silence Chapter and President of said Chapter at the time. He also founded the Louisiana Chapter of the Sons and was overseer for Southeast Florida. He worked very close with Nationals and has the experience necessary to do his job correctly. He is a man of his word and a courageous warrior in the 1% world. He had met Debbie T 20 years earlier when they both worked at a strip bar in Hot Springs.

This is how he came to be involved in our Club. He sent me an email explaining to me how the Sons also had a say in what transpired in Arkansas concerning the MC world and that included our club. His first of many emails follows:

Sun, 21 Sep 2003 12:05:59 -0500 (CDT)
To: hdsadgirl@yahoo.com
From: Brakeline 1% SOS

"Sad Girl, rumors are running rampant about you changing your patch! LOL! Rather than give them or their origin the dignity of repeating them, could you please inform me of the exact nature and details (if any) of what is fact! I have a meeting later this afternoon and this is one of the topics I need to address and getting the facts from the source is the best way. E-mail or call me ASAP. I usually let Murray handle this sort of thing because he has been doing it for so long and doing a good job of it, but the "Sons" also have a final say in these matters now in the State, and with so many calls from other clubs and from members of my own club about this issue, I am looked upon to represent them. Murray is out of town for a funeral so I can't consult with him as we normally do. You know I personally support you and your club so give me some concrete facts to clear this issue up with. Also, I try not to be pushy and swing my weight around but if this is true, you need to consult with me in the future. You know I can be a help and a friend and it is easier to work things out in advance than to fine tune and correct them after the fact.

My life is complicated enough lately with all the other stuff going on in the State. Looking forward to your call or e-mail.

PS: You never came to see me during my 2-week stay on Lake Degray! I was looking forward to a visit from you."

Because of this email, Brakeline became my mentor and we became great friends for many years to follow. I had spoken briefly with him a few weeks earlier but this significant letter began the start of an everlasting bond of trust and syndicated alliance between Brakeline and myself. A liaison between patch holders from two different clubs from the opposite sides of the fence had been formed. From the beginning of my MC travels, an old school biker from the Sons of Silence MC took interest in making sure I did the acceptable protocol and made the right choices.

I responded to him in a positive manner. I apologized to him and his Club expressing that I was unaware of this protocol and that no one informed me of such a procedure. I assured him it would not happen again and thanked him for his information regarding the matter. I made it a priority to learn as much as I could from Brakeline and put his teachings into action. I chose him to be my mentor because he had put his time in the club world. He had proved his statements and had firsthand knowledge of what he was doing. He was friendly with me and not unsettled or resentful of the fact that I was a woman. He was secure in his role and I saw the true character a real biker should have. I saw that he was honest in his judgment and examined every situation carefully before making a decision. This is when I learned that wearing Colors does not make you a biker, but rather… the ability to make a fair judgment based on righteousness, without prejudice to sex, race, color, or religious beliefs. A true biker is able to share his/her experience and the bond of brotherhood/sisterhood, while promoting a peaceful motorcycle community. Wearing colors only makes you part of a specific motorcycle club.

Brakeline's second email came after he saw that neither Debbie T nor I had firsthand knowledge that we needed to consult with the Sons of Silence as well as with the Bandidos in major MC decisions. In addition, we had been seen wearing the actual ARKANSAS bottom rocker on our vest before Murray told me we could not wear it.

To: Debbie T (copy sent to Sadgirl)
From: Brakeline 1% SOS
Sent: Sunday, September 21, 2003 8:53 PM

"Thanks for getting back to me and I'm sorry I missed your phone call. I tried to return it and got your answering machine so I guess we are playing phone tag! The problems were that some clubs had the impression you were putting on an ARKANSAS bottom rocker and a regular MC. In addition, it was put to me that they didn't agree with Murray and didn't think that any Rocker claiming territory was appropriate for a female club. I was trying to find out the facts before making any comments. I went to your website and saw your new design on the webpage and printed it to show at a meeting we held tonight. If your patch is as it appears on your webpage (and I'm told by two of my members who checked it out when they saw you at a gas stop

that it is), than there is no problem with the Sons other than the normal 'male' attitude of some. LOL! City Rocker is pushing it some but if you can stand the heat and keep it, then I guess you deserve it. Don't look for the Sons to support you in this but we will not oppose it either,

I personally offer you my congratulations on both the 1-year anniversary and step up to a three-piece patch with a territorial rocker and a 'WMC'. Just understand that there are a lot of members in several different clubs opposed to it.

As for Murray sanctioning you, that is as it should be, but... he speaks for the Bandidos and any other non 1%'er clubs in Arkansas who support him. Try to work with him and respect his opinions and the way he has run things, but only I can speak for the Sons as to accepting a new club or change of patch in this State. In other words things are a little more complicated now than in the past. I'm not trying to be heavy handed but in the future check with both of us.

Something else to think about. Times are changing. The Sons came into Arkansas with the full agreement of the Bandidos and I worked hard to show everyone that this was not a mistake and that we will contribute to the State and not take away from it. However, the Angels have four Prospects with plans of eventually starting a chapter. Outlaws already have a chapter in Fayetteville. I hate to see it coming but this is going to be difficult for the smaller clubs having to answer to four different 1%'er clubs and get along with all of them. Not much will happen at first but given a few years to grow and they will start to exert their influence. I'm sure you will find Murray and myself fair minded but don't look for that treatment from all parties.

Communication is the key so keep in touch and good luck to you and your club!"

I read and studied his email repeatedly until I understood was he was telling us. This protocol was new to me and I had to learn every behavior pattern, attitude and protocol from scratch, then I had to explain what I learned to the rest of my club members. As I write this, I still question why a Son of Silence took the time and effort to teach me all this when in reality it should have been a Bandido. Two Sons of Silence Club Officers in Arkansas corrected my mistakes and showed me the proper way of doing things in the MC world throughout my time as a patch holder.

Brakeline emailed me after I expressed my sincere apology and things seemed to have smoothed over in the beginning of this new formed alliance between the Arkansas Sons of Silence President and myself.

Date: Tue, 23 Sep 2003 02:45:11 -0500 (CDT)
To: hdsadgirl@yahoo.com
From: Brakeline 1% SOS
Subject: Re: New Patch

"Thanks for the reply. Congrats on the New Patch and 1 year anniversary!!!! You are correct about communication being the key. I know we have it. Take care and ride free! Brakeline SFFS 1%'er."

Some of the established MC clubs in neighboring towns had gotten wind of the newly formed female club called the Highway Chicks. Many of them were not happy with the idea either because they simply did not believe in a women's club or because they had received wrong information concerning our club. We found ourselves constantly defending our actions and having to withstand nasty remarks about who we were. That was something we expected and fully considered a hazardous part of our basic training, per say.

Sons of Silence Brakeline helped us when he paved the road for us so that our ride might be smoother and safer among the many bumps in the road. I'm not talking about an actual road on the highway, but the many bumps and obstacles encountered in the male-controlled political biker world. I was always eager to ask for advice and for direction in my decisions. There were many times that Brakeline saw me going the wrong way and he'd point out the right road. He never told me which way to go, but rather only suggested the way it should be done. He never ordered me to follow an outlined protocol but rather enlighten me in the proper protocol.

Debbie T was the President of our club but I was the public relations/spokesperson for the club. Patch holders preferred to talk to me instead of my President. They called me and informed me of club events and happenings. I did not plan it this way, it just happened. Many patch holders said that they would not talk to Debbie T but only to me. She was OK with this but did not understand why some of the men preferred not to do business with her. I explained to her that perhaps it was because of her sexuality and the fact that many men did not want any type of competition with her. Perhaps it was because I was better at using my communication skills and made it easier for the men to talk with me.

Whatever the reason, it was conceivably better that other club member's deal with me since I wasn't as hot tempered as Debbie T. I had the ability to take a crude and snide remark or comment and use it to my advantage. The Highway Chicks had been inducted into the MC world and sanctioned by the Arkansas Bandidos; therefore, we needed to do what was best for our club.

Towards the end of September 2003, we had recruited new girls into our club. Puddles, a hang around from Jonesboro, and Glitter Girl (Crissy) from Jonesboro as a support member. At the time all new female support members were given an ASSOCIATE bottom rocker for their vest. Support members were those who wanted to hang out with us and wear our support colors but did not have a motorcycle. They would have to be our workforce if they were to be considered club supporters. We were growing at a slow but steady pace and hundreds of eyes were watching and waiting to see the outcome of this female biker club with a three-piece patch and a territorial bottom rocker claiming the turf of Hot Springs.

When the two girls from Jonesboro came aboard our club, it opened new problems for us with the Association Motorcycle Club in Jonesboro, Arkansas.

The Association MC was founded in 1983 to promote brotherhood and a mutual love of motorcycles. The Road Barrons were their sponsors in the beginning. Their President at the time was Mack Newsome, a very kind and serene man who seemed to have no problem with me but wasn't at ease with the rest of the club. I cannot condemn him for this, because some females can be very trying in an attempt to prove their equality with men.

The problem arose when PSC, the girlfriend of an Association MC member (club member's name withheld) was interested in joining the Highway Chicks as an Associate. She was a nice girl and possibly a good trainable instrument, but she talked a little too much. I found this out after she came to Little Rock and met with Debbie T and me at one of the Monday night pool tournaments. She had too much to say about her boyfriend's club and I thought eventually it would be a threat to our club's well being. When she went back to Jonesboro, she told her boyfriend that she would not be joining the Highway Chicks for several different reasons.

She wrote a 3-page email to Debbie T. It was that email which caused problems between both our clubs.

Tue, 23 Sep 2003 17:37:39 -0700 (PDT)
From PSC (email address withheld)

"Well, I guess then my boyfriend felt it safe to let his guard down when I told him I was not joining the Highway Chicks. He said to me that the SOS were pissed because they thought HC (Highway Chicks) were getting an ARKANSAS bottom rocker and they (the SOS) said that was not going to happen. Well they don't have an ARKANSAS bottom rocker so I guess SOS decided they were cool with it. I then told my boyfriend that Crissy was planning on coming to the Association clubhouse Friday night wearing her Highway Chick Colors. My boyfriend asked me 'What is on her bottom rocker?' I said, 'Associate.'

He said that anyone could be an Associate. He asked me if she was already in her Prospect period. I told him I wasn't sure how that worked because we never got that far in conversation with it. He asked, 'What's it going to say after Associate comes off?' I said, 'I really don't know but I would *imagine* it would say JONESBORO since the others say HOT SPRINGS.'

He said that was not an acceptable thing. In mid-sentence when he got pissed and said, 'YOU LISTEN TO ME! If Crissy or ANYONE is seen around town wearing a JONESBORO bottom rocker, they WILL get hurt! That is a threat, not by me but by several other club members. I don't want to see Crissy get hurt but if they are going to have JONESBORO *bottom rocker, there are people who have promised to fight to the end for their territory."*

The problem was that Miss PSC assumed out of ignorance, that one of our Associates would probably wear a JONESBORO bottom rocker. When she told this to her boyfriend who was an active member of the Association MC in Jonesboro, she opened a can of bad, rotten worms for us. I had no intention ever, nor did the thought ever cross my mind of any other bottom rocker other than HOT SPRINGS. As little as I knew about the MC world, I understood it to be common ethical social skills not to invade someone else's territory.

When this assumed, fabricated comment reached the Association members, it caused a big uproar and an elevated state of unnecessary upheaval. Not adding to the fact that it made us look like a bunch of inexperienced bikers, (which we were but we did not need everyone to know this).

I don't know much how the Association reacted and what their measures were to solve this confused matter. They had gotten wind that the Highway Chicks were going to put an ARKANSAS bottom rocker on and then one of their members girlfriend tells them that we are going to put on a JONESBORO bottom rocker. Wow! I would have been angry as well. I do know that once again, Brakeline arbitrated on our behalf in order to keep the peace between everyone. He sent a memorandum to the President of the Association as follows:

From: Brakeline 1% SOS
Date: Sun, 28 Sep 2003 13:54:52 -0500 (CDT)
To: "Beth & Babe" (email address withheld) Re: Highway Chicks

"Thanks for getting right back to me. The prior e-mail was from my position as an officer representing my club. Since you shared your personnel feelings with me, here are mine! LOL Sorry but you kind of opened the door for this one. Ha! Ha!

I've known Debbie T for twenty years. We both came to Arkansas about the same time and I was helping manage a topless club in Hot Springs (The Body Shop) and she worked there. She is a good friend and her being a dyke never bothered me as we chased women together in the clubs and enjoyed it all! This women's club thing is something else. My personnel feelings on this are about the same as when the bra burnings took place years back and 'women's lib' got started. They wanted to move out of the revered position of staying home, not working, raising kids, and keeping house. I felt that along with that also went not opening doors for them, not paying for their meals on dates, etc., and even if the job market was open to them, I felt they should prove themselves able to physically match a man's strength and stamina for the jobs that they wanted which needed this.

Debbie keeps saying she doesn't want confrontation and that she is not competing with the men's clubs (She really means this). Well I don't see it that way. She wants EXACTLY what we have but wants to hide behind the WMC patch so she doesn't have to fight for and earn it! Just like in the late 60's & early 70's when the 1%'ers and those wanting to be 1%'ers all were fighting (and sometimes died) for these rights, the clubs and independents who wanted to fly a real patch but not have to fight for and earn the right to do so, hid behind the Abate and religious name tags to avoid the conflict and 'trial by fire' to have the right to wear their patch. The hard-core element in the lifestyle left them along because hiding behind those institutions to have the right to wear a patch took away the pride and what the patch stood for anyway.

I feel this is exactly what the Highway Chicks are doing. They want what we have but don't want to take the chance of having to fight for it and are taking the SAFE way to a "three piece territorial" patch without earning it or having to back it up. Well the 1%'ers will leave them along just as we do the ABATE, HOG, CMA's and etc., but the patch doesn't carry much of our respect when obtained that way. Not everyone is hardcore and not everyone is pussy's. We have to find our place somewhere that we belong and be proud of it (I can respect this). The Highway Chicks want a position at the top but put in the effort of the bottom. In my opinion, they are exactly where they belong (at least for now).

You can sum my feelings up by asking yourself: Do I want to wear a WMC? If your answer is 'NO!' Then it must not be worth anything! (At least in your opinion but to them it is). So why not let them have it?

I really like a lot of their members and as long as they don't step over the line, I would party with them anytime and give them the respect I honestly feel they deserve, which is indeed some, for all that they have accomplished and the way they conduct themselves, but probably is nowhere close to the respect they want. They have to EARN that! To have true respect they have to fight and die for the patch if needed, ride more than on weekends, go farther than around town or occasionally a couple hundred miles (like going to Sturgis, Daytona, and etc. as a club), keep close ties like family with each member, (attend church regularly, see each other often and etc.); and above all if they want me to respect their patch then they have to respect it themselves first by being picky about who gets it, how easy it is to get, and the quality of their members.

They have only been formed for a year and have plenty of time to make mistakes, correct them, figure out where they are going; change things that aren't working and grow to become what their true potentials are. It is never an overnight thing and takes time, and this is what causes a lot of startup clubs to fail. I've offered to personally consult with Debbie anytime and give advice and the benefit of my 26 years in this lifestyle. After all, if we don't like what they are doing we should work to help them become what we can respect. If we turn our back on them we deserve what we wind up with sharing the highway with us! Like I said at the beginning, this is my opinion. Most of my members just want to scoff at them and fuck them off. Everyone is entitled to their point of view.

Feel free to share this with anyone really interested in my opinion but PLEASE don't take my words out of context and repeat them in a way I hadn't intended. In other words share all of this or none! LOL"

With heartfelt respect, Brakeline.

Once again, we were spared the embarrassment of a club shut down or a mass scolding because one man, belonging to the other side of the fence as far as our allegiance demanded, had a zealous observance concerning the respectable ways of the MC world. His words carried courage, respect, and above all an enthusiasm for the cultural code of behavior in the motorcycle club world.

I emailed Brakeline and thanked him countless number of times for his assistance and well thought out letter to the Association President. I told him that I would always be indebted to him for his gracious and meticulous personal opinion expressed. I said that I agreed with what he had stated and that I would be following his advice as often as needed.

He replied with a supportive email.

From: Brakeline 1% SOS
Date: Mon, 29 Sep 2003 15:41:28 -0500 (CDT)
To: "Sadgirl" <hdsadgirl@yahoo.com>

"I'm glad you understood what I was saying and took no offence. You have a right to be proud of what you have after only a year's work! Large 1%'er clubs take that long or more (Arkansas took me 2 years before we sewed our shit on and another years probation), and we have an entire organization behind us and the ability to "hammer down" any opposition, but it still takes time (if you do it right). Be proud of what you have accomplished and if you wish for more...it's up to you. Slow and steady will get it done. You can't prove yourself overnight but time tells all. Keep up the work, hold your head high, and be worth respecting and you will get it."

I knew I was not alone in the new lifestyle that I had chosen. Brakeline was available to show me the ways of the biker world, and he had no qualms with discipline, correction, or instruction. This was a personal one-on-one mentorship with me. Everything I learned I passed it on to my club but without divulging its source. After all, we were supposed to be under the sanctioned umbrella of Bandido Murray, head of the Red and Gold Nation in Arkansas; however, in actuality I was learning the ways of the biker culture from a club from the other side of the fence, the Sons of Silence.

I was confident that the President for the Sons of Silence in Arkansas would never let me down. The innermost part of my heart told me that he'd show his respect and honor to the end. I was even more convinced when I got an email from him a week later letting me know his high regard.

From: *Brakeline 1% SOS*
Date: Wed, 8 Oct 2003 20:48:07 -0500 (CDT)
To: "Sadgirl" <hdsadgirl@yahoo.com>

"Just got home today a few hours ago from hosting the President's meeting with over 100 Officers from around the nation. I'm exhausted! Congratulations on Monday night's announcement! I know you hold me in confidence the same as I do you. ***I'll never let you down or disappoint you.*** *I'm taking a few days rest if the world lets me! LOL! Later, girl."*

After the Association MC misunderstanding was cleared up, we supported their annual Toy Run party 100%. This was a tradition I had embraced when I rode with the Road Barrons. Many of their members still had a problem with our club, but somehow I managed to secure a good political friendship with the President and several of their members. That was my job and I did it well.

As a Club, we began hosting parties and events in the same pattern as other MC's. I observed how the other club did things, and if the results were good, I would do the same. At least it made my club look like we knew what we were doing.

Our first major event took place at Jones Harley Davidson dealership in Hot Springs, Arkansas. They let us use their facilities and donated many items for use and door prizes. We chose the Garland County Humane Society and raised three thousand dollars for them.

We realized that even though there were only a few of us, we could put together large functions and achieve positive results. I chose Highway Chick ABC to work closest to me for she understood and accepted the MC protocols and knew how to play the political game. What she didn't know, she showed an eagerness to learn and didn't question the business aspect of it. Debbie T was the President but she did not have a clear understanding of the why and how of things when it came to the MC world. She also had difficulty in accepting the fact that most of our incurred actions were based on politics. From the beginning, she had stated that she had formed this club for fun. She did not understand that once we were sanctioned by Bandido Murray as an MC club, and put on the territorial bottom rocker, we fell under the category of patch holders who were accountable to our superiors and the MC lifestyle was not entirely for fun.

Although ABC was new and green, she had enough logic to see where we were headed, and was well trained in human behavior. My education was in the field of communications so between the two of us we began turning gears in the right synchronization so that the club would run as smooth and professional as it was supposed to. For the most part, the MC clubs in Arkansas had to get used to us. They didn't have to like us but they had to respect and accept us since we were inducted as an official MC club by Bandido Murray.

The first local MC club to befriend us was the Outsiders. They were supportive and extremely helpful. They donated many items to our future clubhouse and invited us to ride with them often. The Vietnam Vets and the Boozefighters were supportive by attending our events as well.

The first event we rode to as an MC club was the Swamp Riders MC annual in Prescott, Arkansas. The Swamp Riders are a bunch of good ol' boys from South Arkansas who love to party. I had been to this annual for two years consecutively with the Road Barrons and figured this would be a good showing for us to attend. The faces were familiar, the food was excellent, and the environment non-hostile. I remember it was raining hard but we rode our bikes. We were a WMC and felt it necessary to ride into the wet, muddy campground of the clubhouse. We rode with the Outsiders MC that first time. Once we were there, I spent a lot of my time with the Road Barrons. Old habits are hard to break, especially when the ties seem to be tightly holding you back.

This is the event where we met Tab. She is the daughter of Swamp Rider Jim Barner. She was a nice, quiet girl who was instantly attracted to the Highway Chicks. ABC became extremely interested in her and rode her on the back of her bike for quite some time. Although she did not know how to ride a bike nor did she own one, we took her in as a Highway Chick supporter.

The year had rolled by and we had managed to keep the club going. It was time for our first annual party and Debbie T chose a local bar in Hot Springs for the party. We did not know we could invite everyone, so we only invited those closest to us, including the late Association MC member Sambo. There were five of us girls and we had become great friends as well as sisters.

I remember Glitter Girl received her official Associate and support patches on this day. We all crammed into the girl's bathroom at the bar that was designed for one person. We locked the door behind us and proceeded with our ceremonial order. Debbie T pulled out a bottle of contact cement and slapped in on the back of Glitter Girl's support patch. I laughed so hard because all I could see was a bunch of biker girls "jerry-rigging" a stripe on a new girl. The smell from the glue was overwhelming and we all started getting a little dizzy from it, combined with the heat in the room. We busted out the door like a herd of wild horses as we laughed to our table.

Our first year anniversary had come (September 2003) and we were proud of the small tasks we had accomplished. We had four patch holders, 1 Prospect (Puddles) and four support members. (Bonnie, Felisha, Glitter Girl and Tab). We were proud of the people we had met in the club world and the way we were learning to conduct ourselves. People were getting used to seeing us and from what I heard, had started to expect us to show up at their parties. It was a year of learning rules and regulations, meeting new people, letting people see who we were, trying to win the trust of the local clubs, and principally flying under the other 1% clubs in the State of Arkansas who were not happy with us.

Riding Beside My Boss!

On Veteran's Day of November 2003, it was a custom for the bikers to bring the American flag from Little Rock to Hot Springs, Arkansas, early in the morning and have a brief memorial service at the cemetery. Debbie T and ABC rode with the pack from Little Rock, but because I lived in Hot Springs, I met them at the cemetery. When the service was over, Hector (my very first dear brother) said there was free food at the VFW for everyone. I asked Bandido Murray if he and his Support Club wanted to go and eat.

"There's nothing wrong with free food," he said to me after consulting with the others. I offered to lead the pack since I knew where I was going. He said that would be fine.

I lined up by the stop sign of the cemetery and Highway 70 East with everyone else behind me. When the signal was given, I took off and started towards the VFW for the free food. I was riding on the right side when all of a sudden Bandido Murray came up from the end of the pack and lined up beside me on the left side. I smiled at him and acknowledged his presence. I was honored to ride beside Murray. It was then that I became aware of the fact that this great and important man had respect for me even as a new patch holder. He could have told me to fall back, but he didn't. I rode beside him and I was blessed to have the privilege of this awesome honor. All the other club members following in the back of the pack saw that Bandido Murray and I were riding side by side into the town of Hot Springs. Wow! What a great mark of distinction.

When we arrived at the Hot Springs VFW, we all parked our bikes and Murray and I walked into the building for a helping of the free food. After this day, it seemed that Murray and I had formed a closer friendship and perhaps he would not regret the Highway Chicks as a mistake in the future.

I received an encouraging email from Brakeline.

Date: Wed, 12 Nov 2003 02:00:19 -0600 (CST)
To: hdsadgirl@yahoo.com
From: Brakeline 1% SOS

"You seem to be getting the recognition you deserve and have 'earned'. Riding up front was an honor and I see you recognized it as such! Go Girl!"

My mentorship with Brakeline continued to flourish and I had the confidence to ask him anything that I needed to know in my learning process. In the quiet of my home with just my computer sitting in front of me, I began to think how the accountability burden of the MC world fell strictly on Bandido Murray and SOS Brakeline. I wasn't at the point where I knew or understood all the protocol of the MC world but I had adequate knowledge of human behavior management to know that too much on one person can cause traumatic stress. I was concerned that the consequences of MC activities in Arkansas would strictly fall on these two 1% Presidents. Even though there were no criminal or illegal operations going on that I was ever aware of, the fact remains that the Federal Government considers 1% motorcycle clubs to be outlaw motorcycle gangs. Any possible Federally fabricated crimes could cause the clubs to be charged under the RICO act.

The **Racketeer Influenced and Corrupt Organizations Act** (commonly referred to as **RICO Act** or **RICO**) is a United States federal law that provides for extended penalties for criminal acts performed as part of an ongoing criminal organization. RICO was enacted by section 901(a) of the Organized Crime Control Act of 1970, Pub. L. No. 91-452, 84 Stat. 922 (15 October 1970). RICO is codified as Chapter 96 of Title 18 of the United States Code, 18 U.S.C. & 1961 through 18 U.S.C. & 1968.

I thought about this for months but didn't share it with anyone, including the members from my own club. It was a concern that harbored within my head, for I know the stereotype police place upon bikers and how they are portrayed as criminals or drug trafficking scum. I asked myself repeatedly how Bandido Murray had not thought about this since the Bandidos are considered an outlaw motorcycle club (OMG's) by both the Federal Bureau of Investigations (FBI) and the Criminal Intelligence Service Canada (CISC).

Finally, one afternoon I thought I would ask Brakeline about the possibility of a Coalition of Motorcycle Clubs in Arkansas.

I emailed my mentor with the question.

"Brakeline, I just wanted to ask you why Arkansas does not have a Coalition of Motorcycle Clubs in this State. I mean, it would make it so much easier, especially where decision-making is concerned. All the clubs would be involved and it would take the spotlight off one person or club in particular."

I mentioned my perception of the RICO act also. I told him that I was most likely overstepping my boundaries (which I seem to do rather often), but that as a patch holder I was concerned.

He didn't waste any time in sending me another email with some hope.

From: Brakeline SOS 1%
Date: Sun, 9 Nov 2003 01:09:09 -0600 (CST)
To: "Sadgirl" <hdsadgirl@yahoo.com>

"The Sons firmly support the Confederation of Clubs. We are very active in its running. Murray told me when I mentioned it to him a while back, that 'Arkansas has done well without it and he doesn't see any reason to change things'. It would put a good bit of control into the hands of the Confederation members themselves that he now has.

You really surprise me at the things you notice and pick up on!

The major lawyer Richard Lester who was instrumental in forming the Confederation is also the Sons club lawyer and at the disposal of any of our members anytime. Actually, his law firm usually finds someone local to bail us out and represent us but one call does the trick! LOL! One of my member's "old lady" works part time for Richard Lester here in Arkansas delivering papers, booklets and such to different MC shops that support AIM. I think that you will see a slow trend toward more support for Arkansas to have its own Chapter of the Confederation in the time ahead."

As I read Brakeline's email, I was able to see that the Sons supported a Coalition but it appeared that Bandido Murray did not care to change things. I wrote him back and made an argument that a Coalition would be a good thing, especially for Murray's protection. I also pointed out to him that with a black club in the Coalition (the Hells Lovers) and a women's club also (the Highway Chicks), it would make an excellent spearhead for minority lobbying with the politicians that like to see minorities plead a case. It was my desire that Brakeline present this Coalition idea to Bandido Murray and the rest of the leaders in Central Arkansas. I surely could not have

because I was a new patch holder and a woman on top of that.
Once again, my mentor had an answer for me.

From: Brakeline SOS 1%
Date: Mon, 10 Nov 2003 03:25:24 -0600 (CST)
To: "Sadgirl" <hdsadgirl@yahoo.com>

"Yes, the Confederation started out more as a way to lobby lawmakers. But quickly became a way for clubs on all levels to sit down together, put aside differences, and work together toward the common good. Actually, with the 10-year war going on between the Sons and the Outlaws, we were at a point that we couldn't talk anymore. The Confederation gave us a setting that was conductive to getting communications going again and we were able to put an end to the war; and now I can party in any Outlaw clubhouse across the country! If Arkansas had a Confederation, all the clubs (big and small) could sit down together and decide how things would be and do it democratically. Right now Murray mostly just tells the rest of the State how things will be, but that would change.

Not only does he not tell the SONS what to do, but now the Outlaws are here and they don't take orders from him either, and soon the Angels will have a chapter and they also will be independent. Both the Outlaws and the Angels support the Confederation, as do most of the other Bandido chapters across the nation. With four 1%'er clubs here in Arkansas now, and The Iron Horsemen in Memphis to boot, it will be a definite advantage to have the Confederation going so any problems can be worked out in a good atmosphere before they grow into large problems. THE WRITING IS ON THE WALL."

3
The ARCOMc
Arkansas Coalition of Motorcycle Clubs

On December 14 of 2003, the Presidents of the local motorcycle clubs held their first meeting at the Road Barrons clubhouse in North Little Rock, Arkansas. It was to organize the start up of a Coalition of Motorcycle Clubs. The Highway Chicks were not invited nor informed of the meeting. Whether it was my constant nagging at Brakeline about this Coalition or his vision, or a combination of both that incited the first meeting, well… that I cannot say. Nevertheless, I am sure he lobbied for this Coalition to be incorporated into the MC clubs of Central Arkansas and beyond, and I am glad to have played a silent, but direct part in it.

Topics of discussion in the first meeting were the following: (provided by an attending MC President)

1. The start up of new clubs and the new guidelines they will have to follow.
2. The treatment of each other's Prospects.
3. Picking up Prospects that washed out from another club.
4. Communication between clubs.
5. Handling problems of clubs with black members (the Hells Lovers were present).

6. New laws that could affect us as MC organizations.
7. The forming of an Arkansas Coalition of Motorcycle Clubs (not a COC).

It was a definite and clear understanding that this meeting would be the groundwork and would greatly affect the future of bikers in the State of Arkansas for many years to come.

Early in 2004, ABC and I started attending the Coalition of Clubs (COC) meetings in the State of Mississippi. It was a long and costly ride but I wanted to learn more about the functional and ethical laws of the motorcycle clubs and riding associations.

It is here where we met and became closely affiliated with Bandido Dwayne, President of the Mississippi Bandidos, the Pistoleros MC, the Mississippi Riders RA, Bandido Gunner (GBNF), Southern Cross MC, Dream Riders RA, Dixie Rebels MC, and the Military Vets MC out of Tennessee and Kansas.

The State of Mississippi received the Highway Chicks with more respect than our own home state did. Perhaps it was because they did not have to live with us and share the same back yard, or possibly their mentality was different. They gave us the respect and admiration due to an MC club. We became especially close with the Mississippi Riders, specifically Trigger and Blinky. We rode together; shared meals, partied together, stayed in each other's clubhouse, but mostly had the love, loyalty and respect of brother/sister hood. At least it seemed that way.

I did not understand at the time, that all this devotion to one another was because of a patch. I was too new to comprehend that as long as you were in good standing with the club, everything was alright. When a member was put out in bad standing, the brotherhood and friendship would instantly disappear. It was an instant blackball.

I believed that the devotion to one another was due to genuine friendship and would last no matter what happened in the years to come. Sort of like a marriage, for better or worse, in sickness and in health, for richer or poorer. I did not know that a 'patch' held the bond of friendship and brotherhood together. That is... until it happened to me. That is why I designed the patch "*Love, Loyalty, Respect, por Vida*" for the Highway Chicks. I believed that the association was *por Vida* (for life) and never thought twice about it.

Although Brakeline continued to be my personal mentor and advisor, the Mississippi Red and Gold family would keep us informed of the protocols and procedures in their world. They taught us who, what, when, where, and how of the Bandido Nation and support club protocols. There wasn't the kind of hostility that simmered with the Arkansas Bandidos and the Highway Chicks. Our home state Bandidos did not like or want us. They never greeted us, spoke to us or offered any kind of gesture other than dirty looks. They did not approve of women on bikes and were plain about it. Bandido Murray, nonetheless, was always friendly and courteous with us. He went out of his way many a times to help us in advance. Time and again, he was restricted by his club and could only go so far with us without getting his ass chewed.

ABC and I continued to attend the Mississippi COC (Coalition of Clubs) meetings while introducing our club to as many patch holders and bikers as possible.

The Central Arkansas MC Club Presidents held another meeting on February 15, 2004. This time Debbie T and I were invited to the meeting. Brakeline was also present at that meeting since he was the President for the Sons of Silence in the State. All the Club Presidents unanimously decided to start an Arkansas Coalition of Motorcycle Clubs (ARCOMc) instead of a Coalition of Clubs (COC).

An ARCOMc would function as an independent association governed by the internal appointed laws and bylaws created by each club president as a whole entity, and enforced by the elected officers. The ARCOMc would not be affiliated in any legislative or legal way to the National Coalition of Motorcycles (NCOM).

The first originally elected officers were Bandido Murray as President, Vietnam Vet Beau as Treasurer, and Road Barron Bryan as Secretary. Bandido Murray appointed me as unofficial secretary to take minutes and handle the communications aspect. It was a big step in the history of the Highway Chicks towards Statewide recognition. I mean, if Murray allowed me to participate in the ARCOMc meetings not as a spectator but as a participant, everyone else was apt to stand behind his decision.

I took the minutes for the first ARCOMc meeting on February 15, 2004 and account as follows.

It was a cold afternoon and the piles of snow lay on the ground from the day before. Bikes were scarce but the MC members were not. The Road Barrons clubhouse was abundant with the aroma of pork chops and mashed potatoes cooked by some of their members early that morning.

Most members arrived early. At 1:40 pm, Bandido Murray opened the meeting with the following statement: "Do we want this to go on? Yes!" He answers himself. "This is for the MC clubs of Arkansas only, to help participate, to better ourselves, to get to know each other and get to do things together. We live in Arkansas so we need to have a voice. Let us start with the pool tournament. The reason citizens are shooting in the tournaments is that brothers are not showing up. If you have any pros or cons talk to Kerrdog or Hoppy." End of Murray's statement.

Pool tournament negotiations are talked about by Vietnam Vet Super Dave. The topic includes armbands, discounts and tournaments.

"The pool tournament is run by MC clubs and people need to be involved and participate. The host club has the right to decide what to do.," adds Murray loud and firmly.

"Gators might not stay open so we need to negotiate," says Hoppy.

"We don't want to have to move the pool tournament but we don't want to get fucked," shouts Boozefighter Kerrdog.

"Hosting clubs needs to keep hustlers out." is Vietnam Vet Super Dave's statement.

"The bottom line is to keep all clubs together, getting to know each other. We run it the way we see fit and that's the way it's going to be," says Bandido Murray.

Road Barron Jim stresses that we need to begin the tournament at 8 o'clock sharp. Road Barron President Bryan talks about efficiency and staying on top of the board.

New subject introduced by Bandido Murray.

"What I want to try and do is to get an emergency fund. If you have a wreck and can't pay bills, the fund can do that," he says.

Road Barron Wild makes a proposal. "I think it could start with $100 per club with a three people panel for the Emergency Assistance Fund (EAF), and two benefits per year with donations. The entire benefit will be donated. The MC Representative would be needed if the donation to be made from the EAF were over $200. None of this money is to be paid back. It is a donation. I nominate Selig from the Vietnam Vets MC to be part of the panel."

Boozefighter President Kerrdog asks, "Is the $100 per club or per chapter?"

"It is an initial fee," replies RBR Wild.

"How are you going to get people to commit?" asks Kerrdog.

Murray answers him. "Do you need help getting people off their ass?"

Sons of Silence President Brakeline steps in. "We need to get non patch holders to come to benefits."

"Maybe they will need our help some day," adds Murray.

"Will there be a secretary or a treasurer?" Asks Vietnam Vet Bubba.

Bandido Murray says that the books will be open at all times and announcements can be made at the pool tournaments.

Brakeline raises his hand and questions everyone. "Don't we need to discuss this with our people?"

"We need to know how we feel about it," says Murray.

At this time, there is petty discussion about accounts and money. Kerrdog says that we might have to pay for a band at these fundraisers. The discussion goes on for three minutes and Brakeline puts an end to it.

"We are putting the cart ahead of the horse. We haven't even formed yet. We need to have basic guidelines and get organized. As far as elections, we need to get organized and get a structure, and then go with each individual problem."

The Vietnam Vets talk about Richard Lester. Murray says that everyone voted the attorney down and we can get our own people together. RBR Wild says that this is informal and Kerrdog states, "we sound like ABATE." Everyone laughs.

Murray has the floor. 'This is mainly to give you a voice. If no one wants it, I don't!"

Outsider President Bartman responds. "We got to have a basis to understand."

Brakeline responds. "We all have to put our wagons together. This is not an insurance policy. We as a State decide who is going to ride and who is not. We will have problems we do not anticipate or want. We have thrown out ideas but have not gone anywhere. This is to handle problems we do not anticipate."

Vietnam Vet Bubba asks a question. "So, you're going to pick three representatives out of the nine clubs in Arkansas?"

"A rep does not have to be a president," says Murray.

Further discussion of a State representative floats for several minutes then Hoppy speaks up. "Maybe all clubs should get together and pick a representative."

No one responds and people talk among themselves concerning this topic. The next discussion concerns new clubs joining the ARCOMc and the formation of new clubs. In addition, there is a statement made about articles, publications and stories in magazines. RBR Wild talks about using people's names in stories. Murray ends it by saying that if you are going to write an article and need to use someone's name, get it approved first.

"Go back and tell your people how this is going to work," says Bandido Murray.

Wrap up by SOS Arkansas President Brakeline: "Then we can decide what we are going to do. Take this back to your people and discuss it. We need good individuals to represent us and not a patch. We need to bring the representative to the next meeting so we can meet them. Talk to your people so we can get something going before the riding season. Next meeting is scheduled for March 14th, 2004 at 1:00 pm."

The Arkansas Coalition of Motorcycle Clubs, known as the ARCOMc originally formed and chartered with 11 MC clubs on March 14, 2004. These were the Bandidos MC, Sons of Silence MC, Ozark Riders MC, Thunderheads MC, Association MC, Next of Kin MC, Boozefighters MC, Outsiders MC, Vietnam Vets MC, Road Barrons MC and Highway Chicks WMC. These clubs put their differences aside only if by appearance, to make a better riding place for all bikers in the State of Arkansas. I was proud that the Highway Chicks were a part of this historical thrust, and that I was at the first Charter meeting to witness an event of such magnitude.

The Martyrs were the first club to probate for the ARCOMc and receive their bottom rocker with an MC cube. The ARCOMc members had decided that any riding association wanting to become an MC club would have to probate for a year before they could put on a three-piece patch and an MC cube, and have the majority of votes. They were also required to support other MC events by attending as many functions as possible, including the Monday night pool tournaments.

The ARCOMc did not want any new clubs coming into the State or forming up, however, the Constitution of the United States in the First Amendment states that: *"Congress makes no law respecting an establishment of religion, or prohibiting the free exercise thereof or abridging the freedom of speech, of the press; or the right of the people peaceably to assemble, and to petition the government for a redress of grievances."*

So in reality, we could not stop the start up of new clubs, based on *"...the right of the people peaceably to assemble..."* but we could sure help them in making the right choices.

At the next ARCOMc meeting I asked Bandido Murray if it was possible for the Coalition to have a logo designed that would identify its intent and purpose. He said it would be a good idea and he would bring it up as a proposal at the next meeting.

He explained at the next ARCOMc meeting, the importance of a logo. He asked people to submit a logo design and to bring it to the following meeting so we could choose one and vote on it. Everyone agreed. I was determined to create a logo that could not be turned down. I engaged the service of my son Micah, who was extremely talented in graphic arts and communications. Between the two of us, we designed a logo that was accepted and voted on as the official logo of the Arkansas Coalition of Motorcycle Clubs.

We continued to learn how to become bikers by attending all MC events, asking the right questions, conducting ourselves with respect, abstaining from drugs or alcohol, and associating with the right people in the motorcycle community. Our biggest issue was the Arkansas Bandidos. We did not know who they were other than Murray, and we were cautious not to ask questions about them. I did not want them to think that we were some kind of undercover cops trying to infiltrate their organization because we were not.

I remember today as I look back, that Debbie T and myself would sit down and try to figure out who Bandido Fast and Bandido Wiggs were. We tried for the longest time to put a name with a face. You know, like when you go to primary school and you are supposed to draw a line from an item to its matching article on the worksheet. Well, we had the faces but could not match them with the correct names and were surely not going to ask. Then for the longest time we could not figure out if Bandido Fast and Bandido Eddie were the same person. As I look back through the pages of history a giggle arises within me, but back then, it was a task that made us sweat. We did not want to look like dumb asses so we just let time pass and eventually we figured out who was who.

Subsequent Coalition meetings seemed extremely productive since there seemed to be a genuine concern from the members towards the fraternization of MC clubs in the state. It seemed like it was a good plan for the interpersonal relationships of MC clubs and their members. The 1% Presidents handled any conflict or issue that might have surfaced with other 1% Clubs in the state. The ARCOMc handled any problem or issue that would occur with any non 1%'er clubs. The final decision, nevertheless, with issues directly involving 1% clubs in the state, were promptly handled by 1% State Presidents.

I was taught by my mentor that 1%'ers run the state and that gives them the power to override any non 1%'er regardless of what club they belong to. In Arkansas, we share the state in a triple play. Bandidos, Sons of Silence, and Outlaws. My boss Bandido Murray told me, "If you are going down the highway on your motorcycle wearing your colors and an Outlaw stops you and tells you to take off your Colors, do it. Put them in your saddlebags and if you have a problem with that order, call me."

Therefore, overall, the Arkansas Coalition was a good thing for it freed up the big boys and gave us something to do with our fellow bikers. In addition, I say *us* unreservedly for the Highway Chicks were an official MC club in Arkansas, attending the ARCOMc meetings.

I received an email from Brakeline in July of 2004 with a word of encouragement and praise after my club was inducted into the ARCOMc and my design had been accepted and approved for the official ARCOMc logo.

From: Brakeline 1% SOS
Date: Sun, 25 Jul 2004 14:15:37 -0500
To: hdsadgirl@yahoo.com

"As for yourself, I pointed out that you have never been found to have said or repeated anything that was not exactly the truth and could be counted upon without question, and XXX (name withheld at patch holders request) said that privately, he agreed with me and that you did indeed add strength to the Sons and not take away anything.

As long as you never get caught up in anything that takes away your credibility, I believe you can count on XXX (name withheld at patch holder's request)."

From: Brakeline 1% SOS
Date: Fri, 30 Jul 2004 18:43:56 -0500
To: hdsadgirl@yahoo.com

"You are one of a kind, a benefit to your club, the biker community, and to me as a valued friend, associate, and a spiritual connection I can't really explain but value and cherish none the less. Thanks for being there".

Although the Highway Chicks were a new club, we had met over 400 club members in this short time and had gotten to know at least 30% of those real well. I had a handful of patch holders that I kept on friendly terms. Those who were not associated with my club or the ARCOMc, nevertheless, I found it necessary to keep these doors open for political reasons. My club members did not know how close our solidarity was, for if they did, it may have caused hostility between my club and me. Perhaps, they would not understand that sometimes, moral ethics and peaceful commune could overshadow colors or patches.

It was necessary for my club and me to become friends with all these people in order to achieve our goal as a motorcycle club. As I sit and write this today, I now know that the friendship and bonds established with the majority of them were strictly in direct reference with the patch I wore on my back and/or the Red and Gold colors I represented. However, I did learn over the years that the integrity and valor of the Sons of Silence in Arkansas was genuine and they never flinched at what was truth and what was a lie, and for that knowledge, I was indebted to them.

The next ARCOMc meeting was on August 29, 2004 at the Road Barrons clubhouse. The events occurring that day produced an enormous bolt from the blue, which changed the social status of the Highway Chicks for years to come. There seemed to be some hostility throughout the meeting but never would I have imagined that one club's actions would be so drastic.

In an effort to make things more organized and provide a backbone for the ARCOMc members, I wrote up a set of guidelines for the Coalition that would benefit all the clubs involved. It included the basic operating system for a collective group of people with different ideas under one roof. I incorporated some of the fundamental protocol procedures for the MC world, made several copies and brought them to the meeting. I handed them to Murray and told him my idea.

After he read the guidelines, he was pleased and told me it was a good thing. He passed out a copy to each club president and informed them during the meeting that he wanted everyone to read it and add their input. He told them to bring their comments and written amendments to the next meeting for discussion. He also told the club presidents that I wrote it. If anyone was intimidated or offended at the idea that it was a woman who had written up a set of basic guidelines for the men's MC Coalition, no one said anything or made any suggestions or snide remarks as to voice their opinion.

At the end of the meeting that day, Road Barron Nomad, Ben Taylor stood up and said, "As men, we live by some standards and this is a man's world and we want to keep it that way, so after this meeting the Road Barrons are no longer part of the Coalition."

There was a long period of silence for he caught everyone by surprise. We all knew that Mr. Taylor made this statement because the Highway Chicks were part of the Coalition. After hearing what he had said, a horrendous feeling came over me. I kept taking minutes and never lifted my eyes from my notebook. I knew I was at the bottom of the food chain and had not intended to open my mouth to put in my unwanted opinion and end up with a boot up my ass. Finally without moving my head, I looked at the newly appointed Arkansas Sons of Silence President (name withheld at patch holder's request) to see his reaction. He was just as dumb founded as the rest of the people in that room.

Out of all people to say this, it was Road Barron Ben Taylor, whom I had known for almost two and a half years. He totally surprised me. Ben and I had ridden our bikes side by side down Interstate 30W at 9 o'clock in the freezing rain of February of 2002. We left their clubhouse on the way to meet the rest of the Road Barrons at Denny's Restaurant in Benton, Arkansas for a quick breakfast before heading to the ABATE swap meet at the Expo Center.

My mind flooded with logical reasoning, "There is no way the MC Presidents are going to choose a few girls who mean nothing to them, over a 20-year-old established male MC. I know there is going to be a vote and we are going to be kicked out of the Coalition. We worked our asses off for an entire year, and now we are going to lose it. Some of the guys have been waiting for this opportunity, to get rid of those women trying to be men on motorcycles. The Road Barrons had a clubhouse 20 years ago in Hot Springs and they are old school." All these thoughts came flowing one after the other as fast as running water.

I knew Debbie T was hot tempered and surely enough, she was not going to keep her mouth shut. "Please don't say anything. Please don't say anything. Please don't say anything," I said repeatedly in my head.

Then Bandido Murray, the ARCOMc President cut the silence and told Ben Taylor, "If you pull out, you have no voice in the Coalition. We are in this together but everyone has their opinion on how things should go."

I was stunned and speechless by Murray's response. I mean we were at the Road Barrons clubhouse and they were resigning from the Coalition, and Bandido Murray did not even try to reason with them in order to keep their membership. They were resigning because of the Highway Chicks and Murray's judgment seemed to be partial to us.

No one else said anything. No one gave their opinion. The President's decision was instantly set in stone in front of the MC clubs present. It was a great victory for our club that day and it would go down in history as such. I looked up to where Ben Taylor was standing at the end of the bar beside Road Barron Jim. I looked at him for a few seconds and quickly set my eyes back on the minutes I was taking. I continued to record all the information on paper for I wanted to make sure the minutes were accurate.

But then my worse fear popped up and Debbie T exploded.

"I just have to say that just because I don't have a dick between my legs is why you are acting the way you are, because if I had a dick between my legs you wouldn't have a problem," she firmly said to Mr. Taylor among some other things.

I wanted to curl up and die. I mean it was okay for her to express her opinion and feelings, but unlike me, she has a hard time containing her emotions. She is a very high-strung Sagittarius closely devoted to her circle of friends. When she stated her opinion, I thought we were doomed.

Murray responded to Debbie T's angry statement and said that it was her opinion and that she had said what she wanted to. Ben Taylor looked at Debbie T, put his hand up in a stop motion and firmly said, "Point taken." The Road Barrons were no longer part of the ARCOMc therefore the next meeting was scheduled at a different clubhouse.

After the meeting was adjourned, everyone acted as if nothing had transpired. We all went outside the clubhouse and the Road Barrons acted just as normal as they always did with me. I waited for one of them to come up to me and privately talk with me for we were friends and I knew that eventually someone would say something concerning the situation.

Road Barron Jim motioned at me to walk to the porch where he was standing. He leaned over and whispered in my ear, "We didn't know he was going to do this. He is a Nomad and can speak for any Road Barron anywhere in the country. But we had no idea he was going to do this." I looked at him and told him that I hoped this action would not change our long-term friendship. He assured me that by no means would our personal friendship end.

Debbie T and I stood outside the building totally speechless, waiting for some of the patch holders to come and try to persuade us into stepping down from the Coalition's membership. The Sons of Silence President was standing on the side of the building talking with one of his brothers. He came over to where Debbie T and I were standing and said he needed to talk with us. As you are already imagining I knew this 1%'er would definitely shut us down. He had the power to do so and would unquestionably do it without hesitation. Although Bandido Murray had sanctioned us, this Son of Silence was a 1%'er and did not believe in women MC clubs. He had equal power (due to an established treaty when the Sons came into the state) with Murray, who was the Arkansas State President for the Bandidos as well as the ARCOMc President.

As we walked over to where his bike was, I silently began to create excuses to the biker world for the reason why the Highway Chicks no longer existed. I imagined us showing our face to the world and attempting a philosophical but simple explanation of our termination as a club. I thought about all the money we had spent on patches and t-shirts. I even imagined a memory wall in Debbie T's house.

When we stepped into the area where the bikes were, this 1% president began to speak to us. I was terrified not at the man, but at the man's power. The new Sons of Silence President (name withheld at patch holder's request) did not care for any woman riding a motorcycle and he definitely did not like the Highway Chicks. He publically made it known to anyone in his path. This day was his perfect opportunity to put an end to our club.

As we stopped beside the bikes, he leaned into us and said to Debbie T and me that he was going to stand behind us and that it was too bad that the Road Barrons had made their decision. He said that it was their loss. He also offered to help us if we needed him or his club at any time. He made sure we had his phone number so he gave us his business card.

Debbie T looked at me, I looked at her, and the puzzled looks on our faces went beyond bewilderment. It was one thing for an established club to close their doors on us, but it was definitely a tremendous impact for a 1% club such as the Sons of Silence to accept a club of female patch holders in their own back yard.

From this day forward, I created a bond in my heart with the Sons that would last until the ends of times. I was a Red and Gold supporter and my allegiance was to the Bandidos, but I would never betray the Sons confidence or respect under any circumstance. This was a silent pact I made with myself as the passionate Scorpio that I am. I was not playing double base, but I undeniably knew what friendship was. I was consciously aware of the consequences of betrayal if that comradeship was ever broken.

We thanked the Sons of Silence President for his support and went back into the clubhouse. I wanted to find Bandido Murray and ask his opinion of the whole situation. In light of the fact that the Road Barrons were an established male club and they were in charge of making the yearly calendar for the pool tournament rotations and events, I thought that Murray would have reconsidered his judgment.

"Murray, are you going to kick us out of the Coalition because the Road Barrons pulled out?" I asked my boss.

He looked at me with his reading glasses on the tip of his nose, his frizzy gray hair in a ponytail and his chin tipped down so he can see over his spectacles. "All I can say is that maybe they will see the error of their ways in the future. There are many male chauvinists in the MC world and we cannot do anything about that. But it is their loss."

Then he repeated the final sentence to his statement, "It's their loss."

This had been a day of victory for the Highway Chicks. Days like these were scarce for us and we indulged in its triumph with absolute joy.

That December in spite of Mr. Taylor's attitude, we faithfully attended the Road Barrons traditional Christmas party (except Debbie T) and supported their event whole-heartedly. When I saw Ben Taylor standing near the dancers tent I greeted him with a big hug and gave him the respect one gives another patch holder. He reciprocated. My relationship did not change one bit with the Road Barrons since I was indebted to them for teaching me how to ride with a club and allowing me to ride with their pack for almost two years.

I was fully aware that I had to work three times as hard to accomplish what the men would do in one stroke, but that did not scare me. I knew that my Club would be called names, stared at, made fun at, and belittled. However, it was my full intention to die trying, while winning the trust of these old school bikers who made no room for women bikers, but could not shut us down because Bandido Murray had sanctioned us as an official MC club in the State of Arkansas.

I did remain good friends with the Road Barrons MC since we had known each other for years and it was not the local club's decision to pull out of the Coalition. The only thing that changed was that they did not attend the ARCOMc business meetings, but supported all other events.

4
Damn the Torpedoes, Full Speed Ahead!

ABC and I continued riding to neighboring states and slowly but surely, through stories and pictures, we put the Arkansas MC community on their map. I was playing *secret ambassador* for the ARCOMc in the best interest of all patch holders in an endeavor to expand the political doors of friendship among MC clubs members and other bikers as well.

It was a complex and daringly unauthorized task carried out solely by myself while using some of my club members as innocent contributors. It was just a matter of becoming a safe bridge between different patch holders while constantly inviting and welcoming club members to Arkansas for events and vice versa.

I accomplished this by what I call "duty to reciprocate through perseverance." Sort of like a courtship. The Highway Chicks faithfully and devotedly attended MC events in Mississippi, Tennessee, Alabama and Louisiana. I had hoped it would eventually come the other way around. It was financially draining, leaving no time for personal leisure, and we were dead tired by the time Monday morning rolled in. But two years down the road the results achieved were exhilarating and refreshing, as we watched so many different MC Presidents and Officers in Hot Springs, Arkansas at the junction of Highway 5 and 7 enjoying each other's company and sharing road stories while greeting each other with brotherly hugs.

Was this my job? Absolutely not! Was I out of line in this self-appointed task? I was! Why did I engage in affairs that were generally executed by Red and Gold support clubs in the State of Arkansas, such as the Thunderheads or the Ozark Riders? Why did I engage in a task that was strictly for 1%'ers and their members? Because I chose to make it a personal endeavor based on my gratitude for Bandido Murray for allowing us to have a female MC in Arkansas, specifically for granting me his blessing. I was fully aware that he could have said no and never allowed a WMC in the state. But he did and endured third degree burns on many occasions by his own brothers for it. I was truly indebted to him and this was my own way of saying thank you.

Whether it was right or wrong in the eyes of the MC world officers…, well that depends on who questions it. In my eyes, it was acceptable. Perhaps not my place to do so, but someone had to be the pioneer in broadening the boundaries of the Red and Gold MC community at least for Central and Northern Arkansas.

In the meantime, we worked around the clock to find girls with motorcycles interested in joining the club but were unsuccessful. Most women who appeared attracted in riding with us, just wanted to ride leisurely. I heard excuses like, "I ride with my old man; I have small kids at home; I just want to ride on weekends when it's sunny and just local rides; or I'm not interested in club life." I felt like we were stagnated. Some of the male clubs told us that it was difficult for them to engage new members. I found out that the work and the commitment would have to be three times greater for a women's MC.

I remember telling Thunderhead Big Joe, "I just think people don't want to commit to an MC. It is very demanding and financially draining too. And I also think that the public sees a women's motorcycle club as a dyke club, therefore they tend to stay clear of it."

We had to come up with some form of growth strategy before we would be forced to shut the club down ourselves. The club had only three patch holders, Debbie T, ABC, and me. We had picked up a girl named Tab at a Swamp Riders MC party. She had been with us for about 6 months as an associate but she could not prospect because she did not have a motorcycle and did not know how to ride one. Vickie could no longer be a full patch holder due to medical reasons. We had lost Cheri C due to a motorcycle wreck, and our first Prospect Puddles, had decided that this kind of life was not for her. We were struggling to survive and we could not let our image undergo a dive in the dumps and let the men say 'I told you so.'

We came up with the idea of incorporating official supporters into our club in order to have work force for the parties as well as providing an optical illusion of numbers. We would induct these new lower house members with the same bells and whistles as we did patch holders. We reasoned within ourselves and concluded that if we recruited several supporters and gave them support patches for their vests, support t-shirts, and an official job title, it would make the club appear larger than it really was. If people saw them working at the parties or the pool tournaments, they would think they were our hang arounds.

We had discharged the original support members from their duties due to lack of interest on their part and/or club rule violation. Therefore, when we engaged the new support members, we gave them a full briefing on the operational procedures of the Highway Chicks and the motorcycle club world. We recruited both male and female members.

We did not allow support members to wear full colors so it did not cause a problem with the men. We gave them all the benefits of full club members except voting, wearing full patch, having a voice in public, or by interfering in any type of club business. Our support members did not have to pay dues, but in return for having the privilege to 'play' bikers, they had to work for the club at our request.

In March of 2004, Highway and Hedges Motorcycle Ministry, founder and director Punkin, joined our club. He was the only male honorary officer in the club. He became the official chaplain of the Highway Chicks.

Highways and Hedges Ministry is an Interdenominational biker ministry with the mission of taking the Gospel of Jesus Christ to all people of the world through motorcycling. Highways and Hedges

Ministry is not a Christian motorcycle club, but rather a ministry spreading the light of Jesus into the darkness. When he came aboard our club, his wife, Sweet Baby Rhonda also came with him, and several others of the local members in his ministry.

It must have been a good idea, because slowly but surely, the club had more support members than patch holders. During mid Spring of 2004, The membership was comprised of Pastor Punkin, Chaplain; Vickie, Charter Member; Full Time (male), Events Coordinator; Half Time (female), Crash Van Driver; Kathy, Registration Director; Robbie, Registration Director; Barbara Dee, Janitorial Director; Moe, Security Director; Polish, work crew; Too short, work crew; Moon Raye, work crew; and Tab a hang around. Tab finally got a bike and was in the process of learning to ride it. Our membership was at its highest peak in numbers. There were three patch holders, our new chaplain, nine supporters, and one hang around, a grand total of fourteen. The club seemed to flourish with the new supporters and I had accomplished the image I wanted everyone to see, that the club was strong and healthy.

For the rest of the summer of 2004 we attended as many Red and Gold functions as we could in Alabama, Tennessee, Mississippi and Louisiana. The Highway Chicks were becoming either an icon or an eye sore. Nevertheless, we were becoming.

Bandido Dwayne, President of the Bandidos in Mississippi, was a stern, big man with a by-the-book disposition and a well-respected disposition. ABC and I managed to become good friends with him and eventually our entire club. He was friendly with us and showed us the same respect he gave his support clubs. I can look back and remember that one unforgettable day at Bandido Eating Ed's memorial service in Shreveport, Louisiana. That day, Bandido Dwayne made a remarkable statement to me in front of his brothers. There must have been at least 400 Bandidos at this church, which seemed dwarfed by the many bikers paying their last respects to a "Gone But Never Forgotten" (GBNF) brother. Bandido Dwayne was talking to a group of his brothers in the front steps of the Church. This group included Bandido Wiggs of Arkansas, an official Highway Chick hater.

As we walked past this group into the church, I made sure not to greet Dwayne and thereby avoid an awkward moment. However, as Bandido Dwayne saw us go by, he looked in our direction, loudly and wholeheartedly shouting, "It's the Highway Chicks, once again the only ones representing Arkansas." I playfully but underhandedly slapped him on his left shoulder as we quickly walked into the church. The look on Wigg's face was priceless. Once again, I smiled at the way other states took care of us as far as the MC world was concerned.

That summer of 2004, we developed a good friendship with the Mississippi Riders and the Pistoleros, Red and Gold support clubs for the Mississippi Bandidos. We had met them previously at the Mississippi COC meeting. Unlike our own state, they were very friendly with us and we became good alias and supporters of each other's events. Sort of like a close knit family. We would always attend the same events at other states and usually stick together. In reality, I daresay that the Highway Chicks were the first MC club to leave the State of Arkansas on a continuous basis to attend other Red and Gold events as far as political representation was concerned. We were the first ones to take Arkansas to the Red and Gold regional states as an MC club, for no one else other than one or two patch holders ever attended other MC functions. I am proud of that!

While ABC and I were at one of the COC meetings in Mississippi, I had a brainstorm. I knew that at the time the Highway Chicks were the only ones leaving the State to other MC functions. However, it was not my place to try to bring the Arkansas clubs into other States, but I asked myself, *"What if I bring other clubs into Arkansas and do it in a non threatening way?"* The reasoning was that if others states came into Arkansas, then Arkansas would be ethically compelled to visit their events and thus bring the regional motorcycle community working with each other in a non-threatening manner.

This was when the conception for the MC Officers Dinner was formulated. I knew Debbie T would not be interested in the politics of this idea so I talked to ABC about it on our way back to Arkansas from Mississippi after attending a COC meeting, as we rode in her mother's vehicle. I explained to her the operational strategy of the plan.

My approach was that the MC Officers Dinner would be an event hosted solely by the Highway Chicks, but I would subliminally word the invitation to portray it as a state sponsored event: as a friendly meet and greet party.

"I am going to personally pick out clubs who can benefit from coming to Arkansas as well as those whom we can also gain from. I will send them a personal invitation with an RSVP. I will assign a specific region to every one of our officers so they can follow up. We will invite clubs from different colors. The purpose will be two-fold: first, it will be to persuade Arkansas clubs to be reasonably compelled to visit out of state events, thus broadening the unity of bikers; and second, to continue to make our state a place of greeting and meeting new clubs for peaceful negotiations."

ABC's major concern was persuading Debbie T to accept this proposal because she was the club's President and it needed to go through her.

"Not to worry, ABC. You and I will present it to her as another regular, innocent party hosted by us girls just for fun. She cannot say no to that," I told ABC with a rather sinister tone.

After she heard the idea for the Officers Dinner, she thought it was a great idea and we began to work on our plan. This included repeated visits to Mississippi as frequently as every three weeks. We chose to attend almost every Red and Gold sponsored event and some others as well. We became good allies with Pistolerero President Jaime and his crew and better acquainted with the Alabama Riders MC, Southern Cross MC, the Dixie Renegades MC, the Dream Riders RA, and the Military Veterans MC.

Our home state knew that we had expanded our travels into neighboring states but was not fully aware of my intent and purpose. As long as I was a Highway Chick, I would try to make things better for all MC bikers as I purposely worked behind the scenes in order to accomplish this. People in other states liked us and always commended our manner of conduct as bikers. I was once asked by Bandido Jim 1% Louisiana, late 2004, "Are you the only ones that ever leave the state?"

I made it our main goal to get to know these bikers one-on-one and establish an intricate friendship with not only the Red and Gold clubs, but with as many MC clubs as I possibly could. I followed that old slogan of *"Keep your friends close and your enemies closer."* So even when the Arkansas Red and Gold clubs did not associate with a particular club because they were from the other side of the fence, I made it my goal to befriend them as a patch holder and acquire their comradeship and trust, a successful endeavor that paid off in the end.

In August of 2004, I approached Murray and volunteered to make the calendar of events for the Arkansas Coalition of Motorcycle Clubs. Up to this time, the Road Barrons had made the yearly calendar of events. They hosted a yearly calendar party where every club president or officer posted their events in a large table calendar. This prevented events from running into each other. The Road Barrons calendar party was not an ARCOMc function, but rather a private club party. Now that the Road Barrons were not in the coalition, and I had the graphic skills to put this calendar together, I volunteered the service.

"Murray, I can design the calendar from top to bottom. That includes artwork, design, information gathering, collating, folding, stapling, and distribution. I will guarantee you that it will look better than the previous one and we will sell three times the amount of calendars. It will save us money and all the profits will go to the coalition because I can do all the work myself."

Murray was hesitant but gave me the green light to proceed. I knew I could do this and my club needed the extra boost as far as ARCOMc participation was concerned. I said that we would also have to host the Calendar Party in order to gather the event information. I remember the look on his face to this date. It was kind of a perplexed gaze. He must have thought I was pushing it a little too far, but I had ambition. The kind of driven purpose that Admiral David Glasgow Farragut possessed when he chanted, *"Damn the Torpedoes, Full Speed Ahead."*

In January of 2005, I delivered the first batch of full color ARCOMc calendars to Bandido Murray. I created them from scratch on my kitchen table. However, on the back cover of the calendar it read that the Highway Chicks WMC had published it. This gave the club a much-needed boost.

Before we could catch our breath, September 18, 2004 had rolled in and that meant that the Highway Chicks Second Anniversary party was at hand. We leased a commercial building for our clubhouse. It was located at the junction of Hwy 7 and 5. It was Fountain Lake's first grocery store when the town was first founded. It was a monster of a building and required the same amount of work. It had a bar area, three large rooms, three bathrooms, a four car garage, a bunkhouse, and a basement. The property was large enough for 2 dozen tents. There was a storage building on the north side, and a year round running-water creek adorned the campground. Our lease was $600 per month plus utilities. We worked for 30 straight days painting and digging boats out of the yard that had been sitting for years and overtaken by weeds. Our supporter Robbie painted the inside and outside of the clubhouse in our club colors; blue and gray, with red, and gold accent areas. The only exterior sign was posted on two large glass windows that read "SYLB" (Support Your Local Bandidos). It was a house-warming present from an old friend, Big Rick.

On the building rooftop, side-by-side proudly flapped an American and an Arkansas flag. It was the largest Red and Gold clubhouse in the state. We had it and we were proud of it! The Highway Chicks had a strong optical impression of the presentation we needed to have in order to stay in the political game of the MC culture.

For the second anniversary, we created a themed Mari Gras party and it was an excellent notion. It was a colorful party atmosphere and obviously a different kind of biker party. We had a great turnout and our club seemed larger than it really was due to the number of supporters we had recruited. I had accomplished the visual effects of what I wanted other club members to see, a growing and prosperous club. It was at this party where Tab got her Prospect bottom rocker. After many months of ABC teaching her to ride a bike, she finally got the idea. The Highway Chicks now consisted of three officers, our Chaplain Punkin, one inactive member, one Prospect and nine supporters. A good show of force for any event that made us proud of our accomplishment.

The Arkansas clubs that most supported our events at this time were the Outsiders MC, the Vietnam Vets MC, the Boozefighters MC, and the Road Barrons MC. They would roll in large numbers and party like there was no tomorrow. (This was especially true of the Boozefighters). The other clubs eventually began slowly trickling in larger numbers to attend our events.

Some of the out-of-state clubs that we had been working with in Mississippi and Alabama began to attend our events in Arkansas. It raised the eyebrows of several of our own ARCOMc clubs. The local patch holders wondered why these MC clubs were coming from such long distance on their bikes to attend a Highway Chicks party. It had to be a conjecture on their part for only my boss Bandido Murray and SOS Brakeline, knew that we were expanding into neighboring states where other Red and Gold clubs were.

Upon returning to my home state, I would always bring Murray personal greetings from either the state president or a club officer, a practicing custom of an emissary representing his country. It was my intention from the very beginning to be fully aware that in every action I engaged upon was with all dignity and respect to the Arkansas Bandidos. Murray had appointed me the official secretary for the ARCOMc and as such, I was a proud diplomat.

Tab was a resident in Shreveport, Louisiana and as soon as she got her Prospect rocker, she began attending Bandido and support club events without our permission. As a new patch holder, she took this decision on her own and wandered into events and parties that were off limits to her as a Prospect. She did not inform the club of her non-sanctioned escapades. We were not aware how far she had been wandering off to.

Even with her unconventional behavior, she was an essential tool in our club and through her we met the Louisiana Bandidos and the Gray Ghosts MC. We attended most of their events and they came to Hot Springs for our parties. Eventually we became like brother and sister clubs and had many a good time at different rallies.

5
The Highway Chicks First Heart Patch
"I Support Bandidos MC Worldwide"

Fall had arrived and the trees were beginning to change colors. It was a little windy, but the days were hot and sunny. Arkansas is blessed with late summers. ABC and I continued to attend the Mississippi COC meetings and meet more and more patch holders. We nurtured the friendships we had cultivated that summer and felt more confident in our quest to become the real deal biker club.

During one of the COC meetings in Mississippi, Pistolero Jaime asked me, "Where is your Heart Patch?" ABC looked at me, I looked at her, and the only answer I could think of was, "They are in the process of being made."

"Well if you are a support club for the Bandidos you have to wear a Heart Patch, don't you?" asked Pistolero then, President Jaime, as he stood beside many other patch holders.

Whether he asked it as a challenge wanting to know if indeed we were a Bandido support club, or if he wanted to know why a support club did not have the Heart Patch, I do not know. All I can remember is that he caught me off guard and I did not want to step off into idiot mode. I could not spare at the expense of the Highway Chicks or Murray, that there had been resistance with us having a Heart Patch because we were women.

I had asked my boss, Bandido Murray if indeed we were a support club for the Bandidos in Arkansas. Each time his answer would be the same, "You are a support club." Oh, yes! He was very bold in telling us this; however, when asked by other club members, his answer would be slightly different, "The Highway Chicks support us."

A 1%'er once told me, "Sadgirl, if he would only come out and say, '*Yes, the Highway Chicks are a Bandido Support Club,*' then 50% of his problems would be solved because people would leave you alone. But he won't come out and give a straight answer."

In order to solve this situation, I asked Murray for a Heart Patch for our club in order to proudly show the world who we were, and to gain access into national events without having to have a sponsor. It was embarrassing having to wear a piece of duct tape with our sponsor's name handwritten with a black marker. Everyone knew we were a support club for the Bandidos and our loyalty was applauded by many. We had attended several national events and Bandido Jim always had to sponsor us inside the gate.

Murray took his time on this decision for he had his uncertainties as well. This was a verdict that was very serious and not to be taken light heartedly by anyone. Our own safety was on the line and Bandido Murray would face severe repercussions if the patch was dishonored in any way, but in the end, he granted us permission to sew on the round patch above our heart that read, "I Support Bandidos MC Worldwide". This was in November of 2004.

We were the first women motorcycle club to wear a Bandido Heart Patch. The little WMC out of Arkansas that Debbie T and I established, had accomplished what no other long term, existing female club could not. We wore the Red and Gold Heart Patch. We were an official authorized Bandido Support Club!

We were happier than a kid on Christmas, but many of the old school Bandidos did not share this same happiness with us. They were completely against a female MC to begin with, and even more enraged with the Heart Patch going on our cut. Thus began the continuous warfare between the old school Bandidos in Arkansas and the Highway Chicks WMC.

We did not let this damper our spirits. We continued to become a strong club and show the world we could be just as good as the male clubs. The Confederates MC were having a benefit in Shreveport, Louisiana. I thought it would be a good idea to attend and show off our Heart Patches. The Louisiana Bandidos and the Gray Ghost would be there and since we had become good friends, this would be a good place to go and intermingle with the other clubs and let them see the first female MC with a Bandido Support Heart Patch. With the courage of a thousand men and the disposition of a hungry elephant, we headed to Louisiana to meet Igo and his crew.

It was almost 9:00 pm and it was pouring rain by the time we walked into the bar where the event was taking place. Soaking wet from the long dark ride, we entered the bar and did we make some heads turn! Here were a bunch of girls dripping in rain with Bandido Support Patches on their cuts. It was a "Kodak"™ moment for many folks that night. We were there long enough to greet everyone and take pictures with Bandido Jim and our Heart Patches. He was proud of us and told us that we were deserving of the *ball* because we had worked very hard to earn it. The four of us, Debbie T, ABC, Tab, and I, posed for the momentous occasion. We were 'girls with balls.'

Shortly after that, we proceeded to do what we put down in our history book as "suicide night," and talked about for years to come. The riding order was as follows: Bandidos, Gray Ghosts, and Highway Chicks. The Louisiana Bandidos frequently allowed us to ride with them in the back of the pack. After a while, it became the norm to ride with them and the Gray Ghosts to national events. They did not have issues with us as our home state did.

The *scary* part on suicide night was that it was raining so hard that you could not see the vehicle in front of you. The *scarier* part was that Bandido Jim and his crew took off down the Interstate at 90 mph at 11:00 pm in this torrential down pour. The *scariest* part was that we did not want to be singled out as the Chicks that were not able to keep up, so we took off right behind them. We could not see shit, other than the cloud of water from the swerving biker in front of us with no taillights or rear fender. Talk about suicide! That night was it! It was a stupid and careless decision but the adrenaline was overpowering and by God, we were going to keep up at any costs, and we did! To this day I have never seen rain as awful as that night.

We arrived at the bar soaked, wet, and shivering in our leathers, for it was a cold night as well. We visited with the Louisiana crew and had our usual soft drinks but we never stopped shivering. It did not matter to us because we stood tall with the big boys and our Heart Patches to be seen by all. Suicide night was a productive but scary night for the Highway Chicks. Close to midnight, we all left for Tab's house for a good night's sleep.

In the last quarter of the year, ABC and I finalized the plans for our first officers dinner party at our clubhouse. She had confirmed RSVP's from at least 11 different attending club officers. I was getting a little anxious for I was not sure how Murray would react to this event. Surely, I did not want to get in trouble with my boss over MC presidents coming to our clubhouse from other states, but I was determined to make this happen.

ABC and I worked vigorously around the clock planning the dinner menu with its intent and purpose and we were confident that my motive would surely be carried out in full spectrum. We made sure that every worker understood the importance of this dinner and the manner in which we would serve these men. In the invitation, I specifically worded that the dinner was only for MC Officers and that club members, ol' ladies and prospects were not invited. Later on, we had to make allowances for 1%'er prospects who came to guard their presidents. Overall, the response was favorable with no one judging or criticizing our endeavor – at least openly.

I kept Brakeline informed of my progress, for his guidance and direction were indispensable tools for me in leading the club down the right path. He wrote:

From: Brakeline 1% SOS
Date: Mon, 18 Oct 2004 15:06:51 -0500

"You and your club really are doing an excellent job of bringing the ego maniacs together! LOL! Keep it up."

On the first week of December 2004, we hosted the first calendar party for the ARCOM. It was a gathering where all MC Presidents or Officers in charge brought their club events for the year and listed them in a desktop calendar. Everyone saw each other's events and this prevented stacking of parties. I took all the information home that evening and began the layout and graphic composite of the ARCOMc's first calendar of events. I did everything from my kitchen table and delivered a batch of professional calendar appointment books in January of 2005 to all members of the ARCOMc.

In spite of how well we conducted ourselves and the faithfulness of our devotion to the Arkansas Bandidos, Murray talked to Debbie T and me. He said he was having problems with his club in direct reference to our Heart Patch. His brothers thought that we should not wear it for we were a female club and it wasn't right. I pointed out to him that we had only worn it for two weeks and it wasn't fair to be biased just because we were women. Murray completely agreed with me but he was accountable to his club and had to do what was right in the best interest of his position.

After two weeks of proudly wearing the Heart Patch, we had to surrender it to Murray, who in turned gave them to the Thunderheads MC. At least we had the satisfaction of being the first female MC to wear it. We were extremely saddened and frustrated at having to surrender such a trophy, but I guess the Arkansas Bandidos weren't ready for us quite yet.

We received a better reception in Mississippi. Our website guestbook speaks for itself:

1090105-01-17 at 23:2155
Name: Bandido Probationary Mississippi Jim
Email address: withheld
Location: Jackson, MS

Comments: *Great to have Highway Chicks Sadgirl and ABC visit with us for the Mississippi COC meet in Jackson. Thanks for your support. It's great to see confederations support each other's meetings and spread the word about biker rights. Hope to see ya'll again. Ride hard and safe. Love, Loyalty and Respect, Bandido Probationary Mississippi Jim, Sec/*

Tres., Jackson Chapter, Chairman-Mississippi Confederation of Clubs.

110 0105-01-16 at 23:37:08
Name: Pistolero Kuzz
Email address: withheld
Location: Desoto County, Mississippi

Comments: *Wanted to thank HWY Chicks Sadgirl and ABC for attending the Mississippi COC meet Jan 15. Was good to finally meet and put faces with names. From what I've seen, your club goes beyond the normal call and puts that extra effort out. The HWY Chick will definitely grow with these efforts. Thanks for being with and look forward to many more meets in the future. Love, Loyalty and Respects, & Honor, Pistolero Kuzz, President Desoto County Chapter, Pistoleros MC "SYLB"*

The first MC Officers Dinner took place the second week of February of 2005. The following Club Presidents attended: Sons of Silence MC from Arkansas, Bandidos MC from Louisiana, Gray Ghost MC from Louisiana, Military Veterans MC from Kansas, Mississippi Riders RA from Mississippi, Dream Riders RA from Mississippi, Association MC from Arkansas, Next of Kin MC from Arkansas, Boozefighters MC from Arkansas, Vietnam Vets MC from Arkansas, Martyrs MC from Arkansas, 13 Rebels MC from Arkansas, and Road Barrons MC from Arkansas. There were twelve different MC club Presidents or Officers, including the Highway Chicks.

There weren't any Bandidos from Arkansas present so we (the Highway Chicks) were represented by Sons of Silence Brakeline. He also filled the role of Official Arkansas Diplomat for the out of state clubs that so graciously took time out to come into Arkansas to meet the local 1%'ers and club members. Brakeline greeted them and welcomed them to Arkansas. He took the time to converse with them and show kind hospitality.

All officers had assigned seats and were served a first class dinner and treated with the respect and honor they deserved. My club did a fine job of seeing to that. I remember later on during the month, I selectively made follow-up calls to different presidents to survey their opinion on the MC Officers Dinner. A particular one that stood out was Military Veteran National President, Dogbone. He specifically told me, "It was because of that dinner that we were able to resolve some problems in our home state."

That was later confirmed in an email sent to me by Brakeline.

From: Brakeline 1% SOS
To: hdsadgirl@yahoo.com
Mon, 7 Feb 2005 10:10:09 -0600

"I got a email message from DogBone of the MV and he wants to meet with me again when he comes down in March for your benefit and let me help him figure out how to correct some misunderstandings between his club and ours (out of state), as well as problems he is having with others. I'm sure I can help him, he is willing to listen, and more importantly act. **You can be proud of being responsible for bringing this about.** *If you get down with the blues just remember that the world is a better place for your being in it! Write or call back when and if you are up to it. GET WELL we all love you!"*

Although I was not able to be at the dinner due to being hospitalized for surgery, ABC did a great job of carrying my intent and purpose while turning the helm in the right direction. Brakeline did an exemplary job of representation for the State of Arkansas 1%'ers and MC members. He employed excellent public relations skills.

The Officers Dinner was a success but many Arkansas patch holders did not see the importance of this meet and greet opportunity. They failed to see the future results of the diplomatic target they themselves could have accomplished had they partook in it. I do not understand how an event of such political magnitude could have slipped from the male MC clubs for so long, for this was the first time so many MC presidents were gathered under one roof in an Arkansas clubhouse with a friendly disposition to exchange flyers and conversation. I was proud that the Highway Chicks and I had accomplished this task, but perplexed that the male MC clubs in our state had not attempted such an event in the past.

Of course, there were those critical club members who looked down at us and criticized everything we did. They said that it was not our place to do these kinds of events. They said that it was the job of the long term, male established MC clubs. If that was indeed true, then why had they not done it yet? What were they waiting for? For a bunch of girls to do it? Well, we did!

I was the vice president for our club at the time but had become an expert at over stepping my boundaries and sticking my nose where it did not belong. I did not receive a reprimand from Murray so I carried on with the Highway Chicks, full speed ahead!

As I said previously, I was in surgery as the officers dinner was taking place. I was not only in physical pain but I was heartbroken because I could not be at the dinner. The doctors had removed my left lung due to several untreated pneumonias from riding in the winter and developed a cancerous tumor. This event was the first one I had planned with a specific purpose and I was not there to see the results. I was stuck in ICU for the next 3 days and cried, not because I was in physical pain, but because I had missed the MC Presidents attending my clubhouse.

The first day I spent in a regular hospital room was still hazy due to the vast amount of pain medication I was taking. During the course of the day, there were always bikers in the room. I had never met some of them yet they came to visit. Flowers, plants and gifts adorned that small hospital room that was to be my home for the next two weeks. I vaguely remember falling asleep near or after lunch one afternoon shortly after the surgery. I dozed in and out throughout the day and felt like I would never get well.

I remember waking up and seeing 10 or 15 patch holders around my bed. I did not recognize them so my first thought was, "Great, now I have died and gone to heaven." I was somewhat excited because there were bikers in heaven so I knew it could not be hell. In my weak state, I tried to sit up as I partially smiled at the bikers in heaven. As I looked around the room, I saw ABC and Tab standing beside them.

"If ABC and Tab are here, then it can't be heaven! Damn it!" I said to myself.

Turns out that the Military Veterans MC and others had come to the hospital to personally meet and visit me. I was very glad that they were there although (thanks to the morphine in my I.V.) I do not remember much.

Debbie T insisted in having a benefit for me at the clubhouse and as much as I resisted, she got her way in the end. She hosted a successful benefit on March of 2005 and her effort and success in this endeavor was extremely outstanding. I was not able to work for 3 months and the money she raised covered my bills for that period.

The final count of patch holders, support members, civilians, and friends that came through our clubhouse's door that day for my benefit was 350. That has been the largest number of people at the clubhouse in one day ever. Patch holders attended from Alabama, Mississippi, Louisiana, Tennessee, Kansas, Texas, and of course Arkansas. Some local bar owners could not come to my benefit so they came to my house earlier that morning to bring their financial contribution. It was great to see so much love in the biker community and to see how many people knew who Sadgirl was. Debbie T did an amazing job at hosting this event.

The next day I got an email from Brakeline expressing his opinion about the benefit.

From: Brakeline 1% SOS
Date: Sun, 6 Mar 2005 00:30:07 -0600

"It was GOOD to see you even if for a short time. I enjoyed the party and I think its purpose of raising funds was a success! Let me know if you need ANYTHING! I talked to a lot of people tonight that really think the world of you and were very glad for the opportunity to show it! You can be proud to be the kind of person that inspires that kind of feeling in others. Now get well!"

It was an awesome thing to see so many people that cared about me. There must have been at least twenty different MC clubs at our clubhouse that day for my benefit. All of them were fed and treated with the utmost respect by Debbie T and the Highway Chicks.

Tab finally patched out on this day, March 5 of 2005. It was a brief ceremony at my home in my back yard. The Swamp Riders MC were present to witness the occasion. Her daddy is a member of said club.

The Hard Tail Riders MC and Rusty Spoke Custom Cycle also held a benefit for me at the city plaza in Alpena, Arkansas.

The following month, on April 18, of 2005, the Sons of Silence President introduced a new Support Club for the Sons of Silence in Arkansas, at the Coalition meeting. Brakeline had retired his presidency due to health problems.

"This new support club for the Sons of Silence will be an MC club from the start because that is the way it is done at a national level. They want to be a part of this coalition and even thought they wear the MC patch, they will be expected to do a year probation just as everybody else does. The Sons are responsible for them and they are a support club for the Sons. Brakeline is in charge of looking after the club. The bottom rocker will say CENTRAL ARKANSAS but it is not a done deal. If you have a problem, please come and talk to me," said the new President as he introduced the new club to everyone. (This statement is recorded in the ARCOMc minutes for this month).

I was proud of the Sons and the attitude they assumed. They steadfastly told the ARCOMc the decision they had taken concerning their new support club. They did not ask permission. The Sons of Silence were not like the other clubs. They did what they said and they meant what they said. They never stepped back once a decision was made and their solidarity was solid.

Surprisingly though, a vote was taken that same night and all presidents and representatives at that meeting voted in favor of the Silent Few MC joining the coalition immediately, and without public litigation to the bottom rocker, although our understood and agreed guidelines said that, all new clubs must be on probation for one year without an MC or a bottom rocker.

Brakeline was not able to be at the ARCOMc meeting so I let him know it went well and there was no resistance encountered. He wrote:

From: Brakeline 1% SOS
Date: Tue, 19 Apr 2005 12:08:47 -0500

"I'm finally at the lake, same place as before, site #44. YOU ARE MORE THAN WELCOME! I'll be there till the 27th. Your company would be a pleasure.

The Support club is a done deal; putting on patches as soon as they are made. Miss our talks and sharing of knowledge. You are a rock for me to latch on to in a stormy sea! Love ya!"

The summer of 2005 added some new members to the club. They were all friends of Debbie T except Rattles. She was Brakeline's ex old lady and a former supporter of the Sons of Silence. She wanted to become a prospect for the Highway Chicks and although I knew she would never make it, I did grant her the opportunity to give it a try. Rattles knew that Brakeline and I were very close friends and I believe that in her desperate attempt to win him back, she sacrificed her beliefs and convictions to ingress in a Red and Gold support club. I couldn't condemn her in the effort to win her lost heart, the man she loved, for I would have done the same. I feel that I would not have done her justice if I didn't let her try.

She was with our club for approximately six months before she realized that Brakeline was not giving her the attention she so desperately sought. I sponsored her into the club and the day she quit, she handed me her vest with her Prospect rocker sewed on, as she sat at Lucky's Bar and Grill with tears streaming down her face.

Another new member was Sammy. She was a wild one we named Short Fuse. She was about 5 feet tall with a quick temper and a huge bike. She was so little that when she rode on the Interstate at 85 mph, the wind would toss her back and forth like a ping-pong ball. The others girls were afraid to ride beside her. She was the mule of the club because she was always messing up. This caused her prospect time to extend more and more. She was a good labor hand. She lasted about a year and a half for she could never get out of the prospect period or keep up with her dues. Debbie T and I would humorously tell her that she was going to receive a 10-year prospect pin.

The Highway Chicks seemed to be growing at a fast pace and although it was not healthy, it was what we needed as a club. We had great times together and our friendship appeared to be genuine. Debbie T and I had different goals for our club but our comradeship was tight. At club events we put on a façade but when it was just us girls, we always seem to have a great time and just be ourselves.

6
The Highway Chicks Second Heart Patch
"I Support Bandidos MC Worldwide" *Again*

In the summer of July 2005, we received our second Heart Patch from Bandido Murray. It was just like the previous one except that it had two red roses on the bottom of it. Bandido Stubbs 1% Nomad specifically designed it for the Highway Chicks. We had become good friends with him and he knew where my heart truly was. He knew that we went beyond the call of duty as a Red and Gold support club. Murray had approved it and for the second time we received the long sought-after, visible token of our loyalty to the Bandidos.

These Heart Patches designed distinctively for the Highway Chicks, were once again displayed with ultimate pride. With earnest bliss, we sewed them on our Cut right above the heart position. We even followed the stitch pattern from the previous Heart Patch. Once again, we were the real deal. We were the Highway Chicks WMC, an official Bandido support club (with roses and all). For sure, this time I was convinced we did the right protocol and there was no holding us back.

I kept Brakeline updated on my progress and made sure my decisions and plans were not a breach of protocol. I informed him on the status of our new Heart Patch. His opinion at the Heart Patch ordeal was straightforward at me. I remember him asking me, "Why would you want to support a group of people that don't want your support?" He asked this because he had heard the resistance Murray's brothers were giving him. Personally, I was not aware of how difficult they had made it for Murray causing him so much heartache. I was totally unaware of how much the Arkansas Bandidos did not like us. They were extremely hostile to us whenever they saw us and made sure they showed it.

I had chosen for the Highway Chicks to become a Bandido support club primarily because it was Bandido Murray who stood behind us and sanctioned us to be a motorcycle club. Secondly, I believed that belonging to a franchise (per se) would bestow the needed credibility that a new female MC needed to start with a solid foundation.

My answer to Brakeline was quick and clear-cut. "Because they are the only ones I have found that will take a female support club and we need that regime to stay safe and in the game." He understood my perspective. However, many of the old school bikers did not share his amity towards us and had many negative, insulting remarks towards us. Brakeline shared his perception concerning the Red and Gold Heart Patch in an email he sent me.

From: *Brakeline SOS 1%*
Date: *Fri, 26 Aug 2005 08:09:34 -0500*

"It really seems like the choice is about just how hard core everyone wants to be and what they are willing to do to accomplish it. There are not a lot of choices out there for you to join up with and support in the first place. You can't support a group that will not have your support, and you are lucky that the group you want to be a part of also wants you. Very Lucky! Love romance, and other relationships all depend on a two-way relationship and usually fail because it's not found.

You and the RED and Gold have found that two-way relationship and I'm telling you that it is rare in the 1%'er female support club situation you are in. If that is your goal then you had better go for it and make it work because there may not ever be another chance as good as this one. With that said, everyone should be sure the hardcore style is what they want.

If they really just want a care free, fun loving, ride in the wind with their sisters and not all the problems, trouble, law enforcement hatred, club rivalries, and everything else that goes along with being part of the 1%'er world (even as a support element), then they should back out now and not commit any more that they have, because to let the Red and Gold down later after pledging to support them, would lose the friends you now have. In plain words, make sure you understand and want the commitment and make it or don't make it, but don't wobble back and forth. That would be worse than either choice of wearing or not wearing the Heart Patch."

I completely understood what it meant to be a Bandido Support Club and the entire ladder of accountability. I didn't know the Bandido Nation as a whole but I knew Bandido Murray and he was a good man, and a 35-yr club member. In that perspective, my loyalty to the Red and Gold was principally because of Murray.

It was indeed extremely rare that a 1% club like the Bandidos would allow us this privilege. In reality, it was Murray taking full responsibility for this action, and not his club or his brothers. Brakeline knew the commitment and the honor we were bestowed upon. He knew the consequences and the marking that would follow if we let the Bandidos down. That is why I always tried so hard to do my best.

With our new Heart Patches, we expanded our travels further into our regional states for we were more confident that our host club would stand behind us. It was enthralling that our accountability was to a special group of men, the Bandidos in Arkansas.

The Arkansas bikers directly involved in our circle were getting word of the Highway Chicks "being everywhere." That put some of our brothers into shame, so they also began traveling outside Arkansas. The other Red and Gold Support Clubs in our state did not want to be compared to the Highway Chicks nor did they want us to take their place.

It was intriguing though, the many times we introduced our Arkansas brothers to other patch holders including those not from the Red and Gold world. We were becoming a bridge between Arkansas and the regional states. We had earned the respect of many and we worked very closely with our neighboring states to promote the Red and Gold colors in our home state.

It was kind of funny because at the beginning of the travels of the Red and Gold Arkansas support clubs, they would call me up and ask for the clubhouse location as well as a place to stay. We always made sure that they were taken care of on the other side and had a place to stay that was safe.

Finally! I had achieved what I was after, interpersonal relationships with other MC clubs. Of course, I knew we'd never get the credit but I didn't care. THE RESULTS ACHIEVED WERE GREATER THAN THE GLORY DESERVED! There were many instances where individual brothers would come up to me and privately acknowledge that it was because of the Highway Chicks that they were now leaving the State of Arkansas to attend other club functions. *"You'll never get the credit for the accomplishments you have achieved, but you know that you have done it and that's what is important,"* said Brakeline to me one evening as we casually sat in his media room.

Debbie T still didn't care for the politics and bullshit that came with the title of president, so she let me handle it all. I became the official spokesperson and representative for the club while Debbie T sat back and enjoyed a cold beer. It was a good arrangement for all of us. When I wasn't sure of an action, I would always consult with Brakeline and he'd point me in the right direction. He continued to be my counselor and his guidance was precise, always bringing about the desired results. If no one else knew where I was or what I was doing, Brakeline did. He took the time to school me in the ways of the MC world, for the Arkansas Bandidos other than Murray, did not want to talk to us or even greet us. We tried very hard to be respectful to them and show them that our mission was to support them in any way we could, regardless of their attitude.

Our rags had several Red and Gold patches clearly visible at any angle. That summer I designed a special patch for the Highway Chicks. It was in Bandido colors and it read *"Love, Loyalty, Respect, por Vida."* I chose to add the Spanish words *Por Vida* (for life) because after all "Bandido" is a Spanish word. This patch would be exclusively for our club and we would wear it in a vertical position on the right side of our Cut. It was approved by Murray with the condition that we change the colors to "support" colors. We did. The patch was such a huge success and made such a good impression in the other support clubs that we decided to share it with other Red and Gold Support Clubs. In dealing with other MC clubs, I was very careful not to compromise the integrity of the Arkansas Bandidos or my boss. My mentorship with Brakeline was private and no one knew about it other than Debbie T, so his name or club was never compromised.

All of the Arkansas Bandidos were completely against us getting our Heart Patch except Murray. He went out on a limb for us and respectfully allowed the Highway Chicks to wear it, but was catching too much heat from his brothers for his decision. One evening, as I arrived at the pool tournament in Little Rock, he said he needed to talk to me. As I walked into Long Branch Saloon, I felt that if looks could kill, then I would have died that day, for some of the Red and Gold old school bikers gave me the dirtiest looks only a scolded dog deserves. I could feel the tense hostility as they looked down on me. Murray and I walked to the back of the building. I knew he was having a hard time trying to say what he didn't want to say. Murray knew that we were a hard working club and we went beyond the mile for the Red and Gold Nation in Arkansas. The truth of the matter was that he was accountable to his brothers and he had to do what he had to do.

"I have been taking a lot of slack from my brothers because of the Heart Patch that I gave you. I know you deserve it even more than some of the other support clubs but I am not going to get in a fistfight with my brothers over this, and this is what it seems it's going to come to, Sadgirl. Now…, you might have to take it off for a while until we can figure something out. You are just going to have to keep doing what you're doing and maybe a few years down the road they will see and things will change," he said to me.

"Murray! Not again!" I exclaimed in a whiny tone. "This is the second time we're going to have to do this and it sucks." I added.

"Yeah, I agree. Right now you can keep it on but you might have to take if off again," said Murray in a firm manner. I pouted a bit and made a sad face but told him to keep me updated. I didn't want his brothers to stop me and yank the patch off. He smiled and said that he would most definitely keep me informed. He also told me to be respectful and not have an attitude with any of his brothers that might approach me.

"Me? An attitude?" I said to him as I pointed at myself and laughed. Murray knew me and he knew I could get bossy with the wrong people.

I knew then and there that it would be sooner than later before the stitch holes where the Heart Patch proudly displayed in our Cut, would once again stare at everyone in the face. I did not share this conversation with my club sisters in order to keep a high morale. However, I made sure we took plenty of pictures and had Debbie T plaster them on our website. I wanted everyone to see that the Highway Chicks proudly wore a Heart Patch even if for a short time. It was history in the making and I was proud to be a part of it. It was my endeavor to go to as many places as we could and show off the Heart Patch before it was taken away again.

That month we managed to recruit two new members in our club. Phat Girl was a hang around who lasted only a few months. She did not have a bike and there was too much drama in her life, a virtue that the Highway Chicks did not need or want. She was Debbie T's friend so we made her a supporter and she worked at our events. Eventually she faded away.

Then there was Curve. She was a lovely girl with a soft spirit and completely naïve about the MC world. Debbie T was her sponsor; however, I schooled her in the ways of the MC world. She was a grand asset to the club for her humble spirit made it easy to work with. However, along with her membership in the club came a vast amount of conflict, not directly involving her but her husband.

Labor Day weekend 2005 had rolled in and we arrived at Gilliam, Louisiana for Bandido Jim's Labor Day Blowout racing event on Saturday afternoon. The aroma of hickory-smoked meat being grilled by the Gray Ghost MC was deliciously pleasant. We rolled into the compound and I could see the eyes of patch holders staring in our direction, particularly at the Heart Patch that Bandido Stubbs had designed for us. We dismounted our bikes and walked with pride in the fact that we were the first female Bandido support club with a Heart Patch given to us by Bandido Murray. This time we had complete confidence that we'd gone through the proper channels and protocol. If someone wanted to take our Heart Patch or had a problem with it, they'd have to go through Bandido Murray.

We made our way through the crowd to visit with our Red and Gold family and guests. The band was loud and it didn't seem to bother anyone. Drunken citizens danced aimlessly around the picnic tables and appeared to be having a good time. Couples were also drinking and dancing and those of us who didn't drink sat back and enjoyed the performance.

I had been on the anxious side and I had a feeling something was wrong. It wasn't long after that, just as I had expected—the phone call came in. It was Murray wanting us to wait for him at the party site. He was on his way back from a funeral in Texas. I didn't tell Debbie T my fearful conclusions for I didn't want her to panic and get paranoid about being in the compound. Nevertheless, I knew that Murray was coming to inform us that we had to take our Heart Patches off for the second time.

When he finally arrived at the Gilliam Racetrack, it was almost 11 o'clock at night and he seemed tired and stressed. He said he needed to talk with us.

"Ahhh…, I'm sure you already know what this means." I whispered to Tab as we each grabbed a chair from the barn and made a circle in the field nearby with Bandido Murray in the middle of the circle.

He appeared to be worn out and extremely tired. His voice, full of regret and hesitation, gently journeyed in our direction. He told us that we had to take the Heart Patch off because his brothers just weren't quite ready for the change in women wearing a Bandido Support Heart Patch. He praised us and commended our actions, travels, and effort in conducting ourselves as patch holders. He stressed how some of his brothers were old school who just didn't approve of us. They were making his life miserable for the decision he had taken when he approved our Heart Patch.

Once again, I felt like I had been dropped from a 10,000 feet free fall, and my stomach was one big knot. Here we were back to square one after all the effort we had put into our endeavor. Nevertheless, I knew it was coming and had prepared myself emotionally for it. Debbie T on the other hand, was completely taken by surprise and all she could say to Murray was "I don't understand." The fact of the matter was that she really did not understand. She had made many financial and social sacrifices and did not expect to have the rug pulled out from under her again.

"Can we at least keep the patches on until we get to Tab's house so we can leave here with dignity and not shame?" she asked Murray. He told her yes. I was glad my President made that request for it spared us being the "talk of the town" for years to come. Murray did encourage us to continue to do what we were doing. He said we should prove to his brothers that they were wrong. He told us that it might take years to do this, but if we kept doing what we were doing, they would someday see that we could be a strong club.

That night we rode with our Heart Patches for the last time. When we arrived at Tab's house, we had an informal church meeting and attempted to figure out all the politics of the MC clubs in the men's world. However, no matter what findings we came up with, the fact remained that we had to do as we were told. We did have the choice to stand up, go to war, in order to keep our Heart Patch. Considering that most of us had small children at home, resistance was futile. In actuality, we were not ready to die for our Colors and that was the concrete difference between the old school bikers who established the MC rules and us.

They had proven their Colors and we had not. They had buried many brothers for the sake of their Colors, and we had not. They had fought and earned the right to fly their patch and we had not. That was the concrete difference between them and us, and they were right. We had the luxury of a smooth birth and an easy ride while the old school bikers had ridden the tough and ragged roads sometimes leaving their blood on the pavement.

The extremist Polish Revolutionary, Felix Dzerzhinsky wrote in

September of 1917: "*A revolution, a real profound 'people's' revolution to use Marx's expression, is the incredibly complicated and painful process of the death of the old and the birth of the new social order, of the mode of life of tens of millions of people. Revolution is most intense, furious, desperate class struggle and civil war. Not a great single revolution in history has taken place without the civil war.*" Quoted in George Leggett, The Cheka: Lenin's Political Police (Oxford 1981) p. xxxii.

Mr. Dzerzhinsky's quote is a straight reference to the war, nevertheless, he makes the point that to bring about a new change for a group of people, demands a civil struggle in order to eradicate the old mode of life. The Highway Chicks were not ready for this type of engagement. We talked tough and acted like badass bikers, but none of us were ready to go to war with the Bandidos, much less die for the privilege of wearing that Heart Patch.

The problem was that at the time I did not understand this concept. If only I had studied Brakeline's email to Association MC President, perhaps I would have understood what he meant when he said,

"*Debbie keeps saying she doesn't want confrontation and that she is not competing with the men's clubs. (She really means this). Well I don't see it that way. She wants EXACTLY what we have but wants to hide behind the WMC patch so she doesn't have to fight for and earn it! Just like in the late 60's & early 70's when the 1%'ers and those wanting to be 1%ers all were fighting (and sometimes died) for these rights. The clubs and independents who wanted to fly a real patch, but not have to fight for and earn the right to do so, hid behind the Abate and religious name tags to avoid the conflict and "trial by fire" to have the right to wear their patch. The hard-core element in the lifestyle left them along because hiding behind those institutions to have the right to wear a patch took away the pride and what the patch stood for anyway.*

I feel this is exactly what the Highway Chicks are doing. They want what we have but don't want to take the chance of having to fight for it and are taking the SAFE way to a "three piece territorial" patch without earning it or having to back it up. Well the 1%ers will leave them along just as we do the ABATE, HOG, CMA's and etc. but the patch doesn't carry much of our respect when obtained that way. ...To have true re-

spect, they have to fight and die for the patch if needed…"

Brakeline's email described in detail exactly what the Highway Chicks were: *"A SAFE way to a 'three piece territorial' patch without earning it or having to back it up."* When we didn't stand and fight for our Heart Patch, we fell in the same category as the non-mc clubs. We fell into the category of a safe-zone riding organization. In reality, we were just not ready for the real thing and that was the fact. We proved it when we took our Heart Patch off at Bandido Murray's order. As much as he wanted to help us due to his good-natured will, his brothers were right. The Highway Chicks had not gone through that "trial by fire" that every patch holder earns. I didn't see it at the time but those were the essentials in relation to our club. That day, instead of trying to become stronger, we should have taken our Colors off and retired them with pride, but we fallaciously pressed on to become what we could never be.

ABC was the most upset of all and the only one who had the correct judgment on the situation. She was vocal in stating her opinion and suggested to us not being a Bandido support club at all. She said we should not support anyone and just ride for fun and for ourselves. Debbie T and hang around Curve agreed with her, but Tab and I couldn't. We wanted to remain a Bandido Support Club even without our Heart Patches. The two of us were more determined than ever to continue to wear our Red and Gold patches and even more determined to add more on our rags. I told the club that if we backed out just because our Heart Patch was taken away for the second time, then we'd been known as the girls who quit because they couldn't hang. As long as I was in the club, I was not going to allow it. That night we voted to become stronger supporters of the Bandidos MC and even more devoted in our quest of becoming the first female Bandido support club again (and for the third time).

Before we took off our Heart Patches, we took a last photograph as we proudly stood in Autumn's bedroom. The following Monday I personally turned them in to Murray, all except one, which we kept as proof positive.

I let Brakeline know what had happened. His response was quick.

From: Brakeline SOS 1%
Mon, 5 Sep 2005 12:04:15 -0500

"As for the Heart Patch, I really hate to see it come to having to turn it in, but how can you support a club, and I mean each and everyone in the club, if they don't want your support or maybe in some instance resent your support? An offer of support is more than just pride in wearing the same colors. It is a gift of a promise to watch someone's back and to have that rejected is a serious loss to the person or club who refused the honor. You and your fellow members can take pride in the fact that you kept up your end and failed at nothing. You are still able to say you wore the "Heart Patch" with pride, deserved it, and lost it not for anything lacking on your part but from politics. Life sucks!

I've been kicked in the teeth by my own club for doing what was right more than once, but in the end after the dust settled and hurt feelings had time to heal, others saw that I had risen above doing something just to gain approval and done what was right, and in the end the years of respect it has gained me has been worth it. Don't quit carrying on the way you have been and with time, everyone will see (even if they don't admit it) that you were indeed worthy of that "Heart Patch" regardless of how things turned out. You may share some of these words (but not the whole letter! LOL) with others in your club who may feel let down by all this. You are all tops in my book!"

The reality is that we didn't get the Heart Patch simply because we were women. Had we fought for it, perhaps we would have kept it. Politically, we did everything that was expected of us and beyond. The Arkansas Bandidos had the old school biker mentality that a women's place is in the kitchen or with her old man on the back of his bike.

7
For Better... For Worse!

By the time September 17 of 2005 came around, we were fully staffed and ready for our third annual. The theme for this year would be a Luau. We went overboard buying all kinds of decorations, food and drinks. We spent a lot of time planning for a great turnout. I knew there would be many people that really liked us and we expected them to attend. We hired a band, stripper girls and had a full bar. We were known for "throwing a hell of a party." We knew how to plan an unforgettable event.

Highway and Hedges Motorcycle Ministry did a lot of work for us since at the time they were part of the Highway Chicks. The Gravediggers MC arrived on Friday afternoon, pitched their tents and worked the entire weekend. Other support workers were Curve, Half Breed, Wizard, Kathy, and Robbie. By this time, we had four patch holders, three prospects, four supporters, and Highway and Hedges MM. We appeared to be sailing full speed ahead, strong as ever, except that we no longer wore the Heart Patch. We had a great party and many out of state clubs joined us. Bikers from all over camped out in tents and RV's in the clubhouse's backyard.

Patch holders rolled in by the dozen all wanting that perfect photo opportunity of showmanship. The Boozefighters were supportive and attended in large packs. They always won the trophy for most MC attending in numbers. Conversations were the usual, next events, pool tournaments, who had the balls to fly a patch without permission, who was in control of whom, and so forth. There were the typical private meetings that always seemed to be for power and control. Who had it? Who stole it? And who did it really belong to? Several out of state clubs came just to party with us and others wanted to see Brakeline, but by this time, his health did not permit him to join us.

We had incorporated Red and Gold Colors in our patch. We were determined one way or another to fly the colors. If they wouldn't let us have the Heart Patch, they could at least let us have Red and Gold in our vests.

Tab's visits to Jim's bike shop became frequent. In fact, it seemed that she had the need to visit almost on a daily basis. ABC described her perception of how she began to change as a person and a patch holder.

"Tab started changing the first day we went to see Jim Owens at his shop. She started getting all flirty and interested in hanging around more of the Bandidos. She would tell me she was working late, but she would be out at the shop drinking and hanging out with the boys (or whatever they did in the shop). I have many suspicions that she did more than hang out. She started messing around with Spokes (not his real name to protect club identity), and would not listen to reason. Granted, part of me wanted her to stop because we were still in a relationship. However, the common sense part of me told her to stop because he was trying to be a 1%'er and he was married. I didn't think it looked good. His wife was vocal enough to be a problem and Spokes (not his real name to protect club identity), didn't have the balls it would take to keep her shut up. It blew up as I told her it would. I even tried to talk to her as Sergeant at Arms and let her see that this was not appropriate in light of the world we ran in. She thought she was above harm, above discipline, and just untouchable; and apparently, she was. Giving her another week of probation did nothing but fuel her 'bad girl' opinion of herself. We should have stripped part of the patch off and given her another six months probation or something more. Maybe that would have helped get her in line."

ABC was right. Tab assumed the attitude of invincible and above harm. The power of the patch got to her head and she thought she was a super biker. Debbie T was still the President but she was not in tune to the power struggle that was occurring. I was too busy striving for a spot in the MC world and therefore neglected my own club members. We should have put our priority in our own club before we tried to climb to higher places.

Tab began riding to different MC events by herself. Half the time we didn't know where she was. She did not seek a club officer's permission. She seemed to follow the Louisiana Bandidos and the Gray Ghost MC everywhere they went. She might have been safe with them, but we did not know where she was and that looked bad on our club. Tab appeared to be promoting herself instead of following the appropriate protocol for the Highway Chicks. She got away with it for a long time because her residency was in Shreveport, Louisiana and none of us were there to mentor her. She was retrieving information from them and withholding it to use at her convenience. I saw this as a willful act of insubordination, and a threat to the Highway Chicks. The only good thing that came out of this manner of conduct was that the Louisiana crew became very close comrades with us, especially the Gray Ghosts MC.

Their hospitality and friendship was very comforting compared to the coldness and animosity the Arkansas crew showed us. We utterly enjoyed and took advantage of their kindheartedness. Bandido Jim and Bandido Nomad Stubbs 1% both have a wonderful disposition and excellent experience as 1%'ers. I took full advantage of their alliance and absorbed their knowledge.

I began to see turmoil stirring within our club. It was just as ABC had professed, "Everyone had their own agenda." Debbie T was only interested in riding and partying, I was totally focused in achieving a secure place within the Red and Gold world. Tab's efforts were in promoting herself, and ABC wanted to ride and create a strong sisterhood. All the others followed. This turmoil was too insignificant in my eyes to address the issue. Therefore, it was buried and ignored; a big blunder on my part. I forgot that discipline begins at home while ignoring the golden rule that states, "If your house isn't in order, nothing is."

In October of 2005, Brakeline appointed a new President for the Sons of Silence in Arkansas. The new change of office was good because I considered Mitch to be a very smart and solid man. He understood the ways of the MC world and knew how to handle his club affairs. Many of my brothers hated him and spoke ill of him. That really bothered me because the people who talked about him did not know him. They were only looking at his Colors.

"Mitch is going to be my main man and remain firmly in the driver's seat," said Brakeline with full confidence. Mitch would lead the Sons of Silence Arkansas Chapter into the glory that Brakeline could not because of his health. This was a good change for everyone.

On November of 2005, I headed up to Jonesboro, Arkansas for the Association's annual toy run. I took Prospect Curve and Rattles with me. The event had a great turnout as it did every year. The traveling distance to this Toy Run was three and a half hours. It was a tradition I adapted when riding with the Road Barrons. The Association had great music, excellent food and exceptional southern hospitality, but it also had Road Barron Ben Taylor. The man who told the Arkansas Road Barrons they could no longer be a part of the ARCOMc because we (the Highway Chicks) were in it.

I gave Prospect Curve a quick and condensed overview of who he was just in case there was trouble. I wanted her to be able to know what to do. I knew Mr. Taylor and it was only a matter of time before he spoke to me. And so, I was right. As I was standing outside the clubhouse with my Prospect, Ben signaled me to go where he was. I wasn't in the least bit intimidated or afraid; however, I did deliberate whether I should be friendly or hostile. I chose the friendly conduit since it is the path of least resistance.

I walked to where he was, smiled very big and hugged him. "Good to see you Ben. How you been?" I said in a jolly tone. He took a puff of his joint after hugging me back and said, "Listen, I didn't mean for things to turn out like they did. You have proven yourself and have earned the respect of many. I still believe this is a man's world but I do apologize."

I immediately accepted his apology. I turned and saw the grin on Prospect Curve's face. That meant a lot to me for it takes a real man to admit his shortcomings. We chatted for a few minutes and then we went our separate ways until I saw him once again at the Road Barrons Christmas party in Little Rock.

Christmas in the biker community meant that it was time for the yearly ABATE Toy Run in Little Rock. This event was always included in the ARCOMc calendar. A Toy Run is an organized parade of motorcycles where each rider brings a new unwrapped toy for a child. At the end of the parade, the toy is dropped off and a civic organization distributes them to needy families.

The Arkansas Bandidos have always participated in this yearly event and now it had become an ARCOMc event. On that cool December morning we were to meet Bandido Murray at Long Branch Saloon at 11 am, and catch up with the ABATE parade at the Scott Hamilton I-30 exit. At 11:45. Murray told us to saddle up for it was time to leave. The attendance of ARCOMc members was scarce. The Bandidos were the only 1% club at the meeting location and the Highway Chicks were the only Bandido support club. The only other two clubs were the Martyrs and the Probationary Gravediggers. Legally and by MC protocol, we were the next riding club behind the Bandidos. The departing line up was in the following order: Murray and another Bandido beside him, the Highway Chicks, the Martyrs, the Probationary Gravediggers, and then the citizens. That put me right behind Murray. There were bikes everywhere since many people were on their way to the Toy Run.

We took off and a few miles down the road, we were intercepted by The Sons, The Silent Few, and the Thunderheads. I didn't move my eyes from Murray who was directly in front of me because I figured that this bunch of bikes were citizens on their way to the Toy Run. But it wasn't. Before I had a chance to realize who they were, they forced their way into the front position directly in front of me, by cutting into the line. As soon as I could react, and after swerving to the right to avoid being hit by one of them, I backed off and slowed down enough to allow them to cut in without having to run the whole pack over.

A few Thunderheads followed the Sons but they slowed down and motioned for me to break into their pack. That put me in with the Thunderheads but left the rest of the Highway Chicks in the back.

I didn't think anything of the situation for I knew that it was a technical oversight on my part. I never did take my eyes off Murray to see who the approaching bikers were. It had become my habit throughout the years, not to look over and acknowledge who the biker rolling down the highway was. It was a trademark of the Highway Chick's riding attitude, and therefore not an intentional action to disrespect anyone. But we were accused of disrespecting the 1%'ers intentionally by one women hater. It seems like we were constantly getting in trouble by a few who had refused to accept that women do ride motorcycles in this day and age.

In the following weeks, we continued to work on becoming more and more like the men's MC. We wanted the same merits without the time invested that Murray had asked of us. So in total desperation and acting on the advice of two out of state Bandidos, we put on the '13 Motorcycle' Diamond Patch in our own colors, blue and gray. We didn't ask anyone in our state. At the time, I didn't realize the stink it would cause.

For three weeks, we rode around with our new diamond patch and acted like big shots. We even went to Mississippi and Louisiana with it and unbelievably, were congratulated. But one Monday night at a pool tournament at Long Branch Saloon, a Sons of Silence member whose name I shall omit, noticed it and reported it to his President, Mitch. I was immediately tagged down asked, "Who gave you guys' permission to wear that Diamond?" I told Mitch the names of the two Bandidos who gave us permission.

His reaction was diplomatically firm as he said to me. "Those people are from out of state and you are from Arkansas. Why are you taking orders from people out of state? Did Murray say you can wear it?"

"No. But he's never said anything to me and he's seen me quite a bit," I quickly answered him.

"You got to take it off. That's not going to fly. It's a Diamond and that is for 1%'ers or support clubs only. You got to take it off," said Mitch in a firm tone.

I told him I would talk to Murray about it and insolently walked off. Once again, I was angry at our efforts being shut down especially by a non Red and Gold person. I didn't understand this part of the MC protocol, and therefore embarrassed myself and my club as well as the Red and Gold Nation in Arkansas, by putting on the Diamond Patch without permission.

Looking back, Mitch had every right to demand action of his request. In reality he could have, and should have yanked it off at that moment, but out of respect to Murray, he didn't.

When I got home, my phone rang. The caller ID said "Mitch calling". Once again, he told me that we had to take that patch off. I responded, "Mitch, you are not my boss and I am not taking it off." Then I rudely hung up on him. My insolent respond to his request started a cloud of hostility between the Sons and the Highway Chicks.

Why Mitch didn't shut us down? I don't know. Murray should have pulled us aside and pulled our bottom rocker, but he didn't. We were allowed to get away with much more than, if it were the guys. All Murray told me was that Mitch was a 1%'er and I had to listen to him. I argued with Murray, "But he's not my boss." Murray kept repeating, "But he's a 1%'er". After arguing back and forth, Murray finally told me to take off the 13 Motorcycle Diamond Patch.

We'd lost another patch and this time it wasn't by our brother's hand… but by a patch holder from the opposite side of the fence. This incident quickly spread to regional Red and Gold clubs. I have my suspicions that my one of our members that lived out of state had a lot to do with it because she could not keep her mouth shut.

I had begun a cold war and didn't know it. The Red and Gold Support clubs and some of the neighboring out of state Bandidos wanted to know what was going on with the Sons in Arkansas. They wanted to know why they constantly picked on us and why were they telling us what to do. They also inquired about Murray's role in the whole ordeal. I informed them of the circumstances just as they happened and never added or took away from the facts. In actuality,

I should have told them it was none of their business because it was an Arkansas issue. But I was an ignorant, angry woman and I was determined to make it right for me.

This was one incident where I did not consult Brakeline for his direction. I was so frustrated over losing another patch that I didn't stop to think. I believe that had I done so, I would have understood Mitch's demand and subsided. Perhaps if Murray had taken the time to tell me why we could not wear this patch, it wouldn't have gotten to this point. But I was bitter at the way our efforts were constantly crushed. As I write this, I know that I was forcing unearned merits on our club, merits that we had not earned and not had the right to bear, sort of like buying a Doctor's Degree title from a classified in a cheap tabloid.

At the time, it didn't matter to me. I was totally focused on making the Highway Chicks an icon. We were forced into taking off the "13 Motorcycle" patch and I wasn't happy about it. "Now it was war!" I thought to myself. I constantly argued with and defied Mitch. He said no, I said yes. He said sit; I stood. But it was a personal thing and I kept it at that level. In spite of our constant hostility, I still admired his leadership and quietly accepted his argument.

That same week Mitch came to the bar where I was working. He had Silent Few President, Joker with him. I apologized to him and told him it would never happen again. I told him that my boss had informed me that I had to listen to what he said and keep him informed of everything I did or knew. Mitch told me I was hardheaded and that I needed to quit bucking him. He also told me that if I were a man I would make a good member in his club. I was honored at his comment.

You see, I had learned the Sons philosophy and creed from Brakeline and I had seen them stand by it. I was fond of Mitch's judgment and leadership skills. I was partial to the courage of the Sons in Arkansas because I saw how they stood behind their people and took care of them.

Ever since that day, I kept my word. I kept Mitch informed. I kept him in the loop. I respected him and informed my club, the Highway Chicks that they needed to do the same. Tab refused to respect him. She kept telling me this was a Red and Gold state and she was not going to listen to what Mitch said.

The whole ordeal with the 13 Diamond Patch did put us very close to some of the out of state Bandido and support clubs. They became our protectors, or at least it seemed that way, or maybe we were just being used as monitors, but it appeared to work out to our advantage.

We continued to ride and support other MC events all for that perfect photo opportunity. Our membership had reached a total of sixteen and we were becoming an essential part of the MC community. The Thunderheads and Ozark Riders finally began treating us as a sister club when they heard about my stand with Mitch and the 13 Diamond Patch. They didn't get along with them and they knew we were zealous when it came to the Red and Gold world.

I was the secretary for the ARCOMc and because my phone was listed on the back cover of the calendar, it rang constantly. Many patch holders called seeking direction or Arkansas MC Protocol advice. I would put them in contact with the correct person each time. If their questions concerned general Arkansas MC Protocol, I would answer them. I was looked upon as a leader in the MC world in Arkansas from many out of state patch holders and citizens. I always did show respect to all clubs and offered assistance if ever needed. Never was I rude with other patch holders (except Mitch), and treated all equally.

At the end of November of 2005, we had four new girls added to our club as supporters. They were all from Mississippi. They were Roadkill, Tweety, Tuesday, and Mars. I obtained permission from Bandido Dwayne, President of the Mississippi Bandidos to enlist them into our Arkansas club. The agreement was that after a year of wearing a Probationary bottom rocker, I would renegotiate with him for a Mississippi Chapter of Highway Chicks. Of course, I did not ask Murray's permission. Our bottom rocker said GARLAND COUNTY but the license plates on the bikes read Arkansas, Mississippi, and Louisiana.

As much as I liked the new girls, I didn't have much hope for them as club members, because the time and expense needed to fulfill their commitment to the club was a costly one. Nevertheless, we wanted to expand and these girls wanted to be bikers. Therefore, their enlistment meant that our club could be stronger and our Colors would be seen in another state on a daily basis.

This new endeavor added to the already countless travels, a regular commute to Mississippi and Arkansas. This was an additional strain that our club did not need, nevertheless, wanted. My major struggle was not with the traveling but with Tab's attitude. She did not like the girls because as she put it to me, "I don't trust them." Tab did not trust anyone. She had issues with allowing new members in the club and especially with anyone, she could not control. It is a well-known fact that if one does not trust in themselves, it becomes difficult to trust anyone else.

I put Tuesday in charge of the local supervision in Mississippi. Tab was not happy about this. She did not want new leaders and the girls were too far away to be schooled by her. I talked with Tuesday on a daily basis and had an open line of communication with the Desoto Pistoleros. They kept an eye on the girls as a favor to me. They wanted the best for the Red and Gold in their state and were going to make sure the new Highway Chicks did things right. I couldn't just leave four new girls with our Colors on 200 miles away and not keep in daily contact. Any misconduct with the girls would result in a reprimand directly with the HC. If it was bad for men, it was ten times worse for women, especially a female Bandido Support Club in the making in another state.

In November of 2005, in spite of the trouble we had with the 13 Motorcycle Diamond Patch issue and Mitch, three of the Highway Chicks husbands became hang arounds with the Silent Few MC, a Sons of Silence support club in Arkansas. This move seemed ironic and practically impossible.

There was KB's husband Doobie, Curve's husband Half Breed, and Roadkill's old man G-String. Half Breed had been a patch holder for the Boozefighters MC in the past, so he received his bottom rocker for the Silent Few in a short time. They had a good man for President. Axxel was a Christian with a caring attitude and had been commended by Brakeline to be the Club's President for at least a year under his supervision. He got along well with the Highway Chicks and came to many of our private parties with several other club members, so having our men in his club seemed like a family move. However, Axxel did not finish his commission for he rolled over to his mother club the Sons, and the Silent Few got a new president, Joker. By this time, Brakeline was not able to persuade his duties of the support club's supervision due to health complications, so the Silent Few's guidance was taken over by their mother chapter and new SOS President, Mitch.

Mitch, the high-strung, by the book, exemplary patch holder, enforced the principle that there should not be married clubs. He believed that this caused a conflict of interest, a divided household and most definitely pillow talk. As Club President, I agreed with Mitch 100%, however, my argument was two-fold. First, why were they accepted as hang arounds in the first place? And if they were to continue in the club but the "married club" issue was to be enforced, did it mean that my girls had to be removed from my club?

I would not sacrifice my club members by dismissing them from the Highway Chicks. We were not going to lose our members especially since they had been patch holders before their husbands started hanging around. So the understood question was who is going to step down, TSF or the HC members? I was too stubborn to bow down and get rid of my members and Mitch was not going to ask the Silent Few guys to step down either, for they came into the club before his supervision. This brought about inter personal hostility within our clubs. I never let this situation come between Brakeline and myself and I still kept a decent relationship with Mitch, Sons of Silence President for Arkansas.

One of the biggest problems was that even though our husbands were Silent Few Prospects, they still followed us to events and I put them on the tail of the pack. Word got out to their mother club that they had been riding behind the Highway Chicks and shortly after, they were forbidden to ride with us. Obviously, this was a problem because the husbands wanted to ride with their wives and vice versa. It didn't make sense that we allowed our husbands in a non-Red and Gold club, especially after the 13 Motorcycle Diamond Patch dilemma. But they were happy and felt a wealth of brotherhood in their new club. The best part was that we didn't have to carry them anymore to our events. The girls wanted their alone time and when the husbands followed us, they were obligated to tend to them instead of properly taking care of business at events.

The new Silent Few hang arounds were happy at their new home but always preferred to ride with us. They said we did fun things and rode to many places. Being with the Silent Few was becoming work for them. Later on, they told me they had regretted joining up with a club.

Now that our men were with TSF, the Sons had no choice but to put up with us. We were patch holders but also fell under the 'ol' lady' bracket whenever the girls were with their husbands. Now that was an oddity! Patch holders who were ol' ladies of hang arounds from a club on the other side of the fence.

Mitch constantly told me that married clubs don't work because someone would talk club business and that is a breach of protocol in the MC world. This was a new issue for Mitch and me to argue over. I had two choices: to pull our husbands out of their club or learn to live with the discord. Highway Chick Curve and Silent Few Prospect Half Breed had been married for a long time and their relationship was a loving and committed one. He had resigned from the Boozefighters MC in Arkansas for personal reasons, one of which included the non-approval of his wife's non-conventional behavior. She would not conform to the typical ol' lady conduct and wear a property patch. She rode her own bike and seemed to be more independent than the normal ol' lady was.

When her husband quit the club, he allowed her to become a Highway Chick hang around and subsequently a patch holder. He was supportive of our club and an excellent handyman. He had a great personality and a jovial attitude. We took to him as much as we did Curve and provided a social home for him. He followed us to many functions and didn't care about what people said.

I had been very strict with Curve on club protocol and politics and she did very well with the situation. She was very stressed and worried for her husband and his health. She would talk to me about his medical and emotional health but never shared any pillow talk or comments her husband might have mentioned to her about his club, the Silent Few. I could not convince Mitch to believe this for he always said that eventually it would happen. He adhered to the belief that MC clubs should not be married. Once again, I agreed with him but refused to have Curve resign.

Half Breed did not want to resign because as he put it in his own words, "I have found true brotherhood in this club and I love them. I enjoy myself and have a good time when we are together." He did tell me later on that he would do anything for his wife and that if it came down to her happiness, he would quit the club and let her pursue the road she had taken with the Highway Chicks.

They began putting pressure on the guys that were with us. They were put in a Catch 22. They were not allowed to ride with us anytime we wore our Colors. We could not ride without our Colors and neither could they. That meant we could never ride together – period! At the pool tournaments, they weren't allowed to hang out with us either. That didn't work out quite well. My opinion in the matter was that the Sons were attempting to enforce the correct protocol for the Silent Few but our guys were not ready to become 'club material.'

Joker was a good man but was too much of a people pleaser, which made him very shortcoming when it came to making a solid decision. The situation became a nightmare for both of our club members. We didn't have a problem with it, and I don't think that Joker did either but it was his club and he needed to remedy the state of affairs. I felt sorry for him because he was caught in a hard spot. I knew he really liked the guys and enjoyed their company but his respect and submission to his mother club was indeed first.

Other patch holders began to see the conflict that was brewing between the clubs. People could see the emotional strain within the girls in my club as well as their husbands. Someone who was a close friend of the Sons (not a patch holder at the time) decided that his friendship with me was far more important than all rules and regulations. He called me and said he needed to speak with me concerning some issues. I asked him to come to Lucky's Bar and Grill, my place of employment, and meet with me.

He came down to the bar and sat to talk with me. "What's going on?" I asked. He had a puzzled look in his eye while concern seemed to be at the top of his list. "Sadgirl, I'm not supposed to be telling you this so don't get me in trouble. But XXX (name withheld at patch holder's request) said that if any of you girls ever get in his way on the road, he is going to run you over or shoot you. He is not happy with the Toy Run situation, so please be careful and stay clear out of his way," he said to me.

I politely thanked him for the word of caution but tucked it away as another one of the daily threats we received from the old-school male chauvinist driven bikers. We were used to all kind of insults and crude remarks for being a women's MC. However, a week later another ex patch holder said the same thing to me in an unrelated conversation. He used the same name and stated the descriptive threat exactly as the previous informer. Okay, now it was time to take action. I called a face-to-face meeting with Brakeline and told him what was said to me, by whom it was said, and when it was said. I let him know that it was an unconfirmed rumor, nevertheless, I thought it needed to be handled because the informers did not know the either had communicated with me, and their information matched.

I told him that I personally thought there was not a problem between the Silent Few and my club, but that I believed the problem was with one person in his club. He assured me he'd take care of the problem and evidently, he did. He sent me the copy of an email he sent to the Silent Few. It was how he handled the matter.

From: Brakeline 1% SOS
Date: Sat, Dec 17, 2005, 4:11 pm
Subject: Rumors

"*It has come to my attention that some rumors are circulating concerning the Sons of Silence in Arkansas. I'm writing this notice to put to rest these rumors. I have recently heard that the Sons of Silence in Arkansas does not like and even actively resents the Highway Chicks Motorcycle*

Club and its members. I've even heard that these feelings may be directed toward the Bandidos also. Let me clear this up now, once and for all and make it crystal clear.

While the Sons of Silence does not bow down or step aside for any other club ever, we do respect those clubs who offer us respect. The Bandido MC is a fellow 1%'er club and is given that respect as an equal until some reason comes up to change that. The Highway Chicks as a Bandido support club, is and will be given the respect due a club, which has earned the position they occupy. If ever any problem in protocol ever happens then officers representing the clubs involved will meet to work it out.

If you are wondering, YES I'm talking about the perceived problem of who cut in front of who, and who rides in front of or behind who in the recent toy run! It's all just a bunch of alpha male bullshit and if there were really any problems then they would be worked out by officers of respected clubs. As it is, already too much has been made of it.

Concerning the Highway Chicks in particular, they are a part of the M/C world in Arkansas, a support club for the Bandidos, and officially recognized and ACCEPTED as such by the Sons of Silence. Everyone has the right to like or dislike anyone or any club they chose but only on a personal basis. As a member of a club themselves they have to act in a manner consistent with their club's politics or just stay away from a person or club they do not like.

I'm not sure how each member in TSF feels about the Highway Chicks personally, but can say that XXX (name withheld at patch holder's request) is the only actual "woman hater" in the Arkansas chapter of the Sons. I myself for the record have respect for the Highway Chicks and have seen them strive hard to do things properly in the MC world. As a matter of record any dislike of them should be restricted to a personal level and comments out loud about them should always be in the "I" term and never in the "we". Never should any physical action be taken against ANY M/C club because of a personal attitude or grudge. We represent our club we belong to and our actions reflect on everyone in that club. We don't take any shit but we will never act like a blowhard, loudmouth, school yard bully either.

Anyone who is still unclear about this or the proper way to act, call me and we will meet and I will make sure you understand. Anyone hearing *someone in either the SOS or TSF talking out of line or acting in such a way as to bring disrespect upon either the SOS or TSF should immediately bring it to the attention of an officer in the club or to me personally (especially to me if it is an officer involved). It will be handled. PERIOD.*

Also to be perfectly clear and not to mince words I have heard by "rumor" that XXX (name withheld at patch holder's request) has been spreading some of this. He is not an officer and can only speak for himself and his feelings and attitude only reflect his own person. Also, remember that I am only talking about unfounded rumors that I have heard, not true facts, and am making it clear now exactly how things are. Use your own head and don't be led astray or intimidated into doing something or acting in a way disrespectful of the patch on your back.

We are the best, and will stay the best because our standards and morals are higher than others! We don't have to put others down to make ourselves look or feel important."

Brakeline's letter was to the point and left no room for questionable choices. He knew how to handle club business and he wasn't scared or intimidated by anyone. It was ironic because in private and behind closed doors, the Silent Few and the Highway Chicks had loads of fun in our private parties. We even had sleepovers at our clubhouse. But it was just us, no mother clubs and no high ranking officers other than our two Club Presidents. Colors did not stand in our way and honestly, we had great times of fellowship. However, in public we rarely even spoke. Now how messed up is that?

Sadgirl Becomes Club President

It was publicly obvious that Debbie T was not doing her job as president. The pressure and stress of the politics and conflicts between clubs was driving her crazy. Many patch holders still refused to speak business or negotiations with her. Instead they chose to deal with me. She saw this behavior and decided to step down as president. Debbie T was sitting at my kitchen table when she said, "Sadgirl, do you think I am holding this club back?" Although I knew exactly what she meant I hesitated for a moment and responded,

"What do you mean holding back the club?"

There was a glazed look in her eyes but her honesty was straight forward and to the point. She was resigning as the Highway Chicks WMC President and giving me the helm. I told her that she wasn't good at politics and her communications skills were at a low, but other than that she had been a great president. She told me she was stepping down because she did not want a position that required all the bullshit of politics. My reaction was subtle for I had many questions concerning her role in politics, but her friendship and commitment to the club was beyond question. She is an excellent person. She was the club's co-founder and that respect and honor would always be bestowed upon her. However, it was indeed time for a leader who could interact and negotiate with other club presidents and 1%'ers. I was the vice president so that put me next in line. I accepted the challenge and humbly put on the President stripe for the Highway Chicks WMC. This was at the end of 2005.

Brakeline was the first one to know that this change had occurred. He sent me a short email.

From: Brakeline 1% SOS
Date: Thu, 5 Jan 2006 10:18:30 -0600

"I got a short email letting me know that Debbie stepped down and now you are President; a job you were in all reality already doing anyway; and that she is now VP. It's just my opinion and really none of my business but I think that you two have done the correct thing and that now things are as they should be."

His encouragement was the only thing I needed to hear. Everyone else's opinion although important, wasn't a motivational dynamic of support as Brakeline's was.

In January of 2006 I received an email from Pistolero Kuzz in Mississippi informing me that Pistolero Yankee had a motorcycle wreck and didn't make it. His funeral was to be held in Alabama and the burial site was near the Georgia State line. It was cold in January but I called Tab and Prospect Curve and told them we were riding to Alabama that weekend for the funeral. We didn't know Pistolero Yankee but he was a part of the Red and Gold Nation and that was all that mattered to us.

It was a long, hard and cold unplanned ride for we were fighting the tail winds behind the hurricane that had just passed. (You cannot plan a funeral ride beforehand). That day we rode from Hot Springs, Arkansas to Jackson, Mississippi and bunked at the Mississippi Riders clubhouse. We had to get up at 1:30 am to meet Pistolero Spoons and the rest of the brothers at the Waffle House. Tired was beyond an understatement but we were determined to ride and fly our Colors!

As we were getting ready to leave the next morning, Pistolero President, Al Capone, who would lead the pack, told me to line up beside him and ride at his right side. An honor bestowed upon me that I treasure to this day. Once again it was ironic that an out of state club showed me the respect of an MC President and Bandido Supporter.

We took off and froze our asses off for about 100 miles. The temperature was about 40 degrees with a wind chill of 19. I remember periodically looking at my hands to make sure they were still there. Capone had told us that if we needed to stop, just signal him and he'd pull over. I remembered his words as we were riding in the freezing cold, but by no means was this girl or any Highway Chick going to be the one to pull over first.

How I prayed on that brisk morning for someone from his club to motion him to pull over! I was freezing so much that I was getting lightheaded. I had no sleep the night before and it was dark, But I pressed on. I rode beside Capone and never missed a beat. Finally Mississippi Rider Blinky motioned President Capone to pull over. He had to pee.

I thanked God over and over as I ran to the bathroom and put my hands under the hand dryer. When we were ready to leave as we sat on our bikes, Capone looked over at me and said, "With you, I'd ride to hell and back!" An honor I consider bequeathed on me by a biker.

We made it to Pistolero Yankee's funeral in one piece on our bikes.

We rode like bats out of hell to the burial site. Our poor Prospect I knew would quit and never go near us again once we returned home, for we jammed hundreds and hundreds of miles in just 3 days. It was a Red and Gold motorcycle procession to make a brother proud. There were over 150 bikes and the Alabama Bandidos took pride in manning the traffic lights and intersections. At the burial site I tuned to get an overview of who was there. Thunderhead Big Joe stood right beside me, warm and toasty. "I came in the van," he said to me with a big grin. "We're Highway Chicks so we rode," I responded with another grin.

This is the day I met the Southern Knights MC and Tater for the first time in person. It was a sad event but it was beautiful to see the brotherhood of the Red and Gold family saying goodbye to one of their brothers who was forever to ride with the GBNF (Gone But Never Forgotten) crew. Alabama Pistolero President Big T, acknowledged us publicly for riding all the way from Hot Springs, Arkansas. I looked at Big Joe and spoke to him with my eyes, "Ha! We rode!" He grinned back at me and shook his head as he looked at the ground with his hands folded in front of him.

After it was all said and done, we finally arrived in Arkansas two days later. We had travelled hundreds of miles, were almost blown off the Memphis/Arkansas bridge over the Mississippi River, and got lost in the ghetto downtown part of Memphis at three in the morning. We made a final gas stop in Benton, where we brought a cup of coffee just to defrost our frozen fingers with the warm cup. It was then I met Hell's Lovers Sonny and his brother as they were also in the defrosting process. They were on their way to Texarkana. I introduced myself and gave him a calling card. It was the beginning of a short, but sincere relationship that was cut because of politics.

Hell's Lover Sonny is the President of a powerful, predominantly black Motorcycle Club in Texarkana, Texas. He is a tall, handsome black man with a sweet and kind spirit. When he spoke, his voice had the resonance of a gentle waterfall but the authority of a lion. His silk-like gray hair reached his top rocker and he stood tall among many men. Throughout the years we became good friends as we traveled to each other's club events.

8
Mud on Our Boots

February 2006 was at hand and so was our Second Annual Officer's Dinner. We had put 100% effort and a great deal of finance into making this event a success not only for us but also for the biker community in Arkansas. My goal was for the out of state people to see that Arkansas was a great place to live the MC lifestyle.

I made welcome pamphlets that told a brief history of Al Capone and the boot legging gangsters in Hot Springs in the early 1940's. I included some information from the Hot Springs Genealogical Society of how this town was a neutral meeting place for rival gangsters. Then I suggested how it could be just as good for the MC clubs to do the same. No wonder the H.O.G. organization chose Hot Springs for the official annual State Rally.

I invited Highway and Hedges Ministry to host the opening prayer, serve the food and tend the bar. Sons of Silence Brakeline, and President Mitch represented the State of Arkansas and welcomed the 1%'ers and all out of State MC clubs. I was grateful to them and their devoted passion for club life. They considered it a serious matter and always showed heart towards bikers. There were no Arkansas Bandidos present at this dinner.

The Military Veterans MC National President DogBone presented us with a Certificate of Appreciation for hosting this event. They were extremely appreciative that they were able to solve some political problems in their state (Kansas) because of good advice from Brakeline while at our clubhouse.

The turnout was better than the first one with 20 clubs at our clubhouse. We had Jell-O shots, which I know some people will never forget. There was also great music, bike games, and an admirable show of Colors, but mostly great fellowship. Many Officers were from out of state and we made sure they had a hospitable and unforgettable stay. It was also a good show of our Patch, especially having the new Mississippi crew at hand.

KB got her Prospect rocker on this Second MC Officers Dinner. She had finally learned to ride a bike and purchased one. Her husband Doobie also received his Prospect rocker at our clubhouse with his club The Silent Few, that same night.

Here were two Prospects from different sides of the fence who were legally married. One was a Highway Chick, the other a Silent Few. They had stepped into a new level of commitment and loyalty to their clubs. One was a Bandido supporter, the other a Sons of Silence supporter. Things for us were complicated enough, and now this blissful union put us all directly in the spotlight of for better or worse.

Two clubs from opposite sides of the fence with different colors and different Presidents, hung their vests side by side in their home. A few of my brothers asked me, "Why did your guys join the Silent Few instead of a Red and Gold support club?" The only answer I could offer was that they were offered a friendship not found anywhere else and they were treated as men instead of "ol' men."

I believed that many people did not understand or perhaps were not aware of the political impact and importance of this dinner party. It was obviously evident that to have 20 different MC Presidents, with different Colors under one roof and not have one spat, was a great achievement on its own. This wasn't just another Highway Chick party. This monumental and historical event could have become a State wide ARCOMc sponsored event in the future. The fact that it was my idea and hosted by my club may have been an issue with some people, but I always believed that the results achieved would have overshadowed any political discrepancy. People talked about the Officers Dinner for months. Unaltered photographs don't lie. The ones taken at the MC Officers' Dinner definitely told the accurate story of the peaceful political meeting between different clubs.

The summer days were approaching and many seasonal bikers were getting in gear for the riding season. We had ridden all winter and just wanted a break from going here and there. A free weekend where we could go to the lake and swim or just hang out with our immediate families was my heart's desire. That didn't happen though. We continued to ride to as many events and support all ARCOMc events as humanly possible. These included annuals, funerals, benefits, poker runs, and Bandido National events. If it was happening, the Highway Chicks were there. We wanted to live up to our name and we did.

Our friendship with the Louisiana Bandidos and Gray Ghost MC became tighter. They were aware of the unfairness and cold treatment we had encountered in our home state with the Arkansas Bandidos as well as other conflicts. They always said they'd stand behind us 100% and Bandido Jim welcomed us if we ever decided to move to the State of Louisiana as a motorcycle club. They would be willing to sponsor us and said that if we moved to their state, we might possibly be allowed to wear the Heart Patch and the 13 Motorcycle Diamond Patch. Bandido Jim said it was his state and in his state, he made the decisions. "I don't run Louisiana like Murray runs Arkansas," he said to me in a quiet tone with a half smile.

It was an offer that I considered for a while. I spent many nights agonizing over accepting or declining this offer which seemed like an easy solution to our problems. One of the factors in my deliberation was the notion of not being brushed to the side by the Arkansas Bandidos constantly. I thought about all the comforts of belonging to a true Red and Gold State and being under a Bandido President who was bold in fulfilling his office. We had many church meetings among our club officers and tossed the idea back and forth throughout the year.

After a year of the pros and cons, I decided that we were to remain in Arkansas and tough it out as an MC for the following reason: I could not betray Murray and walk out on him after he'd taken so much slack for us, and truly I wanted to make a difference in Arkansas. I wanted the biker community to get along and promote safe riding. I didn't want to be seen as a quitter by running away to another state. I also considered the fact that I would have to change my residency to Louisiana and I wasn't ready to do so. The Highway Chicks were to remain an MC in Arkansas as long as I was President.

With that thought behind us we tried to become stronger as a club. Tab was spending more time at Jim's Shop in Shreveport and that was a concern because I thought she was becoming too independent. Many other people did not like the fact that she was hanging there all the time either. She did things without consulting the club and made herself inaccessible.

As Club President, I should have executed disciplinary measures and pulled her bottom rocker; placing her on probation for acting as an independent unit. Although she was part of an MC, she was networking on her own. She went as far as to recruit a hang around from Tulsa, Oklahoma and not tell me until she introduced her to me as a Highway Chicks hang around. Perhaps if I had taken the proper corrective measures, I would have avoided much heartache, but I didn't. I let her come and go as she pleased. I trusted her judgment and loyalty to our club. I should have known that her intentions stemmed from the low self esteem she carried while concealing many truths concerning her personal life.

Another pressing issue was her secret suffering love for a Louisiana patch holder. She whimpered over him repeatedly and resented the notion that he chose to stay with his wife and kids over her. She made it seem to us that she had let him go in the best interest of his patch, but if indeed that was the case, she should have restrained herself from hanging out with his club so much, as well as emailing him back and forth. This would have diverted the attention away from herself. Tab had become a handful and no one in the club wanted to deal with her. There were times when we would call her repeatedly but she would not answer her phone or return our messages. Later on, she'd give us the excuse that she'd lock herself in the house with severe depression and did not want to talk to anyone.

I would remind her that as a club member she could not do things like that. We needed to know that she was okay especially while living in another state. We stressed how important it was for her to answer her phone or at least return the phone messages we'd leave her.

Her tardiness to every meet up had become a major problem for us. We always had to wait on her and as a club officer; she was not setting a good example. When I confronted her with the concern, she only laughed about it.

I also had to deal with the guys (our husbands) in the Silent Few MC. They were constantly complaining to me about the rules their club set for them. They didn't understand why they couldn't ride with us and wanted to know why everyone in their club was so uptight. These guys had never been in or around the MC world and knew absolutely nothing about protocol. On the other hand, I had my own club members who were their wives, and wanted to know the why of things. Many times, I felt like a high school guidance counselor.

Personally, I didn't understand why they accepted our men to begin with. It would have been so simple had they been turned down as hang arounds. Our club life was complicated enough and this made matters worse. I don't know if things would have been easier had they joined a Red and Gold club. I do know that as much as they enjoyed the friendship of Joker, Mike, and occasionally Axxel, they were never sure they had made the right decision.

I did take time out of my already hectic schedule to educate them in matters and politics concerning the MC world. These were private meetings at our clubhouse. One of the issues I strongly emphasized to them was that even though some of these club rules set by their own club didn't make sense, they were to be complied with faithfully. Eventually, as they became one with their club and learned the protocols of the MC world, they would soon understand the importance of accountability.

Curve was particularly concerned with her husband's (Half Breed) treatment and respect in the club. He was the outspoken one of the three of them and usually let his mouth get him in trouble. He was the one that said he was going with us to our Red and Gold events and didn't give a damn what any one of his officers thought. He said he could go wherever his wife went because that was his wife. I didn't have a problem with it but I knew his club would. Hey, I got a thrill out of having guys follow and ride behind us.

The problem was that people in other states saw a SOS supporter riding behind us with his Colors on. They called the Arkansas President to report it. This was an insult for a 1%'er, however, we were 1% supporters as well. The difference was that we were from a club of opposite Colors and to top it off, women as well. Damn, did we get mud on our boots!

Half Breed's defiance stirred up discord within his club. This also reflected on the Highway Chicks since his wife was one of our patch holders. Their home became a divided home. The guys began to hate going to their club meetings. They were displeased with the original intention of the club and the outcome. They felt they had been misled in the purpose of the club. This was only their opinion and no one else's.

I knew that the Silent Few was a support club for the Arkansas Sons of Silence and that made them a harvester club. However, our husbands, after hanging out with us for so long, only saw the party side of the Highway Chicks, and thought their club would have the same social behavior. They were not aware that when you become a patch holder, everything is different.

Their direct orders were appropriate and within club protocol guidelines. Therefore, in an attempt to keep the peace between the two clubs, I told the guys they were no longer allowed to go with us. I informed each one of my members that under no circumstance was pillow talk to be considered. "If the guys start talking to you about their club and what goes on, listen and retain, but under no circumstances are you to give your opinion or share our club information with them." I was very firm with my club members. I even threatened to pull bottom rockers if they refused to comply with my orders.

I let Mitch know how I was handling the situation in my club and promised him that I would let him know if information was leaked. He set out a test with the guys. A specific statement that if repeated by the guys to their wives (our club members), I would know who the big mouth was. To this day, and as far as I knew, that test statement never made it to my ears.

Sons of Silence President Mitch and I would meet at the Long Branch Saloon on Mondays to try and resolve the conflict of the divided family. My comment to him was always the same. My girls were first and I was not going to get rid of them in order for the guys to stay in the Silent Few. I was firm with Mitch in my standpoint. He kept telling me repeatedly that he didn't believe in married clubs. I totally agreed with him but I didn't understand why, in spite of this creed, they had allowed our boys in the first place to be a part of the Silent Few if they knew we were a Bandido Support Club. It didn't make sense and the whole ordeal was wearing on our guys as much as it was me.

Our three guys became best friends with each other and built a very close-knit brotherhood amongst them. They tried to become a part of their club like the rest of the other members but always felt like they were different. The private meetings at our clubhouse with them became frequent and it was starting to become a chore. I felt it wasn't my place to educate or console another MC's member and their heartaches, when they had an active President. It was taking away from my duties to my own club.

Half-Breed had already been bumped down to Prospect twice and he was getting fed up with it. I talked with Brakeline concerning the situation. He assured me that our boys were very much liked and a part of the Silent Few. As a club we were down, deep in the muddy corral of the MC politics. Figuratively speaking, our boots were covered in mud, and chunks of dirt seem to sling everywhere, every time we turned around.

On one of the Silent Few club runs to Mississippi, two of the guys broke down (Half-breed and G-String). They called Curve and Roadkill to come and get them with Curve's trailer. As Club President I was annoyed that the Highway Chicks were the ones who had to go rescue The Silent Few stranded members. Of course they were our husbands but I was thinking as a patch holder and not a relative. There had been so much shit said about our club but we were the ones who had to go get their prospects. It didn't make sense to me, but then again a lot of things weren't making sense anymore. I also questioned why their senior officers left them stranded in another state while they returned to Arkansas.

In our Club we would never leave a prospect, a hang around, or a patch on the side of the road until help arrived. These three prospects were left in another state without a patch holder, waiting on the Highway Chicks trailer. "How partial is that," I thought sarcastically. They weren't allowed to ride with us, but they could sure be rescued by us."

I asked Brakeline about the situation and in an email he educated me in reference to this occurrence.

From: Brakeline 1% SOS
Date: Mon, 24 Apr 2006 19:31:44 -0500

"Some clarification is needed though. First: I don't know the situation at the scene so I can't really say if things were done the way I myself may have done it. Second: There are no uniform set of rules or code as to how to treat prospects or what they are allowed to do on their own or how or when to wear their patches. These rules are all made up by the club the prospect is prospecting for and are different for most clubs. A GENERAL CODE OF BEHAVIOR AROUND PATCH HOLDERS AND 1%ers IS PRETTY ADVISABLE FOR A PROSPECTS SELF PRESERVATION. But prospects for the Silent Few go by whatever rules the parent club has made for them and this will certainly be different from the rules a Sons Prospect would have to go by and it would be strange indeed if the rules your prospects followed were the same as TSF. Each club is different and expects different things from a prospect.

I remember your reaction to yours and TSF's prospects being caught out drinking with their prospect patches on. In the Sons generally if a prospect is on his bike he wears his patch. Period. It really doesn't matter if a patch holder is around or not. When I first started in the club before you could get everyone's vote (which had to be 100% to get your patch), you were sent down the road alone, no money, a tank of gas and expected to make it on your own (no ATM cards back then and none of us had a credit card! LOL), across the country to the farthest chapter from your own; prospect for them while there and return home without help. If it was found out you had someone wire you money or something like that, you didn't make it. We were expected to steal, rob, siphon gas, hustle a dancer, or whatever it took to make it on our own just to prove that we didn't need help and were self sufficient and would not be a burden to the club but a self sufficient asset. If bikes broke down on the road it wouldn't be odd for a prospect to sit on the side of the road with the broken bikes in the hot sun waiting on a chase truck or trailer while the patch holder went on down the road to the next air conditioned bar or motel to wait or even on home if it meant being to work on time so he didn't get fired.

That is what a prospect is for. To work, serve, LEARN, become a strong self reliant brother who doesn't need a baby sitter. As for as another club coming along and messing with him..... he would never be abandoned in enemy territory but of course in our lifestyle anything could come up. If he was left alone and someone fucked with him, he would be expected to learn from it and of course we would "fix their wagon" for fucking with OUR prospect! LOL

You mentioned they were left in Mississippi so..... they should have been safe as no one even close to Mississippi would dare to fuck with a Son or a Sons Prospect, (and now it should extend to our support clubs). As for waiting on a trailer from the Highway Chicks, who broke down? Who was responsible for finding a trailer for his broken bike? Was he associated with the HC somehow (friend, old lady)? If I broke down and you were closer to me with a trailer than my own brothers and came to get me, I wouldn't think anything wrong with it. I've almost never (maybe 3 times in 33 years) needed to be picked up on the roadside but many times, I have seen other clubs stop to pick up my brothers and we have done the same. I've gotten calls from as far as Memphis from another club saying they were broken down and were given my name to call, and I took care of them. No one ever felt they should ONLY call upon their own club but rather whoever was available, closer, actually had a truck or trailer.....you get the idea.

My opinion and it's shared by my brothers is that a prospect is there to serve while he learns, and is not to be babied but put to the test and made hard by "trial by fire" and not given a Patch till he grows into it. If he needs something we will be there to help but (and don't take this wrong) if he needs a lift and he can either get it from a brother or use someone else, their time, their money, who are they to use and inconvenience? Should they ask their brother to be inconvenienced or use someone outside the club?"

Once again Brakeline had schooled me in the ways of the MC world. I took my lesson, applied it and taught it to my club as well as the Silent Few members who were our husbands. Things did not improve though. It had become emotionally unbearable for the guys to continue in the club.

On a Sunday afternoon while at a pit stop on one of our runs in May of 2006, Curve got a phone call. It was her husband, Half-Breed. He was calling to inform her that he had quit the club and was on his way to turn in his Colors. She was still on the phone when KB's phone rang. It was her husband Doobie, informing her he was turning in his bottom rocker also. Roadkill wondered about G-String so she called him and he was also quitting the club. The three Silent Few Prospects simultaneously were headed to meet their president and resign from their club. When the girls told me I didn't say anything. It was their decision and I wanted to keep it that way.

Later that evening after we got home they told us that they'd been let out in good standing and that the doors were open to the three of them to return if they ever wanted to belong to the club again.

There was an incident, however, that changed things for them. Half-Breed claimed he had loaned his homemade BBQ grill to his former club. A week after he resigned, he called his former President, Joker and asked for his BBQ grill to be returned. Joker told him that the grill had not been a loan but rather a gift and that such provision did not provide for him taking it back just because he had quit the club. Half-Breed argued that it was only a loan and that he was going to get it back at any cost. This opened the door for a big stink not only for them, but for the Highway Chicks as well.

The following Sunday Half Breed, Doobie and G-String 'packed' their trucks and trailer, and headed north to retrieve the BBQ grill. At this point I didn't care whose BBQ it was. My concern was that now that they were no longer club members, they were Highway Chick 'ol' men' again and we could be liable for their actions.

When they arrived at the house, they told me that they were received in a civil manner and they all shook hands. The Silent Few and several Sons from out of state were present. The guys retrieving the BBQ grill were no longer Silent Few members but the husbands of the Highway Chicks members in pursuit of a stupid BBQ grill.

They retrieved their grill but it came at a high price, for shortly afterward that same Sunday evening, it was posted in the Silent Few website that all three of their 'Out in Good Standing' status had been changed to 'Out in Bad Standings'.

This posed a new problem. In bad standing status they were not allowed to be around us whenever we were at an event. They were not allowed to come to our own events at our clubhouse if any Silent Few or Sons of Silence members were present.

I was faced with a new dilemma and another Catch 22. If I forbade them to attend our events, it was going to cause problems between my club members (their wives) and in turn that would cause problems with my own club. If I allowed them to attend our events, then that would cause a problem with the MC clubs attending, for they were out in bad standing.

Once again the meetings behind closed doors at my clubhouse resumed, but this time it was to help them understand why they could no longer go with their wives to our events. I had to help them understand that they were no longer welcome at MC events and it would be catastrophic for our club if it turned violent.

I was very frustrated and in such a state, I remember telling them as we sat in the clubhouse kitchen, "I told you from the very beginning that you should have gone with a Red and Gold support club. None of us would have these problems tonight if you guys would have listened." That might not necessarily have been true but at the time it felt like the right thing to say.

I called Thunderhead Big Joe and asked if the guys would ever be eligible to hang around a Red and Gold Club even though they were out in bad standing with the Sons of Silence. He said that normally they could not, but said that his club was a Red and Gold Club, so either way it didn't matter. That gave the guys a little hope in the MC world, so they unanimously concurred that for our sakes they would not attend any MC events with us.

I really like these guys for they had worked their ass off at our clubhouse. I remember when Doobie painted our entire clubhouse back in 2004 and worked day and night for almost 4 weeks to get our building ready for our annual. G-String did all the plumbing and much of the hard physical labor, and Half-Breed donated many items and put long hours of work and travel when Curve began hanging around our club. They had also been very generous in materials and labor. So all in all, they were very much appreciated and embraced by me. I was relieved that this conflict appeared to be over, but it was far from over.

One Monday, on the way to the ARCOMc pool tournament, we all stopped at the corner Exxon to get gas and have a short meeting. As we were leaving, Half-Breed and G-String caught up with us and fell in the back of our formation. They were wearing Red and gold support shirts for they had no intention of ever returning to their former club. I greeted them with brotherly love for I had nothing against them, and they were married to my club members. However, they weren't greeted the same way by their former club members. They were approached by Cracker in front of the building. "You can't be here, you are out in bad standing; you've got to leave," he told Half-Breed and G-String.

Half-Breed looked him dead in the eye and calmly said, "I'm not going anywhere. This is a public place and I'm staying."

Before I could look back at Cracker there were punches flying everywhere.

"Not the bikes! Not the bikers! Don't knock the bikes over!" I yelled in frenzy. I thought that it would be worse if the bikes 'dominoed' for that would make a lot of folks real angry.

At this time I looked at Thunderhead Big Joe motioning to him that I needed his help. He was an Enforcer for the Red and Gold Support Clubs of Arkansas, and I was a Red and Gold support club member. He stepped in and got in a fight with Cracker.

A Red and Gold Supporter had stepped in on behalf of the guys who were wearing support shirts that were related to our club. This was the first time in 3 years that we had been publicly defended by our sister club and for the first time I felt like a true Red and Gold club.

Mitch stepped in the fight and continued the hostile, one on one argument with Big Joe. Other patch holders began putting their hands inside their cuts *i.e. (A term derived from the early stages of motorcycle clubs, where the custom of cutting the sleeves (and sometimes the collar) of a leather or denim jacket began. When reference is made to a "Cut" it is refers to the Colors)* near their heart. I stepped away to where our guys were, and Half-Breed told me he was leaving. I told him not to leave until Murray showed up. I didn't want to be left to answer questions about the incident I didn't know. Only Half-Breed and G-String could do that.

Curve jumped in and got in a public display of a one on one argument with Mitch in an effort to defend her husband. "Oh boy! Now we're really in trouble," I thought to myself. Now we were deep in mud and our boots were dirtier than ever. I mean, I've had many one on one arguments with Mitch, but I was the MC President and our quarrels were always in private and respectful. Curve, a Highway Chick, was yelling at the President of the Arkansas Sons of Silence in front of 12 different MC clubs. I waited for the moment where one of the Sons would knock her out cold. But before that happened, Debbie T my Enforcer at the time, picked her up and carried her to the side of the building.

"Where the hell is Murray when I need him most?" I asked myself. I looked around and saw that there were people already on the phone trying to get a hold of him. But I also saw something very unusual near the entrance of the parking lot. There was a gathering of bikers in a tight knit circle with their heads bowed. Some of them were holding hands forming a prayer circle. In the midst of all the hectic confusion, Highway and Hedges Motorcycle Ministry Senior

Pastor Punkin, had gathered his people and then some, to pray. They weren't just praying …. They were praying!

This Christian Godly scene caught my entire focus and developed into a tunnel vision image into my eyes. Like a still frame from a movie, everything froze and all I could see or hear was this group of Christians praying for peace. At that precise time and moment, in a split second, I made my peace with God and rededicated my life to our Heavenly Father. It was remarkable to see how this group of Christians did their job at the right place, at the right time.

Although things were made worse for Big Joe by stepping into the brawl, it was a moment that gave me a sense of truly belonging to the Red and Gold world when their Enforcer came to the defense of our husbands.

Bandido Murray and his wife, Mary pulled up on his bike while the turmoil was still heated. He was as calm as ever and had a very peaceful disposition. He got off the bike, took his goggles off and put his riding gear in his saddle bags as he made a 360 degree visual scope around the perimeter. Mary walked toward the bar and Murray came straight to me without making any pit stops.

"Sadgirl, what's going on?" He firmly asked me.

"You're going to have to talk to Big Joe," I answered him steadfastly and without wavering as I pointed to where he was.

He walked over to where Big Joe and Mitch were in a face to face heated argument and ordered them to follow him to the back of the bar. Everyone backed off each other's face and followed the ARCOMc President. Murray employed excellent diplomatic skills in handling this conflict and everyone respected his command.

Bottom rockers were pulled, eyes were dotted, reprimands were handed out, and the Highway Chicks were put on probation by Mitch for allowing the "out in bad standing" guys to fall into our formation and ride to the bar with us.

I respected Mitch's discipline for us but when I informed Tab over the phone, she was furious and refused to be told what to do by a non Red and Gold patch. I explained to her over and over that Mitch was the President for a 1% club in the State of Arkansas and that gave him authority over any MC patch holder. Furthermore, I explained to her (again) that both Murray and Mitch had informed me that the Bandidos and the Sons of Silence shared equal power in the State and their decisions were unanimous and synchronized. Finally and once again, I explained to her that Murray himself had told me to listen to Mitch and do as he said. She argued with me that Arkansas was a Red and Gold State and she was not going to take orders from Mitch.

She carried all her opinions and perceptions to the Louisiana crew and made things worse for our club. She jeopardized the integrity of the Highway Chicks by disrespecting a 1%'er President in our own home state, and made it difficult for me as club president. From that day on, I was always on the watch making sure she did not piss off our local fellow patch holders.

My loyalty was to the Bandidos but it was also important to maintain a good political liaison with all the clubs. Murray wanted it that way and he was my boss. It was crucial that as Secretary for the ARCOMc, I take the politically correct decisions. Tab was new to the MC world rules and was only familiar with probably 25% of the political rules. As Club President, co-founder of the Highway Chicks, and secretary for the ARCOMc, I was in constant communication with both Murray and Mitch. I received my one-on-one mentorship from Brakeline, a 36-year club member, and founder of several Chapters for the Sons of Silence. Tab, on the other hand had spent most of her time in Louisiana where she resided and was more concerned with her status in the eyes of Bandido Jim and his crew. My interest was the Highway Chicks and the political status that we needed to uphold in the male MC world.

Although Thunderhead Big Joe was reprimanded for engaging in physical contact with another patch holder and paid his dues, it felt good to have a senior patch holder stand up for the Highway Chicks indirect problem.

9
Playing the Political Arena of the MC World
The Louisiana Red and Gold Family

Lost Comrades

In June of 2006, we attended the Annual Bandido Gathering at the Gray Ghost Clubhouse in Shreveport. It was a small, friendly get together of the closest Red and Gold Support Clubs with the parent club. It was an event where we were welcome and felt at ease while having a good time. At this particular one, we had the opportunity to spend quality time with Bandido Stubbs and talk about pressing political issues within our world. He was a major campaign supporter in favor of us receiving our Heart Patch, but he could only lobby so far.

If we were a Louisiana MC, there would perhaps be no problem with the Highway Chicks wearing a Heart Patch. Our immediate superior would have been Bandido Jim and he would have done all in his power to make this happen for us. However, we were an Arkansas WMC and things were different in our home state.

It was at this '06 Bandido Gathering that KB received her full Patch in front of everyone. She was a faithful Highway Chick and the one that worked the hardest in the club. KB was a sweet country girl from Alabama and my neighbor. I met her in 2000 on a friends night out. She had been with us from the beginning and slowly blossomed into a modern day, self-sufficient woman.

Our club seemed to have a good, solid, membership and things appeared to have smoothed out for us somewhat; but in reality, everyone was stressed due to the recent event of the loss of their husband's club status with the Silent Few. The strain proved to be too much for Curve. She resigned from the club. She could not take the stress about having to deal with her husband's cruel treatment. She told me she was emotionally distressed over seeing him psychologically hurt over and over. She said that she did not join the club to bring division into her home but to have fun riding her bike with other girls. She knew I would not let her resign so she went to Debbie T. I was sad to see her leave. She had been an asset to the club and a very good friend to me. She had become the secret friend that every girl needs to have and we got along great.

The Club's downfall did not stop with Curve. By the end of August, we had lost all the girls from Mississippi, except Roadkill, she had moved to Little Rock. It was right after returning from Bandido Eating Ed's funeral in Shreveport, Louisiana. Just as I had predicted, the expense was too demanding. Paying $100 of monthly dues combined with invested time, the cost of fuel to events and other expenses made it very difficult for all the girls, especially the single moms. They did not want all the hassles and obligations of an MC club either. Soon after that, we also lost Prospect Short Fuse. She did not abide by the club's rules so we terminated her prospect period.

Two months later, Debbie T decided to quit the club as well. She was tired of the political bullshit and did not want to be a part of it. She did not want to be a part of something that was not fun and was in a constant state of turmoil. The co-founder and charter member of the Highway Chicks had decided that enough was enough. She had a life to live, a career to pursue and it did not include a bunch of idiotic rules and regulations that did not add or take away from life, as we knew it.

I personally was not in favor of Debbie T quitting the club, so I did not accept her resignation. I did however; grant her a temporary leave of absence of up to a year, with the privilege of returning to the club with full Colors but no rank. She accepted the proposal and we shook over it while drinking Margaritas at Colorado Grill Restaurant.

She never wanted us to be a Bandido support club. She was very much against us wearing the Heart Patch and we argued back and forth about it. Her squabble was... what if we are riding down the highway and some Bandidos that do not like us see us wearing the Heart Patch and decide to shoot us off our bikes? My point was that we were a group of unknown newcomer females that needed a 'franchise' in order to make it in the MC culture, and the Bandidos were known worldwide, so that would be our gateway to recognition. In addition, Bandido Murray made it easy for us by opening the door for us to enter into their world.

After Debbie T quit the club, I promoted Tab to vice president. A decision I was hesitant in making, nevertheless, had no choice since no one else in the club had the time invested to qualify. The other members were new and green in the ways of the MC world. The internal conflicts we were having seemed to send everyone on their own agenda and the struggle with the Silent Few MC made matters worse.

As club president, I was very careful to do things right and follow the correct protocol. I had to employ all of my diplomatic skills in order to keep everyone happy. Mitch scolded me many times for taking the wrong path but he always made sure that I knew why he was telling me how to proceed. He always put me back on the right path and he was the one who repeatedly pounded in the fact that the Highway Chicks were to keep our business in Arkansas and not take orders from other states. I had no choice but to listen to him. First, because he knew what he was talking about and he governed his club in the appropriate manner and secondly, because Murray had instructed me to follow his orders out of respect.

This brought about more resistance from Tab and steered her in her own agenda. Instead of working as a club member, she embarked on an individual mission that would put the spotlight on her as a patch holder instead of the club as a whole. The Highway Chicks were under strain and individual members had been hurt. The club was collapsing from the inside out and the damage seemed to be irreversible. We were down to four members and once again, the struggle for continuance was tremendous. Our dues went up and none of us could afford to pay them. I for one, as much as I loved my club, could not take money away from my mortgage to pay the club dues and neither could the rest of the members.

We were determined to keep the clubhouse building leased because we wanted to show the world that we were strong and powerful, although in reality we were broke ass females trying to survive in a world that was not meant for us.

Roadkill broke up with G-Sting, and KB and Doobie split up ending a 24-year marriage. That left us with no handyman to help with our building maintenance. We were in one great big mess, but I never allowed other club members to see inside our torn down fort. Our emotional walls were burnt, we were broke, our kids were left at home alone, but we pressed on to be the best, or at least to make it seem that way.

In a month's time, we had lost six members and several supporters. It was a devastating loss but I was not going to let it affect the club's image. I continued to keep the lines of communication with all the former members, but it was Curve who was missed the most.

The four of us, Tab, Roadkill, KB and I, began attending more MC events out of state than in Arkansas. We had a better relationship with the Regional Bandidos and support clubs than we did with the Arkansas clubs. We were at every regional Bandido funeral and benefit even if we had to borrow money or max out our credit cards. We gained their grace and acceptance but in return, we lost valuable time with our own personal families, and pushed priorities to the back burner.

I guess that did not matter to us. Our goal was to become an official Bandido Support Club and we were determined to pursue it no matter the cost. Even though there were only four of us, we seemed to have a strong affiliation with Bandido Jim and Bandido Nomad Stubbs. They took the time to talk with us and in their own way advice us concerning the Red and Gold MC world. The Highway Chicks became their protégé in the sense that Bandido Jim sponsored us into the Bandido National Runs. He watched for our safety at these events and we answered to him. The Louisiana Bandidos allowed us to ride behind them and sometimes in the middle of the pack with the Gray Ghosts MC. Our boss, Bandido Murray, was present at these National Events, but it was with the Louisiana Bandidos whom we shared meals, camping and hotel. They had become our family and we felt safe with them. We still answered to Murray but Bandido Jim welcomed us with arms wide open. He showed us the respect due to an MC club. We called him "our other boss."

Things in Arkansas did not change much for us as a club. For me, as an individual and a patch holder it was better. I was the secretary for the ARCOMc and it was my duty to remain as diplomatically courteous as I could and do the right thing in the sight of the entire MC club's membership. It was my duty to come up with strategic actions for Coalition activities in order to promote unity and a harmonious gathering for all the clubs.

I had the honor of coordinating the ARCOMc annual chili cook off and I damn well made sure that every club was put on the list for being a part of that event. I worked with each president to make sure that everyone felt their equal participation in the event, and plenty of money raised for the ARCOMc emergency fund. My dual position was to juggle the way I talked to people while handling things properly. What I said and did, could fall back on the ARCOMc, therefore, the careful use of knowledge and wisdom was crucial. I was diligent not to be partial when acting in my role as secretary.

September 2006 was time for the HC's fourth annual. We had spent a vast amount of money on food, themed decorations, and promotions. We decided on a western theme for this year and new games and prizes to be awarded. The problem was that there were only four Highway Chicks (no one knew that our membership was that low) and hundreds of people to feed and entertain. I had to come up with a way to pull this off and make it a success.

We had all worked fervently to promote the annual and were excitedly awaiting the Red and Gold family that were eager to attend. However, that soon faded when I received a call at work from Thunderhead Big Joe. He told me he believed that if the Bandidos from out of state came to our annual it could cause a big brawl between them and the Sons of Silence at our clubhouse due to the recent hostile events at Long Branch. He thought that in the best interest of all parties involved, that no Red and Gold clubs or support clubs should attend our annual.

I stood there with the phone in my ear, not being able to say a word. You see, I thought he was joking and I was waiting for the 'not' to follow. However, he was not joking. He was serious.

"Joe, how could you? How could you have called all these people and told them not to come to our annual? Do you know how much money we are going to lose?" I said to him, as it was the first thing that came to my mouth.

"Joe, why have you done such a thing?" I said to him in a high-pitched unpleasant tone as I stood in the kitchen of Lucky's Bar & Grill.

He told me that he believed it to be in the best interest of all but that he would check with Murray and see what he thought. "You did this without Murray knowing! Joe, you know better!" I calmly yelled as I paced the kitchen back and forth.

I hung up the phone and I tried to visualize the severity of damage our club would undertake if there were no Red and Gold at our annual. I called Bandido Jim and asked if they were coming to the annual. He told me that he had talked to Big Joe and told him that they would not attend considering the recent events. I let him know if they did not attend, it would only prove to everyone that we had no true support and were totally on our own. I asked him to please reconsider and let me know. He said he would.

When I got home, I sent Bandido Jim an email conveying my standpoint on the matter.

From: *Sadgirl*
To: *Jim 1% President, Louisiana Bandidos*
Sent: *Tuesday, September 12, 2006 10:02 PM*
Subject: *FYI*

"HERE IS MY FINAL DECISION NO MATTER WHAT HAPPENS:

We are going to support the Red and Gold Nation *por vida!* Not to do so.... is not an option. I just hate if our Red and Gold brothers would not come to our 4th year of celebrations because of the others. We have planned and worked for this for 4 hard long years... Thank you for your love."

Highway Chick Sadgirl, President
Love, Loyalty & Respect por Vida

When I opened my email later that evening, there was an email response from Bandido Jim. He had sent this email out before anyone from Arkansas got a chance to call him and tell him the party was still on.

From: "mtbc"
To: Sadgirl <hdsadgirl@yahoo.com>
Re: FYI
Date: Wed, 13 Sep 2006 15:02:53 -0500

"I thought when I talked with Joe I was making the right decision. I do feel Joe is right. It is not going to prove anything to anybody if we are not there to speak for ourselves.

I can't change some people's mind but I can give my understanding of the way I believe things should be.

Your club has been more of a true support club than any of the others, so I will be there with as many of my people as I can. Tell Joe I don't mean this to be to face, since I told him I wouldn't go, but I don't see how I can be heard if I'm not there."

Love Loyalty and Respect
Bandido Jim 1%'er

This day I was truly able to see that Bandido Jim was a man of honor and respect. He was a man of courage and not afraid to be seen or heard. I truly knew that if we ever moved our club to Louisiana that he'd indeed stand behind us as he would any other support club under his leadership. The same would go for Bandido

Nomad Stubbs since they usually hang together and we all know that great minds think alike.

I felt like finally, after 4 years, we were treated with the same respect a true support club gets from a Bandido Club. It was a shame that it had to come from out of state but it was still our Red and Gold family and that is what mattered. If no one from our Red and Gold family would stand and back us up, Bandido Jim and his crew would. There were indeed a few good courageous men left in this world!

The next day Murray called me at work about 4 pm. "Are you still having your annual?" were the first words out of his mouth. "Yes we are, Murray," I answered in a firm but paranoid tone. I was afraid he was getting ready to tell me that we had to cancel it or that he would back up Big Joe's order.

"Well, we will be there!" he exclaimed. He told me that Big Joe was emotional and hot headed, and had taken it upon himself to make those phone calls. He said it was not his place but that he would deal with him. I thanked Murray repeatedly for handling this small internal problem but never said anything negative about Big Joe. He was my brother and I loved him so.

In preparation for the annual, I called on Punkin, Highway and Hedges Motorcycle Ministry Senior Pastor and our Chaplain once again. "Punkin, I need your help. Our annual is coming up soon and we do not have the manpower to pull this party off. I need your crew to stand behind us and help us make this party happen," I said to him in a personal meeting on Monday afternoon at Long Branch Saloon. Punkin did not hesitate for one second and immediately offered his services. They were a blessing for without Highway and Hedges Ministry we could have never had a successful party.

They were the total manpower at our 4th Annual. They did all the work including hospitality committee, traffic control, games, food serving, bartending, door registration, 50/50 sales, and of course prayer. They made the Highway Chicks appear to be 30-member club for they all wore our support shirts.

It was a huge project for a great party and we pulled it off. We were expecting all the ARCOMc clubs to attend as well as many out of state MC clubs. The city of Hot Springs was hosting their Second

Independent Biker Rally and the streets were packed with bikers riding everywhere. Therefore, we were looking forward to a good handful of rally bikers just passing through, to stop in and have a cold beer.

That year had to be the biggest annual ever. There was still tension and hostility between the Silent Few and our club but I was expecting them and I was ready to treat them with the best hospitality and respect ever. As President of the HC WMC, I was not going to show anything less than respect.

Our fourth annual brought over 250 people to our clubhouse that day. It was so crowded that you could not get from one room to another without elbowing someone one else. Every club in the ARCOMc attended, several out of state clubs, and quite a few independent bikers who stopped in when they saw the massive amount of bikes parked in front of the clubhouse. The best sight of all, however, was when Bandido Jim rolled in with his crew, the Gray Ghost MC, and Bandido Stubbs. It was a huge pack and made all heads turn in silence when they pulled into our property.

As club president, I felt like a million dollars. I looked around to see the faces of other patch holders and they were as much impressed as I was. As they pulled into the parking lot, all heads turned to hear the thunder of the Harley's rolling in and the massive amount of Red and Gold patches from Louisiana that pulled up to pay respects to the Highway Chicks WMC. It was a day of accomplishment for me, considering all the politics, hard work and miles I'd put on my bike and my person for the past four years.

Everyone was enjoying themselves talking, drinking, playing bike games and partaking of the great meal we'd cook the night before. My only job as president was to walk around welcoming and socializing with everyone. My enforcer made sure there were no eminent conflicts brewing. With over 20 different patches under one roof, there is always the chance of someone getting out of line whether it was due to alcohol or plain arrogance. However, this time everyone seemed to be mingling and having a good time except the Silent Few. For a while they were isolated gathered outside the north side of the building and were talking among themselves.

It was obvious that they didn't care to mingle with the other patch holders and had attended our annual most likely, because they were told to by their mother club, the Sons of Silence. Several other patch holders noticed their alienated status and questioned me about it. In order to avoid an ugly situation at the annual, I told who ever asked me that they were comfortable enough to have a small church meeting and as soon as they were done, they'd come in and socialize. I don't think I was too credible for many of our Red and Gold brothers kept a low profile while keeping an eye on them, especially the out of town ones.

Bandido Nomad Stubbs approached me close to dinnertime, in the living area of the clubhouse. He leaned into me as he slightly covered his mouth, and whispered into my ear, "Do you want the situation fixed or not?" I immediately responded, "Yes sir, I do."

"That's all I want to know," he said as he walked away to the garage. I followed him from a distance as he went to the back yard near the cold-water running creek with Bandido Murray, several other Arkansas Bandidos, Sons of Silence President Mitch and several of his people. They had a private meeting and after it was over, no one seemed to be in a hostile or tense disposition. Bandido Stubbs walked pass me and said, "Everything will be OK now." I smiled and thanked him.

Honestly, to this day, I do not know what was said in the meeting or the contents of it. I do have my suspicions that it was about the relationship between the Arkansas MC's and the Highway Chicks.

I do know that Bandido Stubbs and his wife, PBOL (Proud Bandido Ol' Lady) Dummy, did a lot of arbitration for our club and they were good to us. That weekend they stayed at my home and even attended the church service offered by Highway and Hedges Motorcycle Ministry the following morning at our clubhouse. Gestures like these leave a good taste behind and do not allow us to forget what friendship is, even though it is because of a patch.

Our fourth annual was a colossal success and an opportunity to show the MC world that the Highway Chicks could be a powerful MC if given the opportunity. The fact that we did not wear a visible Heart Patch did not lessen the devotion we had for our mother club and our boss, Bandido Murray. Nevertheless, it was Bandido Jim and Bandido Stubbs along with the Shreveport, Louisiana crew who showed us true brotherhood and respect.

It was at this annual that I met San Jacinto High Roller Lee and Slow Hand from Texas. They came to our party and had a great time. When they got ready to leave, Slow Hand's throttle cable snapped leaving them no choice but to stay at our clubhouse. They were treated with the utmost hospitality. The next day Grave Digger TomKat and I "trailered" the bike to a local bike mechanic who at my request opened his shop just to repair their bike.

After this day we never again had confrontations with the Silent Few as a club. They showed us respect and we returned it. I continued to have a comfortable liaison with Mitch and learn many lessons from him. He was a smart man and knew what he was doing. I was all about learning to do things the right way so we could stay out of trouble. Tab on the other hand despised him and made it a point to make it difficult for me when it came to following Arkansas protocol.

My goal was to get our Heart Patch back even if it took 10 years but at the same time, I wanted to be sure and keep our boss Murray out of difficult situations by doing the right thing, and having a good political relationship with the other MC clubs. Many of the MC members did not like us and that was OK. I did not expect the majority of MC clubs to be civil to a bunch of girls trying to be like them.

The 2006 Bandido National Turkey Run in Texas was at hand and we had made a decision to attend. I had a family reunion in Texas so I caged it from Austin to Corpus. Tab and Roadkill rode from Shreveport with Bandido Jim, the Louisiana Bandidos and the Gray Ghosts MC.

Once again Bandido Jim sponsored us into the event. We ran into Murray and some of the Arkansas crew, but we spent most of our time with the Louisiana Bandidos, Bandido Stubbs, PBOL Dummy, and the Gray Ghost MC. The host club served a wonderful turkey dinner and we met many Bandidos from other states. It was a good experience, a great fellowship, and we were the only female WMC support club.

I had to return that same day for I had left all my family back in

Austin and I was obligated to spend Thanksgiving with them. I was not comfortable leaving Tab and Roadkill by themselves, but I had no choice. I felt that Tab did not have the club's best interest in her quest, but I needed our Patch to be seen for more than a few hours. We were in this together and we'd gone too far to turn back.

As a club we put a lot of work and sacrifice into it, but it seemed like no matter how much we tried, we were still seen as outsiders. We were a woman's club in a man's world and regardless of how much we accomplished, how much we rode, and how many great parties we put on, we could not cross over to the side of the 1%'er world.

10
The Shepherd on the Other Side of the Fence

The ARCOMc meeting for May 2006 opened a new chapter in my life that day. It was a chapter that changed the entire course of my being, when *he* walked into the meeting.

I remember the first time I saw him. I was sitting at the President's table with Bandido Murray, Sons of Silence Mitch, and Vietnam Vet Beau. Bandido Murray informed the Coalition that there was a man who had moved into the State of Arkansas and wanted permission to fly his Colors. He said his name was Shepherd and he wore a *'Soldiers for Jesus'* patch on his back. Murray introduced him to the Coalition and he stated his intention for moving into Arkansas and wanting to wear his patch.

"I just want to go to school in Hot Springs and do what Jesus wants me to do," he said. His intention and attitude appeared to be sincere. However, Outsider Bartman gave him a hard time by arguing that his intentions were not sincere because he was coming into Arkansas wearing his patch.

I remember looking across the table at Sons of Silence Mitch and signaling to a small patch he wore in the lower right front of his vest. It read "SFFS". I knew that phrase was used by the Sons of Silence in Arkansas and that would be a major problem for him. Later that same evening, Shepherd humbly and immediately, without question removed the patch at the request of the Sons of Silence President.

A few months later, he no longer wore the "Soldiers of Jesus" patch. He showed up at the biker bar as a hang-around for the Sons of Silence Motorcycle Club. Personally, I believed he had taken a detour from the path assigned to him by God and I was very much saddened by his action. I believe that he should have fought for his entitlement to be a Soldier for Jesus and follow the path God had put him on, but instead he chose the passive way and convinced himself that God had opened that door for him, when indeed it was a bypass for the perfect will of God. However, that was only my belief.

I desperately tried not to think of him but it was not working. I knew it was a major breech of club ethics. My colors were Red and Gold and his were Red, Black and White. He was from the other side of the fence. He belonged to the Sons of Silence and I belonged to a Bandido Support Club in the State of Arkansas. Our clubs were not enemies but we were not friends either. At least we were not supposed to be buddy-buddy. We had already engaged in the big blowout with the Silent Few MC, so I definitely did not need the "married clubs' issue resurfaced.

It was not his colors that attracted me to him. It was more like a powerful spiritual magnet that seemed to pull my heart out of my insides and make its way through his blue-piercing eyes, into the depths of his soul. Once inside this spiritual essence I could feel an immense flood of sorrow and spiritual confusion. I felt sadness for him and sympathized in his world. I so desperately wanted to cross over and talk to him but it was forbidden by the unwritten ethical rules of MC protocol.

I cannot seem to stay out of the other side of the fence. I just could not help how mysteriously attractive he was. He had a peaceful disposition about the way he carried himself and never said a lot, at least not to me. I always wondered about him. About his character and his choices, but it always ended in an ambiguity. His aura was very gray but carried no evil. He seemed to be very unhappy in his surroundings and portrayed much to think.

I would find myself distractively starring at him while he stood on the other side of the different patch holders that served as an invisible force. Just a glimpse here and there would make me feel like a high school kid in love for the first time. However, he was on the other side of the fence, the side that was forbidden for me to set foot on. I confessed this ill-fated attraction to my club sisters and they would caution me to stay out of enemy territory.

"Don't even go there," were the orders from my some of my brothers as well.

My commitment to my club and my colors has always been my priority. I am aware that this was my choice and I have always fulfilled my love, loyalty and respect to my club and my boss, Bandido Murray. This however, could not stop me from looking across the room to the Sons of Silence prospect that seemed to have captivated my soul. I was fully aware that as a Red and Gold supporter I was forbidden to intermingle with them publically, especially at a personal level. There was an unspoken code of conduct that called for members of like colors to band together at open events.

One Monday evening towards the end of November 2006, I was at an Exxon gas station in Little Rock waiting for the rest of my club to pull up so we could roll in the Long Branch Saloon for pool tournament night. As I sat on my bike and watched cars go by, a biker pulled up on the other side of the parking lot. The sound of the pipes moved my eyes in that direction. To my surprise, it was him! It was Sons of Silence Prospect Shepherd. He got off his bike and walked into the store. I could not help but to jump at the opportunity of *running into him* at the store.

I quickly made my way inside and we met in the aisle. I was not sure how he would react since I was wearing my Colors and he was wearing his. Nevertheless, our eyes met, fastened, and then, as we both snapped out of the stare, we hugged. It was the first physical encounter we had. Our conversation was brief and general, but it was great. He had a warm and sincere Christian-Godly spirit. I felt a lot of comfort in that short meeting.

Several weeks later, my club and I were at a Sons event called a "Marty Party" at Long Branch Saloon. It was a memorial party for their Chaplain who had passed away the year before. I was in the back room at the bar talking with some of my brothers. As I headed to the front room, I saw Shepherd was standing by a pool table. I stopped and talked casually with him. As we spoke, he grabbed his camera-phone and snapped a picture of us as he put his arm around me. Some my club sisters looked at me as I smiled with joy. They knew that I was engulfed in the moment.

He asked me if I was married. "Yes...," I reluctantly answered.

"Well I never see your ol' man. He never comes around so I'm just wondering," he said.

"This is my world (referring to the MC world) and he is not and will never be a part of it. He does not come to events with me because I do not invite him," was my closing statement. I was brutally honest.

I wanted to tell him the substance of the facts in my marriage but I felt I was justified in answering his question, "Are you married?" Yes, I was married but was separated and miserably unhappy with the man who was a drug addict and a non-patch holder.

We went our separate ways that day. I kept thinking about the sorrow emanating from his presence. I could not understand why this energy was so magnetically strong. The distress in his eyes was almost tangible to my spirit. He seemed so sad and out of balance. In my human reasoning, I concluded that he was just unhappy and probably felt out of place in his new home state. I attempted to dismiss this perception and completely submerged myself into the world of MC politics.

I passionately devoted 100% of my time to the Highway Chicks WMC and the supporting of the Bandidos MC. We traveled, did politics, attended events, met people, got different clubs talking from different states, and rode our bikes everywhere. I put a lot of effort into my role as secretary for the ARCOMc. I organized and planned events for the coalition, kept each club informed of general happenings and continued to put together the calendar of events for the year. I also took care of communicating protocol with the new MC clubs wanting to come into the State of Arkansas and kept them informed of president's decisions and directions. It was a full time job and it kept me busy.

On occasions, at an event, I would run into Shepherd. It was a brief hi and bye but our hugs lasted longer than the normal friendly hug each time. Neither of us wanted to let go but eventually we did. I did not see much of him until January of 2007 at the Highway Chicks clubhouse where he attended a baby shower for Sons of Silence, Brakeline's daughter.

The time I spent with Shepherd at the baby shower was short. I was more concerned with Rachael having all her needs met and attending to my guests. We met in the bar area of the Clubhouse where he said to me, "I had no idea. I had no idea that you were Brakeline's family. You know, you hear things from clubs and sometimes it's just not all true."

I wondered what he had heard from clubs. A picture storyboard ran in my mind of people talking bad stuff about me out of their own prejudice and hatred for women bikers, the kind of talk that should not have traveled into the 21st century. I reassured him that his brother had a high place of esteem in my heart and that we were family and that would never change. We exchanged words briefly and once again, we said goodbye and went our separate ways.

A few weeks later, I was at work at a new job. It was a neighborhood bar on Hwy 5, a scenic highway in Hot Springs, Arkansas. There were no customers so I went in the back room to wash some glasses. A few minutes later, someone called for me. I dried my hands, grinned my teeth and walked to the bar area.

To my total surprise, there stood Shepherd on the other side of the bar (Seems like he was always on the other side). I felt as if God had smiled on me and given me a break from all the pressures and demands of the MC world. He began to make his way around the bar and I met him half way. We hugged..., hugged..., and hugged. It was a comfort to be held by him, but the sadness radiating from his presence still overshadowed my gladness.

"What are you doing here?" I asked.

"Mitch sent me. I heard you've been having problems with a red and white guy. Has he come around? Is he a reasonable man?"

We talked about the situation briefly, and then swiftly began talking about God, the ministry and ourselves. We exchanged life stories and it was no surprise to find out we had so much in common.

The most important element that we learned about each other was that both our spouses had been killed on a Harley Davidson on the highway, my husband in 2000 and his wife in 2003.

It was then that I understood the immense grief in his soul. I saw his wound completely open, bleeding, and overwhelming with emotional pain. I had received closure in my life with my husband's death but he apparently hadn't. We talked for a long time that day. As he was leaving I told him to come around more often so we could visit. I wanted to get to know him at a personal level even though our colors stood between us. I would have to cross over to the side where I could not tread. Was it worth taking the risk of betrayal for love and romance? For the opportunity to serve in the ministry with a man of equal status? Or… was he of equal status?

I knew all the risks that were involved if I began talking with Shepherd at a personal level. As a woman patch holder, I was already in the spotlight. I was fully aware of the reaction of the MC Presidents if I got involved with him. As a woman, I could not help the tangible chemistry that pulled me toward him. I had no choice but to submerge myself in club life completely, hoping that my attraction to him might fade.

Third MC Officers Dinner

With the upcoming third officers dinner at hand, I had to dedicate my entire time for the final preparations of this grand event. February 2007 had the largest and most successful turnout for the Annual MC Officer's Dinner. We had received 23 RSVP's all from different clubs. The enthusiasm from other club officers to attend this dinner was very much anticipated. They were looking forward to the event, many of them inquiring of the event throughout the year. Much club business was to be taken care of at this dinner between individual clubs. It was a 'meet and greet' political affair in hopes of keeping a peaceful liaison between MC clubs.

Tab, KB and I stayed up until 4:30 in the morning preparing and cooking food for 200 plus people. Early that morning we picked up tables and chairs, supplies, and any other item we may have overlooked. We purchased beer, liquor and soft drinks. We had a final club meeting to make sure everything was perfect— and it was! The only missing factor was that Brakeline would not be able to attend due to personal family reasons. In the past, he had represented us and the State of Arkansas and many presidents wanted to talk to him at this dinner.

Bandido Murray would not be attending this year either, but for the first time he sent his Vice President Bandido Fast, accompanied by Bandido Eddie. That was a good political effort. At last, we had the Arkansas Bandidos represent our state, and their recognition as well. Finally on that day, they were able to see that we were a true MC club and could conduct business as well as the male MC clubs. The Arkansas Bandidos met MC Presidents from different clubs that had been in our circle for 3 years now. They finally saw that we did not dream up these people that we talked about for so long. They observed how so many clubs supported us and that made a great difference in the time I remained President.

It was amazing to see how my plan had evolved from an idea I had on the way back from Mississippi several years back, to a great MC gathering of motorcycle club officers. To be able to go from 11 attending clubs to 23 in just 2 years was a great accomplishment for a club such as ours.

Both bikes and cages rolled into our clubhouse that day. MC Officers arrived early hoping to meet and greet other presidents. There were even presidents in crutches (due to bike wrecks) for they were not going to miss this event. Before we knew it, the clubhouse was packed wall to wall with presidents and MC Officers. It was an awesome show of colors and a peaceful gathering. Highway and Hedges MM served and catered to each individual present without prejudice or impartiality.

The clubhouse garage was set up with long tables and elegantly decorated for the male décor. As the MC Presidents sat at their place of choice, Pastor Punkin opened with a word of prayer. A five course meal was individually served to them afterwards. I publically welcomed all clubs to our third MC Officers Dinner. I acknowledged each club by name and gave the respect due. I spoke briefly on the dinner's purpose and thanked everyone, especially the ones that had travelled hundreds of miles. Finally I introduced the guest speakers for the night. Our special guest speaker was Boozefighter Bucket Head from the Mississippi Chapter. Our second guest speaker was Boozefighter 66 Buckskin from Little Rock, Arkansas. They spoke on the political legislation of how government affects bikers. The speeches were informative and supported by literature on the relative topics.

There was plenty to eat, drink and talk about. I was praised by almost every patch holder in that building. It was impressive to see how well organized and structured this year's dinner had turned out. I also observed the positive social aspect and the results achieved. The MC Presidents were amazed on how well this dinner had turned out, but the most overwhelmed of all was San Jacinto High Roller National President, Race. I was standing near the bar when he told me, "Sadgirl, I have been to many events all over the country for many years, but I have never been to one such as this one. This is the most impressed I have been and I congratulate you on hosting it. I will never forget it. I will never forget seeing all these presidents together and everyone getting along."

Words like these made all the effort and hard labor worth it. To see the puzzled faces of people trying to figure out how these girls put on such an event ... To see the glad faces of brothers greeting one another ... To see eyes squinting trying to read the patch of another person ... But most of all to know that this event would make things better for Arkansas in the future was worth every single drop of sweat, and every insult that we endured as an MC Club.

When the dinner was over, I was called into a private meeting with Bandido Fast, Sons of Silence Mitch, and Sons of Silence XXX (name withheld at patch holder's request). I went in the meeting ready to explain why there were so many different patch holders, for I knew I was in trouble. I knew they were going to scold me for putting on an event that was beyond my league and perhaps a little too dangerous. After all it was the first time the Arkansas Bandidos had attended this event.

But for the first time ever, they commended and praised me in the achieved results. I was stunned! I could not believe what I had just heard. I braced myself on the chair's armrest as I waited for the hit, but it never came. For the first time I was given the respect of an MC President by the State's leading 1%'ers (Bandido Murray was not present. He is the head). The only thing they instructed me on was to pre inform them of out of state clubs attending next year. They wanted to know who would be attending. I was jumping for joy when I left the room. After 4 years of being the doormat club, the breakthrough ultimately happened. A good thing had occurred in the MC world in Arkansas and it was because I made it happen through the Highway Chicks.

Club presidents or officers at the dinner were the Bandidos MC from Arkansas; Bandidos MC from Louisiana; Sons of Silence MC, Arkansas; Thunderheads MC (3 Chapters), Arkansas; Ozark Riders MC (3 Chapters), Arkansas; Silent Few MC, Arkansas; Vietnam Vets MC, Arkansas; Boozefighters MC, Arkansas; Boozefighters MC, Mississippi; Back Road Ramblers MC, Arkansas; Martyrs MC, Arkansas; Gravediggers MC, Arkansas; Survivors MC, Arkansas; Outsiders MC, Arkansas; Swamp Riders MC, Arkansas; Pistoleros MC, Tennessee; Pistoleros MC, Gulfport, Mississippi; Gray Ghosts MC, Louisiana; Dixie Renegades MC, Mississippi; Hells Lovers MC, Texas; Road Barrons MC, Arkansas; San Jacinto High Rollers MC, Texas; San Jacinto High Rollers MC, National; Nazarites MC, Texas; Mississippi Riders RA, Mississippi; Southern Cross MC, Tennessee; Military Vets MC, Kansas; Military Vets, National; Highway Chicks WMC, Arkansas; and Highway and Hedges Motorcycle Ministry, Arkansas.

After the dinner was over, Ozark Rider President Wrench called me aside and said that he needed a very special favor from me. He asked me if he could put Ozark Rider Probationary, Swede in my care. "He is going through a divorce. He is in a hard place and is very depressed. I know you can take him into your group and help him go through this. I have respect and confidence in you. I have seen you work with people. I love him for he is my brother and it is breaking my heart to see him suffer emotionally. Would you do this for me?" He asked me in the clubhouse shop area.

I told him I would do my best for a brother must always be taken care of. That day I took him in and put Ozark Rider Swede in the care of Highway Chick Roadkill.

The following week was the first ARCOMc event for 2007. It was a bitter cold and rainy day. The Gravediggers MC hosted the party at Hard Riders Bar in Cabot. KB and I arrived close to 7:00 pm. We caged it because it was freezing and it would be late before we left the bar.

We mingled and did the usual politics before sitting at a table. I got my food, sat down and lo and behold, my phone rang. It was an unknown number. I never answer unknown numbers but I chose to answer this one in particular. It was Shepherd. He had never called me. I was in complete shock and just stared at KB my secretary. He wanted to know what event was going on and where. I told him we were at Hard Riders Bar in Cabot, Arkansas. He said he would be there shortly and hung up the phone.

An hour later, he arrived and sat at my table beside me. I was now past complete shock. He began talking with me as if we had been best of buddies for a long time. I fell in and followed the conversation and flow of the atmosphere. The table was small in diameter so his arm touched mine as we ate and talked. KB noticed the enormous amount of chemistry that was flowing between us and she kept kicking me under the table as she maliciously smiled at me. I kicked her back and told her to quit. She was making me nervous more than he was.

The two of us bought 50/50 raffle tickets and neither of us could see the numbers called over the microphone so we shared his reading glasses. It was so cute. He was actually enjoying himself and having a good time. One of his club brothers, Crash, joined us at the table but it did not seem to hinder the spirits though. His ticket number came up and he won two tee shirts. When he returned to the table, he turned around and gave me one of them.

As it was time to leave, we hugged and as usual, we clung on to each other. We agreed to meet the next day at the Swap Meet in Little Rock, Arkansas.

"You'll have to put up with me all weekend," he said to me as we departed.

I paid attention to what he was really saying, and understood that he wanted to hang out for the next two days. After almost an entire year of waiting, it finally happened! We were going to go somewhere together.

On the way back home, KB and I talked and laughed about the silly, unplanned chain of events. We were being girls about it when my phone rang.

"It's Shep. Is he calling you already?" She hollered at me immediately.

"Nah, it's not going to be him," I said as I reached for my phone.

I looked at the caller ID and recognized the number. It was him calling me! I was in awe. I motioned for her to be quiet so I could talk with him.

"I just want you to know that I had a good time this evening and I enjoyed the conversation," he said.

"Well I did to. It was nice talking with you," I replied.

He told me he would be at the swap meet and that he would look for me. Everything seemed to be happening so fast considering the fact that I had waited an entire year to be able to talk with him. I felt overtaken with joy like a whirlwind from the north. One day we were complete strangers glancing at each other across the room and the next we were making plans to go to an event. I giggled all the way home with KB and talked about this fresh new happening.

The next day did not come soon enough. As I walked into the fairgrounds for the Swap Meet, I immediately spotted him. He was standing guard by his President, Mitch. I walked up to Mitch and talked with him but did not pay much attention to Shepherd. I did not want to get him in trouble by distracting him.

We went about our club business until 5:00 pm. The vendors had begun to close down and the crowd was scarce. It was a cold day and many of the bikers left as the sun was going down. As we were ready to leave, he approached me and asked me where I was going.

"We are going to the Thunderheads MC After-Swap Meet Party," I said.

He acted as if he wanted to go with us, however, I was concerned because all but one of his club members were there. Our Protocol said that at least two patch holders must attend an event together, especially if it is not your club-sponsored event. He was a probate and I was under the impression that he could not attend a different colors event, particularly by himself. However, I was not going to tell a 1% probate what to do so I did not say anything.

As we were leaving he said, "Do you want to ride with me?"

He was driving his pickup truck and I had ridden in KB's truck with her. I looked at KB, she looked at me and said, "Go ahead."

"OK. I'll ride with you," I told Shepherd.

KB and I walked to her truck so I could get my purse. "Oh my God! I can't believe he invited me to ride with him. I'm so gonna die!" I said to KB as I grabbed her arm and yanked her back and forth repeatedly.

"Have fun," was all she could tell me.

I got in his truck with him and headed to the Thunderheads clubhouse with my club. I could not understand how he just went with us to a Red and Gold party without consulting with his patch or any of his officers. I am glad that he did go for on this date we became a couple.

We had a long conversation about many different things on the way to Garner, Arkansas. One distinct question still echoes in my mind, "Do you think you can make a good pastor's wife?"

It wasn't ten minutes into the drive when he asked me this question. "This is the fastest proposal I've ever had," I thought to myself. Was I super irresistible or was he moving too fast? It was intriguing though, for I wasn't expecting something so profound to emerge in our casual conversation.

He told me that he did not pursue me because I was married and he was a Christian man. He also told me that did not believe in sex before marriage. He was upfront and honest about his moral convictions.

"Okay, I can live with that for a while," I said to myself.

As we were riding in his truck to the Thunderheads Clubhouse and our conversation was becoming intense, I noticed him looking in his rear view mirror often but refused to comment about it. Finally he said, "Well, Axxel is right behind us and you ARE noticeable. I had told him I was going home so I don't know if he'll pull us over." (Axxel was at the time an Arkansas Sons of Silence). I acted semi-indifferent towards his comment but in reality I was secretly panicking. He was riding with an MC club member of opposite colors, and not going where he had told his Patch. He was riding with the Highway Chicks WMC, the club one of his brothers hated so much.

After about 5 minutes of passive pursuit he pulled up beside us on his bike and made sure we saw him. He passed the two trucks of Highway Chicks in front of us and went on. It was one of those moments in my life where I exhaled, relaxed, and thanked God we were not in trouble just yet.

We arrived at the Red and Gold Clubhouse in Garner 35 minutes later and as we walked in, my brothers gave me a point-blank stare. Their eyes spoke to me and their silent question was... what is he doing here?

They all knew he was a Sons of Silence probate and the immediate reaction would be to accuse us of bringing a spy. I reassured some of my brothers that it was OK and that he was with me. He was not wearing his cut just a support shirt. He sat at the Highway Chicks table beside me. Bandidos, Thunderheads, Ozark Riders, Martyrs, Boozefighters, and a few citizens filled the clubhouse. I made my rounds but remained with Shepherd for the most part. He was my guest and I did not want him to feel awkward.

I sat beside him and gave him my undivided attention although I made it appear otherwise to everyone else. I was the President for my club and had to be diplomatically courteous with all other patch holders, especially the Oklahoma Bandidos that were present. The band began playing a slow song. Shep turned towards me and asked, "Do you want to dance?"

I didn't think twice. "Yes!" I said as I smiled at my sisters. He reached and picked up the camera we were taking pictures with and put it in his pocket. "Damn, he's a smart man," I said to myself as we made our way to the dance floor.

That was the first time he held me in his arms. It felt great. As we danced, everyone starred at us and wondered what was going on. It was an intimate encounter between two obvious lovers on the dance floor, who couldn't hide their feelings for each other. Our patches did not seem to matter for we were engulfed in the moment as we followed the rhythm of the music and everyone starred at us. This was one dance I wanted to last forever. However, I knew all good things must end, and so it did. When we sat back at our table, my sisters were giving me the 'you troublemaker' look. Tab was furious that he had accompanied me in the first place. She was hating on me and made it obvious. This time, I did not care what she thought. I was overtaken by this man whom I had admired afar off for a year.

That night he drove me home. I invited him to come inside and gave him a tour of my home. He looked around and said, "You have a lot of things and I have a lot of things. Who is going to get rid of what?" I smiled. We talked for a few hours and I expressed my concern of how I believed his president would not approve of us being a couple. It wasn't long that Mitch and I had the conflict of "married clubs" and it was still fresh. We had said this would never again happen; nevertheless, Shepherd reassured me that it would be OK. He said not to worry about it.

He knew I lived alone so he asked me, "What do you have for protection?

"You know, now that you mention it, I cannot find my gun. So either my ex took it, or I hid it and can't remember where I put it," I said to him.

He pulled a gun out of his inside vest pocket, took it out of the hoister, unloaded it, and gave it to me.

"You need protection," he said as he showed me how to use his hand held small weapon. I looked at him in astonishment. I had never had a stand up man show his true colors. He asked me about my divorce. "What's holding you up?"

"Finances," I answered.

"Divorce is not an option. I will give you the money," he firmly stated.

OK, someone wake me up. I thought to myself. The man that I'd admired for almost a year was in my living room in my house sharing his feelings with me. The same man I'd been hesitant to approach due to his club colors.

I was quickly getting involved in a dangerous love triangle. A triangle because we both belonged to MC clubs and were both accountable to our leaders. The situation we were getting into was a political risk for all parties involved but we could not resist the attraction and chemistry that prevailed over the politics of the MC world.

That week he called his club president and asked for his blessing to date me. Although Mitch was not very happy with the idea, he gave him his blessing. He also went to Brakeline and asked for his blessing and guidance. Last, but not least in the same week, he went to Bandido Murray, my boss, and asked for his blessing. Bandido Murray told him that he needed to treat me right and that it was OK to date me. Shepherd had secured permission from the three men in charge of the 1% clubs in Arkansas. That gave me the impression that his intentions were serious and long term.

He said to me, "I feel like I'm dating the Godfather's daughter." That was a sweet and true statement. Murray was like a father to me.

Shep gave me Bandido One Wire's business card and told me to call him and check his references. One Wire is the Chaplain for the Bandido Austin Chapter and secretary for the Texas Coalition of Motorcycle Clubs. He is also his very close friend. I called One Wire a couple of days later, introduced myself, and explained my intentions with his brother. I informed him of my status in the MC world as well.

In the weeks to come, we continued to spend time getting to know each other. We went on several dates and worked on our relationship around our scheduled club events, never letting one overshadow the other. My position in the ARCOMc was very demanding and my phone rang constantly. Shepherd was learning to deal with me being a patch holder and I had to learn not to be one whenever we were together. I still feared the fact that we wore different Colors and hoped that none of our Presidents would interfere too much in our relationship.

Sons of Silence Mitch informed him that we could not ride together wearing our Colors. He said it would be an insult. I did not have a problem with Mitch's order. There were bigger things at stake and riding together was not one of them, at least not for now. We continued attending church and getting to know each other more. I had filed for divorce and was anxiously awaiting the Judge's decision. Until my divorce was final, I was not eligible to be his woman. That was his choice and I respected him for that honor bestowed unto me. Shepherd told me he needed his small loaner gun back because it fit perfectly in his vest pocket but that he would give me another one instead. He invited me into his bedroom and took seven or eight different pistols out of his safe. He laid them on his desk and asked me to pick one. I sat down and carefully picked up each pistol one by one and examined them. I felt the weight, balance and anything else that I thought I would like. In reality, I didn't know anything about guns but I didn't want to look stupid. I finally picked out one that I thought I would like. I picked it because it was big and pretty. He showed me how to handle the gun and the specifics about it. "Are you sure this is the one you want?" he said to me as he stood beside his desk. "Yea, I kind of like this one. It's so big!" I exclaimed.

"That's a Springfield 45 ACP. It's a good one. Are you sure that's the one you want?"

"Yes I am. I like this one."

"Well, OK, if this is the one you like, then it's yours," he firmly said to me with a chuckle while taking the others back to the safe.

I thanked him as I sat there in total amazement of how much he cared for me. I took a few minutes to ponder as I looked out his bedroom window at the tree tops on that beautiful sunny day. I took the gun home and always kept it close to me.

I continued to travel into Alabama, Mississippi, Louisiana and Texas with the Highway Chicks. After the success of the MC Officer's Dinner, it seemed that doors were opening left and right. The little free time that I had, I spent with my new boyfriend from the other side of the fence. He was good to me and helped finance some of my trips.

Shepherd was interested in purchasing some real estate for investment purposes. He had seen a bar for sale adjacent to the lake. It was called Kat's Bar and Grill. We drove to the property and spoke to the bar manager, looked at the property and examined the building. I tried to get the feel of it but could not get a good feeling about it. Work and bar managing was not a problem for me. I had been a bar manager for several years and knew the operational procedures of bar management. Shepherd said he would work the bar with me but I just could not see myself stepping into this line of work with him. It felt like God's spirit was not agreeing with mine.

"If you had the choice of going into business, what would you choose? What would you do?" He asked me as we in his pickup driving down Central Avenue, Hot Springs.

I contemplated and tossed back and forth my response. It culminated in my most honest respond. "I'd like to do full time ministry. That would have to be my choice."

It was what I wanted. For the past ten months, ever since I re-committed my life to God at the Long Branch parking lot, I had been struggling with my calling to the ministry. The burden to return to the teaching ministry was aglow and strong, but I knew that I had to wait on God's time. He would send someone my way to balance the work. For me, it seemed that God's time was at hand. Every piece of the puzzle was falling into place. I had surrendered to God and given Him complete control of my will.

Shepherd's heart was for the lost and needy while mine was for defeated Christians. He preached to the lost and I taught to the body of believers. We were both at God's disposal willing and ready for the work of the Gospel. We had the perfect balance. He was a preacher, I a teacher. He had compassion; I had command. He had a mission; I had a vision. He was a biker and so was I.

The Arkansas Coalition of Motorcycle Clubs pool tournaments started back up in March of 2007. Every Monday night a different MC club would host the tournament. Our club ethics did not allow us to fraternize during the tournaments or during any MC club event, but that did not unsettle us for we understood there had to be give-and-take.

"We can glance at each other across the room or touch our hands as we walk near each other," he said to me in an effort to encourage me. He was letting me know he would be thinking about me. In reality, we always managed to spend time talking with each other regardless of the rules of engagement.

Tab hated to see us privately talking. She would roll her eyes and make crude remarks. It seemed to me that she was upset that it wasn't her who had been love-stricken. She reacted the same way when KB got her a boyfriend.

Being with Shepherd did not cause me to change my social behavior with my club, my boss or the MC family. This was my personal life and as far as I was concerned – my happiness for the rest of my days. My fervor and loyalty to the Red and Gold world was stronger than ever. My admiration of courage and valor for the Sons of Arkansas was just as fervent. I had hoped against hope that the "marriage" of our colors would not affect or interfere with our clubs, but I knew better. I knew in my heart that sooner or later one of us would fall as the fatal victim of the forbidden love between two patches of opposite colors.

He arrived at my house the next day, and when he walked in the door he starred at me.

"What?" I asked with a puzzled look on my face.

"I saw a building for sale. It is a church building and they only want $190.000 for it. It's in the Historic District of Downtown Hot Springs and it's beautiful," he said as he held out his hands, palms facing up.

We sat down to dinner and talked about the building he had seen. After dinner, we sat on the couch to watch a movie but the church building had consumed his entire focus. He could not stop thinking about it. Suddenly he put his boots back on and said "Put your shoes on, let's go see it." We headed out the door for a 10-minute drive to Whittington Street. It was the old Haven United Methodist Church building.

It was indeed an architectural splendor of glory. Its magnificent historical outer brick walls implored the need for worshippers. It reflected a certain holiness that can only be tangible in an old church building. At least that was the impression I got from it. He began calling the real estate agent so we could see it inside. He must have called four times before he finally got a response.

"I'm right here at the church and I would like to see the inside of it if you are in the neighborhood," he said to the agent on his cell phone as he paced back and forth in the drizzling rain.

As we waited for the realtor, we walked around the building and looked at every corner and crevice. We walked every square foot of the property and I imagined the kind of ministry we could run out of this place. Was this a possibility? Was God going to allow us to work in the ministry of the Word? I asked myself.

The rain came down harder but it didn't seem to bother us. We were extremely excited about God's work for us and anticipating our future as a ministerial couple. While standing at the front steps at the main entrance, I grabbed a hold of his soaking wet arm and said, "You pray and I'll agree."

He began to pray, "Lord, I don't even know how to begin to pray for something like this. But if it is your will, give it to us. Give us this church so that we could reach the lost in the community for Jesus." I was beside him agreeing with him and completely trusting God.

The real estate agent finally showed up and introduced himself, he turned towards me and while shaking my hand he said, "I know you. You are my hero. You ride a purple bike."

"Oh great! Here we go again. No matter where I go, someone knows who I am," I thought to myself. It was a humorous unexpected episode where I realized how well known I was in my town. The brief introduction was amicable and funny but the mood quickly changed when the agent opened the front door and we entered into the building.

It was a beautiful nostalgic classic foyer. The first thing my eyes caught was the antique well used curved wooden pews laid out sparingly in front of the sanctuary. Adjacent sat an oversized pipe organ, a ravishing work of art that echoed hundreds of hymns from retired songbooks under the elegant cathedral ceiling. I could not believe that the magnificence of this lovely structure could possibly be the headquarters for our ministry.

The agent continued with the tour. There were little rooms scattered throughout the basement once used as Sunday school rooms, nursery and prayer rooms when the church was in her full splendor. There was a pastor's study, a green room, a choir room and many other chambers that emerged a moldy staleness of pleasant antiquated atmosphere. The kitchen was oversized and all the appliances were in perfect condition. I was fascinated by the white one-piece porcelain classic kitchen sink in tiptop shape.

I could hear the clattering of plates as godly Methodist women washed them in the early 1900's and visualized all the great Sunday picnic dinners. The bathrooms were throne rooms for the toilets sat on an elevated concrete slab. This architectural structure was indeed an enormous space and a mighty project.

Was this what God wanted for us? Was this the building set aside for us to begin our ministry in? That I was not sure of, however, the one thing I did know was that it was every preacher's dream church house. A structure of this magnificent glory was indeed a gift from God.

We prayed for God's will to have priority in our lives for we were sure that ministry was not an option. We knew that our ministry was on the verge of exploding and location was not as important as purpose. It was only a matter of choosing the building that would house the people.

"Do you think they will accept $175.000 for the Church?" Shepherd asked the real estate agent.

"Are you making an offer?" was his quirky response.

"Well, yes. I do want to make an offer." There was no hesitation in his voice as he plainly made the statement to the realtor.

I was in awe. His decision was sudden and without hesitation. His words carried assurance and substance. I was a bit surprised at the suddenness of his determination, while fearful of the impulse of which he made decisions. This compulsive drive may have been an indication of being double-minded and that frightened me. I did see that his objectivity, nevertheless, showed a capacity for humanity and this was his ambition.

After the tour we immediately went to the real estate office and the agent pulled up the contract from his laptop. He signed the necessary papers and wrote a $1000 check for earnest money. We never did get to have our movie night but this was far better. This was the real deal and it was happening right under our roof.

11
Patch Holders are People Too

March 16, 2007 rolled in and good news along with it. The building owners had accepted the offer Shepherd made. We had a dinner date that night at Hard Riders Bar and Grill in Cabot, Arkansas. It was the same place where he sat at my table exactly thirty days ago and made first contact with me. There he shared the good news. "My offer has been accepted and it has been signed, sealed and delivered." I smiled and acknowledged how well he had handled the business end of the deal. I was proud of the wisdom he employed while dealing with the agent.

Thirty days prior, the beginning of our relationship had commenced, and 30 days later the beginning of our ministry followed, all in the same bar. We were two patch holders from two different sides of the fence who had united our hearts and hoped to bring MC clubs together through example, and win lost souls for Jesus.

My club had to go on a trip to Birmingham, Alabama that weekend. We promised to attend the Pistoleros MC party and show Arkansas Red and Gold support. KB and I left early that Saturday morning to our brother's clubhouse. It was a difficult trip for it seemed that the spiritual enemy had opened a full one-on-one attack against me. Everything that could have gone wrong went wrong, from mechanical breakdown to bodily injury. I pressed on and recognized that a personal spiritual attack had been launched against me. My Pastor, Punkin, was a great spiritual supporter and a great source of encouragement, and always prayed with me whenever I needed him to.

Shepherd and I continued to try to become best friends and enjoy each other's company. He wasn't a fun friend for he was always tired and never did anything exciting. Watching movies and going to church were the height of his excitement. I on the other hand thrived on fun, excitement, and adventure, and had a circle of close friends around me that were not part of the MC world.

One of these friends was his 23-year-old son, Wish. He was a timid but smart ex Marine who as any young man wanted to enjoy life at its fullest. I took on the mission of becoming his friend.

April Fool's Day came along with a full moon and it did not make a good day for us. It was a day full of turmoil and confusion brought about by the enemy of God's people. Shepherd wrecked his bike on a slippery black top road. He had some cuts, scrapes, and minor damage to his bike. But on Sunday morning, he picked me up for the morning service. I wore a cherry-patterned black sundress with a pair of casual shoes. It was the first time he had seen me in a dress.

"Wow! You look nice," he said as his eyes traveled from my head to my toes. I really did not expect a reaction from this Virgo man but I welcomed his compliment.

We weren't accustomed to regular clothing. Our everyday dress was our colors with jeans, club support shirts and riding boots. We looked like bikers because we were bikers. I submerged myself so much into the MC life that somehow I quit living my life as a person. I was a patch holder even when I slept. All my decisions, all my actions, centered around my club colors and MC protocol. I eliminated many good people from my life because they were not patch holders. Other than my Home Crew friends, my circle of trust was comprised solely of MC people. I applied this principle to my own club members and lost some good girls because they could not comply with the rigid protocol standards I set for them. Their actions and problems were judged by MC protocol and I executed no mercy or compassion when they most needed it. I had forgotten that patch holders are people too.

That Sunday we arrived at church and were happier than ever. We had communion and were looking forward to Selena's wedding later that evening. She was a church member who had become my friend. After the morning service, the bride and groom asked me if we would go on a ride with them after the wedding. They were planning to ride the motorcycle in their wedding attire and wanted us to go with them. I told them I would gladly accept if it was OK with Shepherd. I also told them that we could not ride behind them because we were patch holders and those were our club rules. They were fine with the stipulation so I called Shepherd to obtain his approval. This would mean that we would have to go home and change clothes and get our bikes, but it was a minor inconvenience in exchange for making their special day happier.

After church, we went to our homes and were back at church by 3:30 pm for the wedding. As we sat next to each other during the ceremony, our souls embraced every word as if it was intended for us. He put his right arm around me and clenched my shoulder as I reached with my left hand and interlaced my fingers with his. It was a wonderful feeling of love and security that overwhelmed our souls, a feeling of two people sharing one love. It was an unspoken commitment that we made to each other that day through body language as we sat in that last pew of the United Methodist Church with our colors on. It was a beautiful unspoken union of sincere love shared by patch holders of opposite sides.

After the reception, the bride and groom climbed on their bikes for a photo shoot and I noticed that Shepherd seemed uneasy about riding. He expressed his concern about being seen riding together.

"I don't have a problem with it. My club does not have those kinds of issues," I said to him as I reached in my saddlebags for my gloves. I was getting rather annoyed that he was always so afraid to do things. I reached in my saddlebag to find my gloves and put my purse away. I looked to him but he was around the corner on the phone. I knew that his conscious had gotten to him and he was talking to his club president requesting permission to ride with me.

He came around the corner and with a tone of anxiety said, "It's OK for us to ride since it's an escort. Mitch said that if any, you could fall back to where my rear tire begins. It's going to be OK. I'm not worried about it."

At that moment, a terrible feeling of sadness came over me. Amongst all those people in the parking lot taking pictures and watching for our bikes to pull out with the wedding party, I felt very sad. It was as if I was deaf to the people's laughter and I was caught up in a cloud of silence. I could hear nothing but a deep sadness.

How was I able to hear sadness? I do not know. I do know that it was a sick sinking feeling in the middle of my stomach as if someone had punched me with all their might. A heavy-hearted gloom that made my arms and legs seem like they were floating.

I remember I pulled out and stopped in the middle of the parking lot to give the bride and groom space to position themselves. Shepherd leaned towards me and asked me, "Where are we going?"

"We are going Highway 7 North via downtown towards Lake Nimrod. I know how to get there."

"OK, then I'll stay with you," he said in an insecure tone and a quirky smile. I understood this to imply that I was going to lead since I knew the destination. So as soon as the bride and groom were positioned behind us, we rolled out of the parking lot side by side, I on the left.

It was not a club ride. It was not a club event, but a private favor for fellow church members. There were no politics involved other than leading the bride and groom. I rode my bike the way I always ride, with confidence and frolic recreation. The thought of club politics, never at any given time crossed my mind or even hinted at it. This was a friendly act of kindness towards our fellow church members.

Shortly after we took off, I noticed that I was way ahead of Shepherd. I looked at my speedometer thinking that I was speeding exceedingly but it wasn't so. I was doing 40 mph and he lagged behind about an eighth of a mile.

"What is wrong? Maybe he is having a mechanical problem with his bike," I thought to myself.

For the next nine or ten miles, he kept falling behind further and further. I remember slowing down to almost 25 mph to allow him to catch up. Traffic was backed up behind us with everyone wanting to pass. It was embarrassing to ride so slow. I questioned him as I lined up beside him at the traffic light, "Is everything OK?" I could not understand why he was falling behind so far off.

"Oh yea, I'm just waiting for them," He said as he pointed to the bride and groom. However, they were directly behind him. "Well, they're supposed to stay with us so they'll be OK," I said to him.

He nodded as if we were on the same page but once again, he fell back quite a distance from me. I was still under the impression that because I knew where the couple wanted to go, I was leading the non-club event ride. I am used to leading a pack. I know the hand signals and the safety rules. Shepherd had previously shared with me that he'd always been in the tail of the pack and did not lead. Therefore, with an honest minded attitude, I continued to ride at a steady and reasonable pace of approximately 50-55 mph on the country roads until we reached our destination (my normal riding speed was 65 mph on these roads).

At the intercession of Hwy 7 & 5, I signaled the riders to pull into the parking lot of a Phillips 66 gas station. I strongly believed that he was having mechanical problems with his bike since he was still falling behind quite a bit.

I got off my bike, shut it off and pointed at the bride and groom. "Is everything alright?" I asked.

"Yes, everything is great! Take us anywhere you want!" Exclaimed the bride in joy as she threw her hands up in the air.

"Florida, here we come!" I said in a joking tone.

"I turned to Shepherd and asked the same question. "Is everything alright?"

I really wish he had told me at that checkpoint stop that he was offended because I rode ahead of him. I would have rectified it immediately; nevertheless, he said everything was OK. We got back on the road to our destination. When we arrived, he took some pictures of the bride and groom, and talked with them for a little while. It was getting cold so the newlyweds got on the bike and headed to their honeymoon.

"I guess Will and I are going to take Glazy Peau over to Denisha's

(She is his young niece) house to see her," he said to me but looking at his son Will who had followed us in his pickup

He was cold and rude towards me. He had never acted this way and his indifference hurt me. Once again, that same feeling of sadness I felt at the church parking lot came over me and my soul was deeply suppressed.

He sat on his bike ready to take off. As he turned the ignition switch on, I asked, "Is everything OK?"

"No, everything is not OK." He answered in a cold and distant tone.

"What is wrong?" I asked.

"You know what's wrong. You took off and left me." He said to me in a whiny tone.

I could not respond because I had no idea what was going on and no notion of his offense. I had thoroughly enjoyed the ride because we had ridden together. The concept of him and I riding together overshadowed any club rules in my mind. It was indeed a joyous time for me. However, he was upset about it and I had no clue why.

Was he distressed because his club had forbidden him to ride with me? They said it was disrespectful and they did not want to see it. It was tough not being able to do what you love with the one you love; nevertheless, I had to accept this fact because we were from opposite clubs. Was he offended because I refused to ride 15 mph in my town with my colors? Or, was it because a woman rode a bike in front of him? This particular day was special for me because we were going to get to ride together. That was… until the glitch of club rules and male ego got in his way.

I was standing beside him still not knowing how to respond to his words. He turned his engine on and said, "We'll talk about it later. This was for them anyway." He took off immediately without saying goodbye.I stood there…, stood there…, and stood there, trying to figure out what the hell had just happened.

"We had our colors on so that made it a club ride. You disrespected me by going ahead of me," he said in a high-pitched tone on the phone close to 10 pm that night.

I explained to him how it was not my intent or premeditated

plan on how to ride, which turns to take, what speed to do, etc…

"I am sorry. I apologize for disrespecting you. It will never happen again," I told him in a regretful voice over the phone. I wasn't sorry for riding in front of him for I was an MC President and it was my right to ride in the place of honor I did. He was a 1% probate but his riding skills were too delicate for me. I had ridden with the Louisiana Bandidos, the Gray Ghost MC and other Red and Gold Support Clubs. We rode fast and hard. We didn't do any sightseeing riding and we didn't play games on the bikes. These were my everyday riding habits.

After trying to dissect the matter, I concluded that me riding in front of him was not about club colors. It was strictly about his feelings. It had absolutely nothing to do with me. I arrived at the hypothesis that perhaps a memory trigger was activated in his mind and may have been the reason without even realizing, why he fell back so far. I remembered the story of how his wife died. She was riding her motorcycle on the highway in front of him when she crashed and instantly left his side.

Was it indeed possible that when I rode in front of him it triggered a subconscious memory of her accident? Did the possibility exist that he had an involuntary flashback of her death?

That seemed like a perfect and logical explanation of his sudden change in character. Hypothetically, I assumed that he was not aware of this memory activation but acted to it because to every action there is a reaction. The action was me riding in front of him, and the reaction was his wife's death. "This could be the only possible explanation of the onset of his cold rage towards me," I reasoned within myself.

"You will never be a patch holder to me and I will never be a patch holder to you. You will be my lady, my wife, and I will be your man, your husband. We cannot ride together right now but that will change. I am not worried about that. Our relationship is personal and we want to keep it that way," said the probate named Shep. He had shared with me on different occasions that if he were president for his club, he would change the riding rules.

This statement was very confusing to me. If we were not patch holders to each other, then why did it matter to him that I rode in front of him? If that was the case, then it was only his lady riding in front of him and not a patch holder. I knew that as long as we were on opposite sides of the fence our clubs would always be involved in our lives and politics would always have an upper hand. I also knew that he would always remain under the microscopic lens of the Sons of Silence as long as we remained a couple. This was partly because of one man in the Arkansas club that hated any woman who could ride her own bike, especially if she had a patch, especially me!

The next thing that happened was what would undoubtedly change my life forever. We leisurely walked into the kitchen. He abruptly stopped in front of the sink, looked straight into my eyes and with every confidence in the world asked the question I could never imagine.

"Do you want a property belt?"

A property belt is the engagement symbol that a Sons of Silence patch holder gives his old lady, girlfriend or wife. It is a black leather belt embossed with the club's colors and says "Property of" (the patch holder's name is inserted). The property belt is worn in the same manner as the property patch is worn in other 1% clubs.

With a blank stare, not sure of what I had just heard, I attempted to answer. I tried to process the answer logically, but it seemed like the bedazzling effect of this question was dynamically more overpowering than my reasoning. This was something I never expected him to ask, at least not at this point and time. Was his reasoning overmastered by his emotions, or was this the opportunity for him to sacrifice his reasoning for his emotions?

The woman inside of me screamed out "Yes! Yes! Yes!" I wanted that belt more than anything for I knew it was a public display of our commitment and the token that would legally bind us together in the MC world.

This went against our club rules for we could not mix colors or wear property patches, so I said the first thought that came to my mind in a slow-motioned tone, "I t-h-i-n-k... I m-i-g-h-t h-a-v-e t-o t-a-l-k t-o M-u-r-r-a-y a-b-o-u-t t-h-i-s...."

Then, I stopped mid sentence and realized the extent of his offer.

His heart, his club and everything that he loved seemed to be linked to that belt. I looked at him and firmly said, "I would be honored to wear your property belt."

"Oh, OK. I will order one for you," intoned his startled, impressed voice.

"Thank you for that," he said as he pulled me toward him, embracing my entire being. Happiness once again filled my soul and I felt we'd reach another level in our relationship.

I was completely aware (for I wrote and compiled them) that our laws and bylaws said:

(1) A person who wears a "property patch" from another motorcycle club cannot be a member of the HC.

(2) HC do not wear property patches from other clubs. To do so is a violation of our laws and bylaws.

I reasoned and remembered that our laws could at any given time be superseded by my boss Bandido Murray; however, given the fact that he had given us permission to date was in itself a substantial overruling of this HC bylaw.

Therefore, if I stand guilty of accepting a property belt from Sons of Silence Shepherd, then my condemnation was bestowed to me whether by negligence or intention, by the State President of the Arkansas Bandidos.

Either way, I was realized that even though I was a patch holder, I was a person also, a person that needed to love and be loved, a person that needed and wanted a family life and I was entitled to it. I was happy to be a girl in love even though I was the President of the Highway Chicks WMC. I didn't think of any political repercussions in accepting his property belt. It was an honor to belong to a patch holder from the other side of the fence.... to belong to Shep.

Thursday, April 5th of 2007, I went over his home and for the first time he asked me to nestle in bed with him. As he held me in that bedroom, I could feel the passion of his energy flowing and the undeniable chemistry between us. The serene and pleasant atmosphere was like the smell of dogwood flowers after a springtime rain. The energy in the room shifted from masculine to a balanced female-male energy. I knew that instant embraced by my man. that I was finally secure and safe. I was with Shep.

"This is the first time we've laid together in bed," he said in a gentle, soft-spoken voice, as he repositioned his strong arms around me holding me tighter. I could feel the unspoken love his heart was screaming out. I could hear the silent cry emerging from the deepest and most secret place of his heart. I closed my eyes and envisioned our essence intertwining in the spiritual realm. It was like a picture perfect montage of our souls making love in the purest of intimate affection in order to merge our spirits as one. It wasn't a sexual sensation, but rather a spiritual one; a beautiful, comforting ardor of emotion leaving us completely drained of energy in a post-orgasmic state. It was a most tranquil ambience that reflected the stillness of a glass ocean. It wasn't long afterwards we were asleep in each other's arms resting in the peace and quietness of his home.

My club was scheduled to host the next pool tournament on April 9. There was a good turnout that night and everything seemed to be going smoothly. The Arkansas Sons of Silence treated my club with more respect and appeared to be more sociable as a club than in the past. This was a major breakthrough between our clubs considering the enormous amount of hostility with the male/female, married biker issue.

I was not sure, if their friendship with me had evolved over time or if it was because I was dating one of their members. Either way, I was glad that the bickering had stopped. Life was simpler for all of us.

On that night, my boss, Bandido Murray, said he needed to talk to me. We walked to the back of the bar where we met with Sons of Silence Arkansas President Mitch, and Sons of Silence XXX (name withheld at patch holder's request). After a brief political meeting concerning general ARCOM business, Murray looked at me and said, "When he came and asked me to date you (referring to Shep) I did not know who he was. Now I know who he is and I'm concerned that he can put you in a bad spot."

"Murray, everything is fine. We do not talk club business other than what is out for the public to know. We get along good and I want to keep it that way," I said to my boss.

"How close are you guys getting?" asked Sons of Silence Mitch.

"Very close," was my firm immediate response.

"My only concern is for your safety. I don't want you to get in a situation where it can get dangerous for you," said Bandido Murray.

"He said you wanted a belt. Do you want a belt?" said Mitch, as he looked straight into my eyes in the pitch black of the night while the four of us stood in the back of the bar.

"When he asked me if I wanted a property belt, I did not want to hurt his feelings, so my first and immediate response was 'I think I have to talk to Murray about that,' I said to all three 1%'ers as we further discussed the issue.

"You can go and call him into this meeting and asked him to confirm what I just said. I am sure he will not lie. I told him I wanted the belt because I did not want to hurt his feelings, but then, after I thought about it for a minute, I told him that I would be honored to have his belt."

After a few seconds of silence, XXX (name withheld at patch holder's request) said, "You cannot wear the belt and your colors at the same time."

"Of course not! I would never do that. I would only wear that belt as his lady and NEVER as a patch holder, and NEVER with my Red and Gold colors, and NEVER in the State of Arkansas," I firmly said to him.

"So many people know you, not only in Arkansas but everywhere and maybe that could be a problem with one of our Nationals. I mean, maybe... if they see you with your colors and then with his belt, they could lose respect for you or him and that would be bad. You are who you are and he is a Son, a probate. He will ascend but you will always be who you are, so that is something to consider," said his President.

"I just don't want you to get in a bad situation and get in trouble because it will come back on me," said Murray.

I had committed my love to my colors and my club. I had sacrificed most of my personal life for five years to the MC world because I loved my colors and the Bandidos. I knew what commitment was and I understood how to be devoted to my choices. But I still made the decision to dive into the other side of the fence while maintaining my loyalty to the Red and Gold. This was my personal life and I hoped it could be separated from my club life.

"OK, guys, this is what I'm going to suggest," I said to all three of them as I put my hands out in a surrender mode.

"I mean, this is what I'm going to ask of you guys. Let us work this out and make it happen. The moment it causes any problem with any of our clubs, then at that time we will deal with it. Until then, I ask that you give us the opportunity to make it work. I know in the past it did not work with the other person, but he was a hothead and talked too much. I am very secure in whom I am, and non-emotional. I can assure you that it will not cause a problem." I said with the greatest assurance I was able to pull out my entire sleeve.

"OK. That is fine with me," said Bandido Murray.

I was able to relax every muscle in my body. I felt like I had faced a firing squad of three 1%'ers for the love of a man. I have to assume that when both Mitch and Murray gave us permission to date, they expected it to be an overnight screw. They did not anticipate a property belt to appear in the picture. But one thing no one could deny was that both of us did obtain actual consent from both Murray and Mitch to date; the two 1%'ers in charge of the state.

I had no regrets for it was my hope that he would soon hold me in his arms in front of the nations and tell me he loved me. Every inch of my insides cried out in silence to him 'hold me tight and never let go,' but the absence of his passion ran through my blood like untamed horses stampeding in the open field. I felt he was dreadfully afraid to reach out and love another woman.

I treasured the little amount of love that I did receive from him and cherished every moment we shared. However, in my heart I knew that eventually either the politics of club colors or the absence of his love would tear us apart. It was only a matter of time.

The Broken Pact

It was a clear cool night on a Wednesday afternoon as we stood in a church parking of the United Methodist Church in Hot Springs, Arkansas. You could hear the loud argument of people fighting in their homes in the background. Once more, Shepherd began to state his case with the same lack of self-esteem, complex-filled statements. "You are a strong, independent women and I don't know if that is going to work out with us in the future. I don't want you to change me. I don't want to wear a certain brand of pants. I like what I wear. I just don't know if we are going to work out as a couple and I am concerned about the church. Can we work a church together if we are not a couple? I am not in love. I mean, cultivating love takes time and I am not in love. Let's take our time. Don't rush me to the altar just yet. Don't go buying me rings. I want to be your best friend. I want to marry my best friend. I mean, I am not breaking up with you. I want to be your best friend."

His words hit me like a raging bull running full speed into me. I was confused at the way he talked to me and how it all poured out from him in less than one minute. However, I wasn't shocked, for I felt something bad would happen that night. I was devastated when it finally hit me in the form of reality. I had worked so hard to please him and be the kind of women he wanted but his only concern was I…, I…, and I.

Personally, I did not want to be his friend for he was a lousy friend. He did not like to go out and have fun. He didn't like to dance or go to nightclubs. He didn't like fun games or friends and he slept too much. He rode his motorcycle too slow and always stayed behind. He was very critical of people and quick to judge their behavior. As a friend, he sucked. I wanted him to be my boyfriend. I want him to be my man. I wanted him to be my husband.

I felt he was so concerned with his fears, drama, insecurities, and his everlasting grief, that he had failed to see how he was badgering the women God had sent him. I remember reaching with my hand and holding onto the passenger's seat of his bike as I heard him tell me that he wasn't in love with me. A feeling of impending doom had overcome me.

I could not handle another break up with someone I loved. I am strong-willed, and with this character, I had made the decision not to have my heart broken ever again by any man. That was never going to happen again! I refused to be the victim who locked herself in her house and cried all day. That would never happen again!

I should have listened to my heart at the time I was writing this, for down deep in the innermost part of my heart, I felt Shepherd and I would never be a couple. He was too weak for me and I was too strong for him. I knew that in his own lack of self-confidence, he had the need to control a woman in order to make him feel secure and whole.

On Thursday, April 9, Shepherd patched out with the Sons of Silence Motorcycle Club in Arkansas. He called me to inform me of his ascension to full patch at 10:49 p.m. He seemed extremely proud of his achievement. I was genuinely happy for him. It made him feel good and lifted his spirits. This was something he'd been waiting for and had worked hard for it. An entire year of prospect/probation for the Sons of Silence MC is a mission not to be taking lighthearted. Shepherd had become a 1%'er patch holder.

The next Monday night's pool tournament was hosted by the Boozefighters MC. Shepherd would be attending for the first time as a full patch holder. I was proud to see him roll in and be a little more sociable with the Red and Gold support clubs. That same night I learned that Highway and Hedges Chappy would soon become the chaplain for the Ozark Riders MC, a Bandido support club for the state of Arkansas. Also, Wish had officially become a hang around for the Martyrs MC, a Red and Gold unofficial support club. Good things were happening in the Coalition because Bandido Murray was an excellent President and because people like Shepherd and I were working with all our might to make things better for the biker community.

I had recruited a new Prospect for the HC. Magic was an independent, soft-spoken girl who rode a Heritage Soft Tail. She had been around us for three years but continuously declined all invitations to ride with us. In April of 2007, she finally decided to make the plunge and become a Highway Chick. I took her in and met with her at 2720 Club in Hot Springs, to inform her of all hang around duties and my expectations for her. I told her that my purpose in the HC was to make a safe place for women to ride as patch holders, but she had to understand that family was first.

"If we do not have peace at home, our journey in the club will be a hard one," I said to her during the prospect orientation period. I had learned throughout the years as a patch holder that putting our blood family on the back burner was a sacrifice not worth making.

Her concerned was for her husband. She wanted him to be able to ride with us to events and not feel left out. I assured her that he would be able to ride with us to open events and he would be a part of our family. I was her Patch so I made myself available 24/7 to her not only as president but also as a friend.

Monday night at the pool tournament was a quiet, causal one. The usual politics and show of colors went on like it did every Monday. Bandido Murray made the weekly announcements and shortly afterwards, the crowd was sparse. The week had passed and I hadn't heard from Shep. Wish didn't know what was going on either. The suspense of not knowing where he was and what was going on tied my stomach in knots; nevertheless, I waited for him to call as I kept busy with matters pertaining to my club.

In the process of this ordeal, I learned that love is the most painful emotion a human being can experience. People come into existence because of love and many times die for it. Love is the sphere for the cause and effect of the human race, their motives and intentions. If love did not exist, the world as we know it would be an unpopulated planet void and without form.

We were created to love and to be loved and when this decree is violated, chaos settles in the heart and disrupts the established pattern for the human soul. I truly wish there was an escape clause for the nonexistence of this passion, for perhaps life would be easier and complications absent from the heart. There wouldn't be the need for crime and war would be eradicated. But since love is the groundwork of the human heart, we must learn to live with the pain of it while reaping the joy and gratification if only for a moment.

When I finally met up with Shepherd, he broke off our relationship in a very cold fashion. I knew it was coming and had to prepare myself emotionally. The Bible study was over on that one summer night and mostly everyone had left. I taught the lesson that week in place of the pastor who was out of town. In the same tone and spirit as he did the previous Wednesday, he said he needed to talk to me. It was then that my wariness was confirmed. My emotions were closed, my heart was solemn as I prepared myself emotionally for the pain Shep was about to put me through.

As we sat in his pickup truck in the parking lot, I had a flashback of the first time we were riding in the truck two months earlier when he asked me if I'd make a good pastor's wife. Now, in the same truck he was telling me he was detaching himself from my life.

"You are a celebrity. Everyone knows who you are, Sadgirl. I cannot ask you to change and to continue in this relationship would be a disaster. You have worked very hard to get where you are and have accomplished a lot. When you enter into a room you radiate that you are a strong leader. You are a peacekeeper. I commend that but I do not want it in a romantic relationship. Even though you are a woman, the 1% men respect you because you have worked hard to get where you are in the motorcycle community and with your club. Do not make any drastic changes because of this. Continue to do what you are doing for it is a good thing. I have too much insecurity to deal with this. I am sick. I am not well. I still love my wife Debby and am not done grieving. I have to get well and I feel I am moving forward but I don't think this relationship is going to work. I am not in love with you." He said as he put his hand over his heart and emphasized his statement.

"Permission to speak freely?" I asked.

"Go ahead," he replied.

"First and foremost, let me say that if you would have loved me the way I love you, I would have surrendered everything to spend the rest of my days loving and serving you. But I see that is not the fact," I said to him in a cold tone as I sat beside him in the truck.

"I got close to you because you invited me into your life. I mean, you made statements like 'Do you think you could make a good pastor's wife?' That is an open invitation! 'You have a lot of things and I have a lot of things. Who is going to get rid of what?' That is an open invitation! 'Divorce is not an option. I will give you the money.' That is an open invitation! You took me on a road trip to Flagstaff, Arizona and introduced me to your children and grandchildren. That is an open invitation.

You had me meet your entire family and even said I can call your mother mom. That is an open invitation! That is why I got close to you. You invited me into your life with the expectation of a lifetime commitment," I said to him as I held back the anger and exercised complete self-control.

"I am sorry. I should have not made those statements and you have opened my eyes to that," was the only thing he could say.

Was he aware that being sorry did not fix things? The feeling of impending doom hovered over me. I felt like I was being dumped off on the side of the road with a bag of pots and pans. I could not cry. I could not smile. I could not be angry. I sat there and listened to his sorry excuse for not wanting to keep the women God had sent him to love, nurture, and take care of. He hurt me and insulted my loyalty to him. The fact that he was sorry did not fix things. The fact that he was sorry did not change the pain he had just put in my heart. The fact that he was sorry was not going to fix the life he had built up with so many promises and in less than ten minutes tore completely down.

These were his final words to me. He didn't reach out to console me and never tried to make sense of his actions. I didn't cry because I couldn't. I knew this was the last time I would sit beside him in the truck. This was the last memory I'd share with him. The reminiscence of our first kiss in this very same place surfaced as he was walking out of my life.

"Well, I think it's time for me to go," I said as I reached for the door handle of his white Chevy pickup. He walked me to my truck. We hugged. I reach for his hand but it was gone. The man whom I had fallen in love with was walking away forever.

You see, it wasn't just about Shep and Sadgirl. It was about bringing together MC clubs and uniting hearts. It was about creating a biker church where all patches would come together under the same roof to worship one God. It was about being an example to the nation that indeed God loves us all equally. And finally, it was about the phoenix rising from the ashes of grief into the ministry.

After Shepherd broke off our relationship, I still had my club, my brothers and the ARCOMc family. I took comfort in the fact that my MC family would always be with me, for the bond of brotherhood was for life. Or was it? I wasn't completely alone but surrounded by a group of people that loved me for who I was. Or did they?

12
Out in Bad Standing?
Highway Chicks WMC vs. Highway Chick President Sadgirl

Sunday, April 29 2007, 11: 41 p.m.
This weekend threw a curveball at me in the most unexpected fashion that no human being deserves. The sun was warm as we rolled on Interstate 30 East at a cruising speed of 80 miles an hour. There were eight bikes in the pack that I proudly led from Texas to Arkansas

I was on my way home from a trip on Sunday afternoon with the Highway Chicks. The weekend was spent in Longview, Texas at Mom's Bar with the local Bandidos and the Red and Gold support clubs. The bar celebrated their 22nd annual crawfish boil. It was the last trip I would take with the Highway Chicks, the Red and Gold, or any ARCOMc club as a patch holder.

While we were at Mom's Bar, I felt a large amount of hostility with my club officers, especially with Tab and Roadkill. I dismissed this perception as my own personal mixed emotions as I was still grieving for my severed relationship with Shepherd.

The Arkansas Bandidos were at Mom's Bar and I had the opportunity to spend some time talking with my boss, Bandido Murray. He was in a very good mood and our conversation was general and pleasing. He introduced me to Bandido Ed, whom I had previously met at the Pistoleros clubhouse in Birmingham, Alabama.

I distinctly remember Murray telling Bandido Ed, "We've had some bumps in the road but all is good now." He laughed about it and he patted me on the back.

The three of us stood in front of Mom's Bar that night and talked for approximately 45 minutes. We talked about our experiences on the road and the different ways we all got speeding tickets throughout our travels across the US highways. We laughed, and had a laid-back good time.

Once again, I failed to listen to my own advice: the heart never lies. If I had listened to my heart, I would have foreseen the events about to unfold with my club, the Highway Chicks.

When I got home from the Texas trip, I took a shower, ate dinner, and went to my daughter Tabeel's home to watch the sitcom Desperate Housewives® with her. A weekly tradition for the past two years that we could not give up. I would occasionally find myself speeding home on Sundays from a weekend event just to see this show.

After the show was over, I left her home to return to my house. I immediately went to the computer to continue writing the manuscript of this book. I sat at my computer chair and I saw that my computer was missing. I freaked out and went crazy! I called the last known person that had been in my home, my son Shalom. He had come to take back his printer, which he had loaned me. Therefore, I assume that in the process he took my CPU.

I begged him, "Shalom, please bring my computer back. The book I am writing is there. I need to have my files. Come take the rest of the computer or anything that you want, just give me back my computer so I can copy my files."

That computer contained personal family pictures, club pictures, my son's recent wedding pictures, pictures of Shep and I, all the ARCOMc minutes since 2003, my writings, my poetry, and pretty much everything that I used on a daily basis.

"Mom, I only took the printer. I do not have the computer," he said in an angry tone as he hung up the phone on me.

I was frustrated and had lost complete control of myself when the notion of losing the manuscript to this book occurred. My only concern was the contents of this book, but then I remembered I had given Shepherd a 61-page hard copy draft of the manuscript for him to read.

I went to the place where I hid the backup disks for all my files and programs that were in the stolen computer. They were still there, untouched and unseen by the perpetrators. I put the stack of disks on my nightstand and beside them the 45 pistol Shep had given me.

I went to my bedroom, shut the door and began to pray. I felt hopeless and without direction. The last time I felt this way was right before Jerry died. It was like an uncontrolled, powerless sense of falling. I literally saw myself free falling in slow motion off a mountain cliff side.

I began pacing uncontrollably from the living room to the back porch. It was then that I noticed my Colors missing from my tool cart where I have hung them for the past five years. There was no second-guessing and no doubt. Someone had deliberately broken into my home and taken everything that pertained to the Highway Chicks, the Bandidos, and the Red and Gold world. All my Bandido support shirts from my bedroom closet were missing. My Red and Gold stickers and personnel items were missing as well.

But who? Why? I was clueless. I stopped at the back door, put my hand over my head and searched for answers as I rested my head on the porch banister. More than ever, I was alone. I needed Jochebed, my twin soul, and she wasn't there. She was the only one person in the world who I've felt could help me, but she wasn't there. I hadn't felt so alone since the death Jerry.

Why would someone take my Colors? Hundreds of questions and possible answers flooded my mind. Should I call the police? Should I call my brothers? Should I call Debbie T? I anxiously paced the floor in the dark as I attempted to come to terms with what had happened.

Was it ATF or Drug Task Enforcement or something of the sort, just because of my association with the Bandidos? But I knew there was nothing that could link me to any illegal activity. I was never involved with any illegal activity and was not aware of such actions with the Bandidos or any motorcycle club I associated with.

From the beginning, my only job with the Red and Gold world and the Coalition in the State of Arkansas was to be a public relations, peacekeeper person, and I did that with pride.

I knew that I had never been disloyal to my boss, Bandido Murray or to the Red and Gold Nation, so the thought that my own brothers having done this never crossed my mind. I picked up my phone and called Tab. She was my enforcer and vice president.

"Where are you?" I asked.

"Little Rock," she replied

"Someone broke into my home and stole my computer," I said to her in a monotone. "They also took my Colors," I added.

There was a brief silence.

"They are in a safe place," She said.

"You broke into my home and took my shit?" I asked.

"We as a club took a vote and decided it was in the best interest of the club to remove you from the club," she said with an arrogant snare.

Tab proceeded to inform me of the reason she decided to revolt the club against me.

"We feel you are not loyal to the Red and Gold. You have not paid dues for two months. You had a party at the clubhouse without informing the club. You took liquor from the club. Since you started dating Shep, you do not wear your Colors when you go with him to a Sons event in his truck, and you go in the truck so you won't have to wear your Colors. You do work for Mitch and you get several phone calls from him on a daily basis. They are personal phone calls. You are writing a book about the Red and Gold world and you do not have that right. You are out in bad standings".

"How dare you? Whatever happened to sisterhood? If you had a feeling, an emotion or problem with me, you should have approached me instead of breaking into my home and stealing my personal property. You broke into my home where I pay my mortgage and took my computer and my tee shirts out of my closet that I paid money for. That is breaking the law. You had no right to do that. You invaded the sanctity of my home because you had a feeling? A feeling without proof, an accusation stemming from jealousy." I calmly said to her on the phone as I sat in my back porch in the uneasy still of the night. I could not believe that she had the audacity to think that she could do this to the president of the club and not have any repercussions.

After I heard her accusation on the telephone, I closed my ears and quit listening to her stupidity. That is exactly what it was. The stupidity of a jealous woman that was in desperate need of power and glory.

Out in bad standings? I do not think so. Read on and see for yourself how this case will end, for justice will always prevail even when the system fails to do what is right in the eyes of society.

IN THE CASE OF #0429-07

HIGHWAY CHICKS WMC AND TAB, *PLAINTIFF*
vs.
HIGHWAY CHICK PRESIDENT SADGIRL, *DEFENDANT*

Plaintiff accuses Defendant of, "We <u>feel</u> you are not loyal to the Red and Gold...."

Defendant writes:

How dare she create a presumption and question my loyalty to the Bandido Nation? She, out of all people knew the sacrifice and total commitment all of us (not just me) had put into the club. She knew all the ridicule and humiliation Debbie T and I endured from the Arkansas Bandidos, and in spite of it we still wore the Heart Patch along with Red and Gold support patches on our cut. This "feeling" of her accusation carried no validation because there wasn't any proof of my disloyalty to my superiors.

> I. "We <u>feel</u> you are not loyal to the Red and Gold..." is not valid grounds, nor does it reflect or contain evidence of a legal verdict (decision) for the club's actions against the Defendant.

Plaintiff accuses Defendant of, "*You have not paid dues for two months....*"

Defendant writes:

Did Tab forget that I had made seven consecutive payments out of my pocket for the clubhouse refrigerator? Payments that covered my dues for at least four months. Did she fail to understand that I had proof of all payments made to the leasing company?

> **II.** *"You have not paid dues for two months...."* is not valid grounds, nor does it reflect or contain evidence of a legal verdict (decision) for the club's actions against the Defendant.

Plaintiff accuses Defendant of, *"You had a party at the clubhouse without informing the Club...."*
Defendant writes:
Did Tab forget that I was the president of the club and therefore entitled to use the clubhouse anytime there weren't club events or functions? I used it for a small family wedding for my son. There wasn't any profit and it wasn't a club function. The building was used by a club officer in the same manner that she used it as personal sleeping quarters for her without asking. What's the difference? Did she conveniently forget that?

> **III.** *"You had a party at the clubhouse without informing the Club..."* is not valid grounds, nor does it reflect or contain evidence of a legal verdict (decision) for the club's actions against the Defendant.

Plaintiff accuses Defendant of, *"You took liquor from the club...."*
Defendant writes:
Did Tab look at her inventory papers correctly to know that the booze for the wedding was purchased by my son?

> **IV.** *"You took liquor from the club...."* is not valid grounds, nor does it reflect or contain evidence of a legal verdict (decision) for the club's actions against the Defendant.

Plaintiff accuses Defendant of, *"Since you started dating Shep, you do not wear your Colors when you go with him to a Sons event in the truck...."*

Defendant writes:

OK, now this accusation is the stupidest of all. It shows her desperate attempt to bring a finger pointing charge against me. No 1%'er or patch holder ever wears their colors in a cage or when not riding a motorcycle. Neither Shep nor I wore our colors anytime we rode in the truck. In addition, we are grown adults and we can ride in our vehicles anytime we chose to. We obtained that privilege when we purchased insurance and registration from the State of Arkansas.

> V. *"Since you started dating Shep, you do not wear your Colors when you go with him to a Sons event in the truck…"* is not valid grounds, nor does it reflect or contain evidence of a legal verdict (decision) for the club's actions against the Defendant.

Plaintiff accuses Defendant of, "*You go in the truck so you won't have to wear your Colors.*"

Defendant writes:

This isn't even a valid allegation. It is a ridiculous subjective assumption fabricated by a jealous girl who had no clue what she was talking about. My colors was the most important personal belonging of my life. Anyone who knew me could validate this. I was even fired from a long-term job because of enduring faithful to my club and colors. Shep and I traveled in his truck anytime we wanted to because once again, we are adults and we live in the USA, which is a free country. We rode in his truck because we damn well felt like it!

> VI. *"You go in the truck so you won't have to wear your colors"* is not valid grounds, nor does it reflect or contain evidence of a legal verdict (decision) for the club's actions against the Defendant.

Plaintiff accuses Defendant of, "*You do work for Mitch….*"

Defendant writes:

This is a serious accusation for the following reasons: Who gave her the facts for her to state: "You do work for Mitch." Has she been prying in the SOS business affairs? Did she get this information from inside the SOS? If so, is Tab suggesting to the public that there is a snitch in the Sons? What is she implying? What basis does she have to substantiate this accusation – not only against me, but against the Sons of Silence President of the Arkansas Chapter?

> **VII.** *"You do work for Mitch...."* is not valid grounds, nor does it reflect or contain evidence of a legal verdict (decision) for the club's actions against the Defendant.

Plaintiff accuses Defendant of, *"...You get several phone calls from him on a daily basis...."*
Defendant writes:
How can she prove this? Does she have access to my phone logs, and if so, did she have the legal permits to access the FCC records? Did she access Mitch's phone? Is she a cop or associated with cops in order to retrieve this data? Has Tab tapped my phone? Has she tapped into Mitch's phone? What solid fact does she have to prove that I get these alleged phone calls from Mitch on a daily basis?

> **VIII.** *"...You get several phone calls from him on a daily basis...."* are not valid grounds, nor does it reflect or contain evidence of a legal verdict (decision) for the club's actions against the Defendant.

Plaintiff accuses Defendant of, *"They are personal phone calls...."*
Defendant writes:
Did she tap into Mitch's phone and record the conversations in order for her to say they are personal? Did she tap into my phone and record the conversations in order for her to say they are personal?
Let's assume for a minute, hypothetically, that Mitch and I had "personal" conversations on the phone. If this were true, then it was indeed my personal business, and had absolutely nothing to do with club business or being disloyal to the Red and Gold Nation. It was personal and therefore she could not use it against me.
She not only slandered my name, but the name of the Sons of

Silence President for Arkansas and that is a very serious matter!

> IX. *"They are personal phone calls...."* is not valid grounds, nor does it reflect or contain evidence of a legal verdict (decision) for the club's actions against the Defendant.

Plaintiff accuses Defendant of, *"You are writing a book about the Red and Gold world...."*
Defendant writes:
She had not read my manuscript nor had any idea of the contents of the book, for if she would have, she would have realized that the book I was writing at the time was of a love affair between two people from two different motorcycle clubs. She would have realized that it was the story of how God redeemed two souls out of grief into the ministry. She did not know that the book I was writing was about the forbidden love affair between Shep and Sadgirl. She made a scrupulous assumption without having any facts or knowledge of the contents of my manuscript.

> X. *"You are writing a book about the Red and Gold world...."* is not valid grounds, nor does it reflect or contain evidence of a legal verdict (decision) for the club's actions against the Defendant.

Plaintiff accuses Defendant of, *"...You do not have that right...."*
Defendant writes:
My question to my fellow man is, did she have the right to make an assumption about the Red and Gold world when she, herself was not a Red and Gold patch holder? Who gave her the right? Who gave her the authority to tell the President of the Highway Chicks that I did not have that privilege? Did she self-appoint her grandiose persona to the seat of judge? Was she walking in Murray's boots? This in itself appears to be a very serious violation on her part.

> XI. *"...You do not have that right...."* is not valid grounds, nor does it reflect or contain evidence of a legal verdict (deci-

sion) for the club's actions against the Defendant.

PROCEEDING FINDINGS:

THE COURT has found that the Plaintiff's accusations are not valid grounds, nor does it reflect or contain evidence of a legal verdict (decision) for the club's actions against the Defendant for the flowing reasons:

1. Allegations I, V, VI, VII, VIII, and IX are subjective. A personal opinion cannot be used as a charge against a person, unless slander or defamation is intended.
2. The remaining allegations cannot be proven and therefore must be dismissed due to lack of substantiated evidence against the Defendant.
3. The Defendant's character witness for the duration of her 5 years as a patch holder has been unimpeachable, and her integrity has been above reproach. She has executed her duties as Secretary for the Coalition of Motorcycle Clubs in the State of Arkansas in a non-bias, professional manner.

FUTHERMORE THE COURT FINDS THAT:

4. The Plaintiff failed duly exercise due process to the Defendant. The Plaintiff violated their own Laws and Bylaws, *i.e.* ARTICLE # 12; Resignation or Suspension of an Officer: Explicit Quote:

   A. *After a thorough investigation of the Officer, the Executive Director can suspend an officer of any events or activities of concern for thirty (30) days.*
   B. *If suspension is needed to be permanent, a letter must be submitted to the Executive Board requesting suspension within five (5) working days from date of suspension.*
   C. The officer under suspension must request an appeal in writing within five (5) days to the Executive Board from date

of notification by registered letter.
   1). If no appeal is requested the suspension becomes permanent.
   2). If an appeal is requested, a hearing will be scheduled within ten (10) days from the date he/she received registered letter to investigate and make a ruling on the matter.

5. The Defendant was not offered a 30 day suspension. (12:A)
6. Defendant did not receive a letter informing her of her permanent suspension as a club member or as President of the club. (12:B)
7. Defendant was not able to appeal the suspension because the Plaintiff did not mail a letter informing the Defendant of the suspension. (12:C) i.e. *A member may be expelled, or have their membership suspended, for conduct unbecoming a member of HIGHWAY CHICKS. A warning letter must be sent to the member by the Officers before any suspension or expulsion proceeding occur.* (12: H) **instead**, the Plaintiff burglarized the Defendant's home and criminally seized her Colors and personal property items.

In light of the above-mentioned seven (7) findings, THIS COURT finds that the Defendant, Highway Chick Sadgirl is found NOT GUILTY of all charges brought against her by the Plaintiff.

THE COURT orders a complete absolution from her label "Out in Bad Standing" and orders absolute restitution of all privileges rightfully due a full patch holder.

The above case is a clear example of how my superiors should have handled my case. My boss should have given me the opportunity of a hearing, but he did not. He was misled by my vice president who took full advantage of his kind heart; all because I fell in love with a man from the other side of the fence....

I wonder… if this injustice was allowed to me, the active secretary for the ARCOMc, a friend of Murray, and President of a Bandido Support Club, then what chance do regular club members have? What chance do prospects and probationary members have?

13
Blood on the Barbwire

I loved the Arkansas Sons and I was not going to let anyone, especially Tab, use them as a culprit. She had no right to talk about something she was ignorant about. Sons of Silence Mitch and I had many disagreements and arguments in the past, but I was grateful and in debt to him for allowing Shepherd to the date me, and for the time he took to become my friend. I harbored no resentment or grief towards him. I had actually begun to enjoy his company for I learned he was a standup man and one to honor his word. I respected him because he was a 1%'er and I had gotten to know him as a person. This by no means meant that I was disloyal to the Red and Gold world as Tab had accused me of.

I distinctly remember telling her one day after listening to her ramble about Mitch, "You know, if I ever get in a situation where I need someone to stand up for me, I think that I would have to call Mitch because he backs up what he says."

That did not go well with her but I didn't care because I had to get along with everyone. Those were Bandido Murray's instructions. He always preached, "We have to get along."

As I write this book, I truly believe that this girl thinks she is or will someday be a Bandido. I truly believe that in her quest to achieve power and glory, she has committed a great injustice not only to her sister, but to the Highway Chicks, the ARCOMc and the MC community. She could never walk in my footsteps. She could never be Sadgirl. I earned that name, position, and title and she took it from me. The day she took my colors was the day she set in motion the slow destruction of the Highway Chicks WMC. It is my objective opinion that Tab craved the powerful spotlight as well as the fresh and adventurous love I had with a patch holder.

It was my job at Murray's request for me to get along with everyone in the MC world. I knew my politics and did it well. My phone conversation with Tab, the day she took my colors, ended when she hung up on me. I unsuccessfully tried to call her back. I called Murray in an effort to understand what had just happened. He wasn't too empathetic on the phone.

"Murray, what is going on? Have you talked to Tab?" I asked.

"You crossed the line," he said.

"What are you talking about? I don't have a clue what's going on," I said to him.

"I'm taking care of another matter. I'll talk to you in person later," he said in a cold tone. It seemed like he did not want to talk to me and I couldn't understand why. I called Big Joe also but he said he was sleeping.

I hung up the phone in a completely dumbfounded state. I felt I was left to rot on a desert island with no food or water. My own club sisters had condemned and sentenced me to death without a trial and without honor to our code of ethics: Love, Loyalty and Respect.

The most important thing to me was the matter of the heart. When I started dating Shep, I knew there were political club risks involved. I was fully aware of all the reprimands and repercussions I might have to face, but I expected it either from Mitch or Murray. I never expected my own club to crinkle me up and toss me in the trash can because my heart chose to love a man from the other side of the fence. I never expected to be slammed into the barbwire and minced into it to the point of causing emotional bleeding.

My sisters did not understand that a Scorpio never betrays their loyalty to any one even to their own harm. We are strong-willed and able to get things done when no one else can. Tab thought that by taking my computer, they would stop the writing of this book, but little did they know that it only motivated me more to continue writing words on these pages. Their actions only added additional chapters taking different twist and turns that would involve MC clubs and their procedures. Twist and turns that could have been avoided if the man in charge would have upheld his office as a righteous judge and not condemned me without a trial. If he had known that my vice president's accusations and charges carried no evidence, then perhaps a lot of heartache and embarrassment would have been avoided.

I made a decision I needed to make three years ago. I was going to move from Arkansas for a while and take a breather while I finished writing this book. I needed to get away from Jerry's home, the grief, and most of all I needed to detach myself from Shepherd. I realized this when at the last MC event I attended in Longview, Texas; I'd see phantom images of his persona as I observed other patch holders. It seemed that now I was grieving his loss as he grieved the loss of his wife.

True love unfolds when one completely surrenders to it and confidently lies in its infinite power. Although Shepherd did not love me, the passion in my heart was sufficient for the ultimate sacrifice of mortality. Just like the ending of all true love stories and the forbidden love between two people, a fatality is inescapable. That night in the solitude of my home, I died! I became the sacrificial lover that lost it all because I loved a man from the other side of the fence. My life had taken a sudden turn without any visible warning signs.

I didn't know where all this was supposed to take me. I did know that all things work together for good for them that love God, who are called according to his purpose. I knew God had a purpose for me. I was just not able to pinpoint it and didn't have a glimpse of what it was. It was frustrating to know that the church we were planning to start was not going to happen. I thought of all the bikers that were supposed to be saved under our ministry. Would we be held accountable for that?

I had many questions but no answers. I had no guidance and no way of knowing what my next step would be. I had to trust God. It was a hard thing to do, for my heart was involved in a whirlwind of circumstance. In the same week, I had lost my boyfriend, my colors, my club, my brothers and my dignity. I stood empty handed leaning on the barb wire fence that separated me from my brothers. I stood before God and asked, "What now? Where do I go from here?"

I wanted Shepherd to know firsthand what happened. I searched my heart and found enough courage to call him. There had been no contact between us for five days; however, these were extraordinary circumstances far above my control.

Sunday, April 29 at 10:27 pm, I pushed speed dial number seven on my cell phone. Shep answered the call.

"The reason I'm calling is because I want to tell you firsthand and directly from me what happened. I do not want you to hear it from a third-party," I said to him.

I told him everything, undiluted as it had occurred. I was not angry but frustrated. I spoke with this 1%'er and freely informed him of Tab's hatred and hostility towards the Sons of Silence. He was angry. He could not understand the way this woman had taken matters into a mutiny, from an emotional assumption she conceived. He assured me that the book I was writing was not about any club in particular but of the Romeo/Juliet love affair of two people from different MC clubs. He informed me that his President had called him and inquired if he knew I was writing a book. He told him that he was the one who had given me the idea to write the book. He assured Mitch that it was not about MC clubs. Shepherd asked my permission to let Mitch and Murray read the draft copy. We spoke on the phone for about 45 minutes. He said he'd read my manuscript and was able to see things different.

There was a brief moment of quietness. He was still trying to make sense of the whole situation, of how this woman disrespected my home and my position. The phone conversation with Shep ended on a good note that night. I assured him that everything on the manuscript that I had given him was everything that I wanted to tell him but never had the opportunity to do so. He seemed to be very upset of how the matter with my club politics had been handled. He told me he would do everything he could to have the situation fixed and he would do some investigating of his own.

Tab had accused me of not being loyal to the Red and Gold world because I dated a Son of Silence and because I received personal phone calls from their President, Mitch. She had made an unscrupulous assumption based on her emotionally, unstable life and personal unhappiness. She did not understand that I was not only the President of the Highway Chicks WMC but also worked as peacekeeper to make my home state a great place to live and ride. I worked very hard behind the scenes with club members and presidents to keep lines of communication open between patch holders while at the same time indirectly and quietly smoothing out any possibly hostile situations that could occur.

As a woman, it was easy to talk to these guys and offer solutions to simple MC protocol, or just interpersonal relations advice. I guess that either I was real smart or a non-threat. I'd like to think it was the first one.

I engaged in many tasks behind the scenes within a five-year period. The credit always went to the ARCOMc or to Bandido Murray and that was how it was intended to be. I wanted it that way.

I can specifically remember when one of the coalition clubs, Next of Kin MC, lost all their members but one, their President Doc. He was disappointed and practically gave up on the club. My job behind the scenes was to encourage him and keep his spirits lifted until he was ready to reactivate his dormant club. For two years, I called or e-mailed him every two weeks or as often as I could. I kept him informed of ARCOMc meetings and events, personally encouraging him when it seemed he'd lost hope. No one asked me to do this but I loved my brother. My singleness of purpose was to meet the needs of the people and if I was able to be of assistance to someone, then by God, I was going to do it.

After two years of keeping Next of Kin Doc in the loop, in February of 2007, he attended his first Coalition meeting and engaged Toothpick as his first prospect. He was well on the road to social MC recovery and I was glad to have been a part of it.

It took excellent communication skills, charisma and discernment of people's characters to perform this kind of work. None of my club members knew the extent of the work I did because I never told them. All they saw was my performance as their president. Tab did not have a clue of why I visited bars where non-Red and Gold club members hung out and talked with 1%'ers and other club members. She never knew the devoted work I did for the ARCOMc. Where I went, how I went, and why I went to non-Bandido bars was oblivious to her and many others. She never knew the risks I put myself in or the chances I took in the process of meeting people; all for the sake of peace in the MC world in Arkansas, and in an effort to gain the trust and respect of the 1%'ers, not only for myself but for the Highway Chicks as well. Riding a motorcycle was only a marginal benefit of pleasure. The real purpose of having a patch on my back was to be a constructive link in the chain that outlined and kept the ARCOMc together as a peaceful organization.

I can take the next 10 pages and list all of the things I did for the ARCOMc and my superiors, but I feel it would be pointless because somewhere, somebody would invest all their energy in proving me wrong. When I first started writing this book my intention was to write about the forbidden love between an SOS patch holder and a Highway Chick President. How God brought us out of the ashes of grief into the ministry of his Word. Our desire was to bring clubs together and prove to the nation that two people from two different clubs, from opposite sides of the fence could form a love relationship, a ministry, and still maintain a good standing status with their respective clubs.

The ARCOMc in the state of Arkansas is a good thing. Bandido Murray has done an excellent job as President of such. He has done an exceptional job in co-existing with the Sons of Silence and in sharing the state power, as peace is kept between different 1% and MC clubs. As ARCOMc Secretary, I shared this vision. I made sure to the best of my ability that I played my part in promoting unity and safe riding.

So for Tab to make the accusation against me of being disloyal to the Red and Gold world was the highest form of betrayal conceived. Especially since, she instigated a club vote against me without even attempting to talk to me first. I believed that her actions were based solemnly on resentful and envious personal feelings. She desired the position, the power and the attention I had. She exhibited the typical jealous behavior of a power-hungry, insecure person and initiated a mutiny against me. She wanted my job and was determined to get it at any cost.

After she called everyone and told them I was out in bad standings, I could obviously not attend the pool tournament that Monday night. Highway Chick Hang Around Sparkles, and Martyrs hang around Wish, came to my home. Although they were only hang arounds, they were very upset at what had been done to me. They were not going to attend the pool tournament but I told them they needed to go and let me know what was going on.

Sparkles had been one of my best friends since the year 2000. Her loyalty was to me and no one else. She relayed information to me as it occurred at the pool tournament that night. I received my first phone call with an information update. "No Bandidos had yet arrived, neither had or Mitch." No one is saying anything. No one is talking or volunteering information. That Tab girl did have a meeting with Mitch and XXX (name withheld at patch holder's request) in the back and the patch holders were told that, they were not allowed to talk to Sadgirl. There seems to be a lot of tension."

After the pool tournament was over, Sparkles and Wish came to my house. Sparkles said she did not want to be a hang around for the Highway Chicks anymore. She saw that their actions were unjust and she did not want any part of the group of people like that. She also stated that she was with them because of me and since I no longer was a part of them, she wanted nothing to do with them.

I also got a call from hang around Martyrs, Andy. He also heard what had happened and decided not to be a part of the Martyrs motorcycle club either.

"I am not going to have someone tell me who I can talk to and who my friends are. You and I have been friends for 10 years. I have only known these people for two months," said Andy to me.

I also received a call from Highway Chick hang around, Connie. She informed me that she would be turning in her support patches as well. She was not happy with the way the club treated their president. "I am your friend and will always be your friend," she said to me.

I received a call from Highway and Hedges Senior Pastor, Punkin. He was an Honorary Officer for the Highway Chicks WMC. He was not happy with the situation either.

"I am going to call Tab and tell her that I do not want any part of the Highway Chicks any more. I will still perform my spiritual duties but I do not want to wear the Honorary Officers Patch. What they did was wrong," he said to me.

Monday night passed and no one called me other than the ones mentioned above. Out of among 200 so-called brothers in Arkansas, not one of them called to check on me. Not one of them had the courtesy to say goodbye. Makes me wonder and I ask myself, "Were they really my brothers? Were they really my friends? Did they love me for who I was? Or did they love me because of the patch I wore on my back?"

My heart was heavily flooded with sorrow due to the loss of who I thought were my brothers, my family. Five years of love, loyalty and respect seemed to be oblivious because of one woman's unsubstantiated accusations. I didn't blame Shep for the situation I was in for it was my choice to date him. However, if I would not have dated him I would probably still be President of the Highway Chicks. But then again, maybe it was meant to happen the way it did. Only time will tell.

That night, a Red and Gold patch holder informed me that Tab posted a bulletin on the internet informing everyone that I was out in bad standing for life with the Highway Chicks. The club that Debbie T and I had founded decided to rid themselves of their president.

On Tuesday morning, I received a call from San Jacinto High Roller, Vice President Lee. He was in Texas. He called to say hello and inform me of his whereabouts. I informed him of the recent chain of events. He professed to be my friend and that no one was going to tell him that he could not talk to me. He was extremely angry. He told me that if they did not remove my bad standing tag, he had a feeling he and his club would be pulling out of the Coalition.

"Come to my club, Sadgirl. Would you become a San Jacinto High Roller? We will be more than glad to take you into our club in Texas. You would wear the exact same patch that we wear. The only difference is that you would be an honorary member because you are a woman," he said.

"Lee, I cannot join any club if I'm out in bad standing with Murray. I just wish I knew why I was out in bad standing. Hell, I just wish I knew why I was out period!" I said to him.

"Well, I will keep you informed on what is going on. I will also give Allen a call and let him know what is going on. You are my friend. You worked very hard for us and I will not forget that," said Lee.

Being out in bad standing with the Highway Chicks was not a concern or a problem for me because I was a founder and charter member. The club only had three members and was a local fading club. On the other hand, being out in bad standing with Murray and the Bandidos was a different situation. Then I reasoned within myself. How could I be put out in bad standing with the Bandidos if I was never a Bandido? If I was never in, I could never be out! Therefore my status with all other clubs was good, other than the Highway Chicks and the clubs that perhaps befriended them, and could not (or would not) stand on their own integrity.

Later during the week, San Jacinto High Roller Slow Hand, out of Houston, Texas called me. He wanted to know the events that unfolded and led to my situation. He told me he would talk to Bandido Fast and find out what was going on and he would let me know. San Jacinto High Roller, Lee, did call to check on me. He offered his friendship – That, I will never forget!

Highway and Hedges LeAnn, who is also my prayer partner, called and offered her support. "They cannot tell me who can be my friend. I am not an MC. You are my friend and my prayer partner and that will never change."

It was the weekend of May 4. My first weekend as a non-patch holder. I still didn't know why I had been put out in bad standing. I still hadn't heard from Murray. No one was able to say what the charges against me were. Was there a possibility that someone realized the charges Tab made against me were fictitious? Or because there was no proof of her accusations? Was there a possibility the Bandido officers had made a hasty decision based on the whims of the jealous female?

I sat in my living room by myself, my only companion, loneliness. My club sisters were gone, my brothers had cut me off, and so did the man I thought would spend the rest of his days with me, not even a phone call. The feeling of being alone had hovered itself over me. The house was empty my phone was silent. I waited and waited, but none of my Red and Gold family reached out to me.

The sorrow of loneliness gave me the feeling of being stranded on an island with no life form. I had done so much for so many people and now I was able to see how they have forgotten. In my heart, I knew I could call Brakeline and he would talk to me, but I did not want to compromise or put him in a situation where he would be reprimanded by his club members. I did have the comfort that he would understand and not excommunicate me like everyone else. I knew our friendship went beyond the shallow rules and regulations any motorcycle club could have for we were family.

I found myself on the other side of the fence, but this time, I was alone without any colors. I had been put out of the MC unit to the unprotected side where patch holders do not tread. I was forced to look to God as my true Shepherd. I looked to Him for comfort and direction. I looked to God the Father for strength joy and. More than ever, I needed to trust my Heavenly Father and stay focused on his plan and purpose for my life. My body was weak, my soul emotionally drained, but my faith had not failed. I could not let my faith crash, for it was the only thing holding me up and allowing me to continue to live. I did not want to wake up each morning but I did. Why did life have to be so cruel and prolong its existence within my soul? Why did God not give us a 'get out of life' card that we could use at crucial times?

Losing my patch may have been an insignificant matter for many people, but for me it was devastating. When I lost my patch, I lost the purpose in my life because my patch was my purpose. When I lost Shep, I lost the life of my purpose because Shep was my life.

I wanted to quit, I wanted to give up. I wanted to get on my motorcycle and ride to the end of the road, never returning to this cruel society that I had been a part of. It must have been my brothers and sisters from Highway and Hedges Motorcycle Ministry praying for me at the time, which gave me that small lifeline to hang on to. They had indeed shown true Christian love for they never failed to call and check on me. I had fallen into a heavy state of depression and no one but God my Father knew about it. There was a little flame of faith that kept my spirit alive. My kids most of all, and old friends from the Home Crew did come to my aid. Andy, Bubba, Sparkles, and now Wish had proven to be my true friends and brothers.

I was sitting in my back porch talking with my daughter, Tabeel. I was telling her my plans for the move and the deadline I'd set for myself. At 9:50 pm, I received a phone call from Kansas. It was from DogBone, National President of the Military Vets MC. He wanted to share his grief and sorrow with me of the death of Bandido Gunner, from Texas.

"I had no idea he had died. Thank you for informing me. I am so sorry he was a great brother," I said to him.

On another note, have you heard what happened to me?" I asked him.

"No, I haven't. What's happened?"

I told him everything that happened with me and my club. It took longer than usual for he kept interrupting me by cussing and yelling at what he was hearing. He was angry and could not believe where the sisterhood of the Highway Chicks had gone.

"Sadgirl, you have done so much for these clubs, not only in Arkansas but in other states as well. The Sons of Silence began talking and having relations with us because of you. What you have done with the MC Officers Dinner is incredible. What the fuck is going on? Why the fuck would they not tell you anything? How could they commit such an injustice and get away with it? I am going to make some phone calls. I am not going to let this go by. You have earned too much respect throughout the years and have brought too many clubs together to allow this accusation to be brought against you. I know that you have been nothing but loyal to the Bandidos, and to the Red and Gold world. I will make some phone calls and see what is going on. This will be fixed," he said to me extremely frustrated.

He called approximately half an hour later and said, "I called Pistolero Kuzz. I arranged to have a meeting with him on Sunday evening. He does not know what is going on either but we are going to talk and find out what is going on and why they have acted in such manner. There is no way you can be out in bad standing. There is no way you could be out. I will call you tomorrow night and talk to you. I love you sister."

You know, I felt a lot of love there. A National President from the State of Kansas was concerned with what was going on in Arkansas with me. A brother that was not from the Red and Gold world was willing to open up a can of worms with Red and Gold brothers and attempt to correct the injustice that had been done against me. It felt good to know that at least for now, someone cared.

I received a call Sunday, May 6, at 9:08 am. It was my Chaplain. He wanted me to know that he had seen Shepherd at the Ozark Riders Birthday Party in Cabot, Arkansas. "He did ask me about you and wanted you to know that he did."

I am glad that he did ask about me but very disappointed that he had not contacted me. Had he also condemned me without a trial like my brothers did? Was he aware that perhaps all this ordeal took place because I was dating him and he was a Son of Silence? People did not understand that I had fallen in love with him as a man and, not with the patch he wore on his back. If the patch on his back were a "Hell's Angels" patch or a "Gypsy Joker" patch or a "CMA" patch, or whatever patch. If he never had a patch it would not have mattered to me because I fell in love with the man and not the patch.

Punkin said, "I talked to Roadkill and Debbie T. They were acting different. KB seemed to be the same. Tab was not there. I'm still going to talk to Tab and turn in my patch. I do not want to be a part of what they did. I am blessed at the way you have handled this. You have shown a true Christian attitude."

Another call came in at 12:20 p.m. It was Highway Chick hang around Connie. She just wanted to remind me of her friendship and loyalty to me and reassured me that come Monday evening, she would be turning in her support patch.

As I sit here, I know I can assume the badass biker attitude and take a violent approach towards the whole situation. I know I can get my Springfield 45 ACP and go cap this women who disrupted my life and, maybe serve a couple years in prison. That would not be a hard thing. I have many friends who are labeled "thugs" that I know owe me many favors and would not have a problem taking care of things for me. I have the ability to retaliate and start a war. However, this time I have chosen to remain calm. I feel that the self-control in me has overpowered my angry emotions, and although I am extremely angry and upset at the way things turned out, there is an unexplained calmness in me, which is beyond my understanding. I know that my heavenly Father has a plan and a purpose for me. I have no idea what it is but I do know I must not fret, but wait on Him. I must patiently wait and see how God unfolds the steps in my life at the next phase of my life.

This week I understood the value and the importance of human life. I realized that the past five years of my life had been wholeheartedly invested in things that had no eternal value. I became conscious of the fact that to live in this planet is a privilege allowed by God and could be taken away at any given moment and time. I became aware of the reality that we have been put on this planet as a link in the human chain. Every link no matter how good or how bad has some form of love attached to it. I learned there is good love and there is bad love. The good love is the God kind of love that embraces, accepts, sacrifices, and most of all forgives. The bad kind of love, even though it is based on goodness, pushes people away, hates, is selfish, and most of all, never forgives but lives with grudges.

I remember the last time I spoke with Tab on the phone after I heard her accusations, I told her, "Tab, I want you to know that I forgive you, and I hope you take the girls where they were intended to go. Once again, I forgive you and may God bless you." I hung up the phone as I vaguely remembered that three years ago she didn't even know how to ride a motorcycle. I never again spoke to her and I truly did indeed forgive her for her bogus conspiracy against me.

I realized that the things of eternal value were more significant than any other element in this world. A three-piece patch; club colors; events; rules and regulations; protocol; among many other rudiments, was what had been of importance to me for the past six years; elements that I would never be able to take with me when I died, rudiments that didn't mean anything to anyone other than those involved in that world.

That Sunday evening as I walked down my driveway, I saw a vehicle smash into two bikers. In a twinkling of an eye, their bodies were twirling through the air to an unconscious state as they fell to the ground. Two people who were leisurely riding their motorcycles on a warm Sunday afternoon were suddenly stopped by an unplanned sequence of events. It was just a matter of time before there were ambulances, fire trucks, and bystanders all trying to help.

"What was really important in these people lives at that time? Was it the clothes they were wearing? Was it the motorcycles they rode? Was it the type of leather vests they had on? Was it how much money they had in their wallet?" I asked myself as I watched the chaos standing beside my mailbox.

I realized that what was really important were the people they loved, and the people that loved them. I did not want to spend the rest of my life fighting over colors, turf, friendships, or even respect. That had no eternal value and no love.It was then that I understood why I was willing to sacrifice everything for Shep. It had nothing to do with my club, my colors, my motorcycle, or my lifestyle. It had to do with love, and even though he did not love me, that did not change things. I had committed myself to love and that was far more superior than any club protocol could ever be. I even understood why I had sacrificed six years of my life for my club and the Red and Gold world. It was because I truly loved them, and because of this love I knew that I would NEVER betray them or be disloyal to them in any matter.

In the end, that is all that I was left with, love and the memory of love; memories that I would cherish for the rest of my days on earth. Memories of a genuine love that existed only in the motorcycle world and only if you had their patch on. Memories of love as long as you were not out of their club in bad standing. All the favors, all the work, all the friendships built on love, loyalty, and respect, all the hugs, all the photos, all the verbal commitments, were nothing more than memories. Memories that I would never forget, commitments I would never betray, because my love to the Red and Gold world was genuine and from the heart.

The grieving process had begun for me, bringing with it the most devastating painful emotion human beings regret: loneliness. But it was time to say goodbye. It was time to eliminate the Arkansas MC lifestyle out of existence in the same manner you erase a chalkboard.

As for Shepherd, I was totally able to see that he was haunted by the ghosts of his past, too many to compete against me. He was happy living with his phantoms and he was not ready to let go of his deceased wife. No matter how many times he tried to part with her, he never could, not because he couldn't, but because he wouldn't.

Tuesday, May the 8th.

Sparkles and Wish came over the house at 1:00 am. Wish bought a message from Thunderhead Prospect Sam. "He wants you to know that because he and Big Joe are so close he cannot call you. He wants you to know that he misses you very much and thanks you for being there for him."

"You know, Wish," I said to him with a heartfelt tone. "I really miss Lucky, Sam and Mitch. Those are the three people I miss the most. Not necessarily in the correct order, but I really miss them."

He brought with him a Colt 380 pistol that his dad (Shep) sent to me. He wanted to trade it for the Springfield .45 ACP he had given me three months prior. I could not part with the .45 pistol. It was a gift from his daddy and it was the only physical memory I had left from him. We did shoot the 380 and although it was a nice gun, I told Wish to tell him, it was a "no deal." I would be keeping the gun as a treasured gift from him.

"Bandido One Wire will be in town today. Are you going to see him?" asked Wish.

"Until they remove this bad standing label, I will not be able to talk to him either," I said to him with a frown.

"Does he know you are out?"

"It doesn't matter if he knows or not. I will not violate protocol. I am too respectful of Murray to do so," I said to him.

"Bandido Murray mentioned your name in a good way at the Ozark Riders MC Birthday Party on Saturday," said Wish.

"Really! What did he have to say? I eagerly asked.

"Axxel got kinda pisssed at me. I told him his bike was purple. He didn't like it and told me, 'It's not purple!' I turned around and Murray was standing behind me. I asked Murray 'Isn't that bike purple?' He responded, 'almost as purple as Sadgirl's."

I know that deep down in the quiet place of Bandido Murray's heart he knew all the shit that was said about me was not true. He is a sincere man and I truly think he got caught up in the moment and made a swift judgment. He knew me too well and I believed in my heart that he knew I was not the kind of person Tab accused me of.

Phone calls were starting to come in mainly from ministry clubs and patch holders wanting to express their discontentment with the situation. I had already made the decision to relocate and take a much-needed vacation. I needed a fresh start as a non-patch holder. I was fully aware that it would be hard for me to ride as a citizen but I had no choice, at least not for now.

I rode, conducted myself, and thought like a patch holder. Not to do so would take years of deprogramming my attitude. I hoped that things would be cleared up in the near future and people would know that Tab's accusations had no substance or proof. But for now, I had to rely 100% on God's Spirit to strengthen my life and guide me in the direction He had planned for me. More than ever I believed Romans 8:28, *"And we know that all things work together for good to those who love God, to those who are the called according to His purpose."*

So no matter how bad the state of affairs that I was in seemed, I knew that in the end it was God's plan and purpose that would be fulfilled in my life. The hard part was the waiting and going through the situation, without being separated from the love of Christ due to an angry attitude because of the abandonment from my MC family.

The feeling of loneliness and desertion from losing my club family was excruciating. I had to adhere to the promise of Romans 8:33 to 35, and apply it to my life in order to keep my sanity.

"Who shall bring a charge against God's elect? It is God who justifies."

"Who is he who condemns? It is Christ who died, and furthermore is also risen, who is even at the right hand of God, who also makes intercession for us."

"Who shall separate us from the love of Christ? Shall tribulation, or distress, or persecution, or famine, or nakedness, or peril, or sword?"

Saturday, May 12, 2007.

Today I chose to accept Tabitha Tatum's invitation to her graduation. She is Brakeline's oldest daughter, a great friend and family member. I knew her dad would be there and this would be the perfect opportunity to see if Brakeline was still on family/friendly terms with me. He is a retired SOS member, and has the option to choose who his friends are.

As I arrived at the small, crowded parking lot of the Malvern High School, I began thinking about all the good times I'd had with Brakeline and wondered if he knew what happened with me. My hands were sweaty and shaky as I parked my black F-150 Harley Davidson pick up on the grass beside one of the educational buildings. I prayed to God that our relationship would not change. Our friendship, from the beginning was built on trust and honesty, and it had proven to be so over the years.

I walked into the crowded school auditorium from one end to the other with eager family members wanting to see their kids graduate. There was no place to sit so I leaned on the back wall with my camera in hand ready to take pictures of Tabitha Brakeline Tatum as she walked down the aisle. As I looked around for the rest of the family, I saw Nathan her husband, and Sissy her mother, sitting three rows from where I stood. She waved at me while motioning me to sit beside her. "I was saving this seat. Come sit with us," she enthusiastically said. Sissy said that Brakeline was sitting in the upper box with Sons of Silence XXX (name withheld at patch holder's request). We were glad to see each other and we talked for the duration of the ceremony. I am sure the people around us were irritated at our conversations as we were kind of loud.

After the ceremony was over, we waited for the rest of the family to join us. We pushed our way to the front of the building and took some pictures. As we walked towards the area where Tabitha was, I saw Brakeline standing beside his daughter. I saw him look at me and in a split second look back down at the camera he was tinkering with. When he realized it was me coming towards him, he swiftly looked twice. When we finally met we hugged and I was so glad to see him. I exchanged a verbal hello with XXX (name withheld at patch holder's request) and his wife but we did not shake hands. That was OK with me. I was satisfied with his greeting.

I had not told Brakeline what happened with my club's decision to overthrow my rank. I did however; notice the concerned look in his eyes when he saw me.

"What are you doing here?" he asked me in total amazement.

"Tabitha invited me to her graduation."

"Oh... I didn't know. No one told me," he said.

"No one ever tells you anything," I said to him in a joking matter.

"I heard the bad news last night. We have to talk. I had no idea until XXX (name withheld at patch holder's request) came over last night and told me what happened; but that is just one side of the story," he said to me as he squinted his eyes with worry.

"I will get with you and tell you everything. I'm going with Tabitha and her mom to the graduation dinner and then I will get a hold of you."

Later that evening I called Brakeline and told him my side of the story. He seemed to think that what happened was an internal power play from my own club. His opinion was that my own club had initiated the removal of my person based on one person's jealousy. It was interesting that he discerned this even in his retired status for there were other people saying this very same thing.

"The Bandidos and the Highway Chicks have put you out in bad standings but the Sons of Silence will not give you that label because there is no proof of anything they have said. We are not like that.

So until any proof surfaces, you are not out in bad standing with the Sons," said Sons of Silence Brakeline.

It was a relief to hear him say this. I was very concerned with Mitch's opinion about me as a person and patch holder. I had worked very hard to gain his respect for this was important to me, and I was not about to lose it because of some accusation without proof. I asked him to please, make sure Mitch was completely aware that none of my actions ever reflected any disrespect or dishonor to the Bandidos, to Murray or to him. I wanted him to be conscious of the fact that my intentions in the club world were honest and trustworthy, especially towards him.

On Monday evening I went to Brakeline's home for a final meeting before I left and to bring him the registration for the party barge I had given him. Sparkles and Wish accompanied me since they had been staying with me for the last month being a strong support and comfort. When we arrive at Brakeline's house I opened the front door and called for him. I introduced my friends and we went into his media room for a private conversation.

"Where are you headed?" he asked after I told him everything that had occurred.

"I am going to Florida but I do not want anyone to know just yet. I don't want people calling down there and sending hate messages," I said to him in a serious tone.

He promised me that no one would know of my whereabouts, but I needed to stay in touch with him and give him an address. He understood the feeling of loneliness that had overwhelmed me for he too had survived the feeling of not belonging to anything at one time.

"It feels like you have lost everything. Like there is nothing left for you. It happened to me when I retired. That is not as your situation, but for two years I felt I was lost not knowing where to belong," he said to me.

"Has anything changed with your club?" I asked him with a genuine concern. "Are they keeping you in the loop like they should?"

"Yes! They are now. As a matter of fact just the other day they called me with a small problem and asked my advice. Everything is fine now," he said to me.

I explained to him how my major concern was that Mitch understood the value of my integrity and the loyalty to my club. Brakeline assured me that he would talk with him and relay my message. He informed me that in his conversation with other patch holders, he was told that I overstepped my boundaries many times in an attempt to keep peace with the MC clubs within the state of Arkansas, over and beyond the 1%'ers. They told him that I was delusional in thinking that I could accomplish this.

"In all honesty Brakeline, there was many times where I worked behind the scenes to improve interpersonal relations with clubs. I am aware of that! It was not my mission in life or my goal, but a job I performed not for me, but to make things easier for my boss, Bandido Murray. And in the same token there were many times where I've withheld information from him in order to keep things running smooth. No! This was not my obsession but a token of appreciation for my boss for taking me on his ship and steering me under his flag. Did I overstep my boundaries? Of course I did. I always do and have become an expert at it." I was honest and straightforward with him as I always am.

"I personally know that this is correct but you will never get the credit for it," he said. "You and I talked and I saw how you worked. I remember you sitting in the chair where you are right now, and asking me directions where protocol was concerned. You actually listened to what I said. You were not a know-it-all. At one time for about two years you were the only one keeping me informed of club events and happenings in the state of Arkansas. Just remember you will never get the credit," said Brakeline to me in a firm but dissatisfied tone.

"I am okay with that because I know who I am. I am confident and satisfied with the work I performed for the past five years. My only concern is the one I mentioned earlier. It is for Sons of Silence, President Mitch to know this."

"Don't worry, I will take care that. I promise." He reassured me. "I don't want you to disappear out of my life," said my personal friend and mentor.

I assured him that would never happen. I let him know if that I had to choose one person to stay in contact with in the state of Arkansas, it would be him. I also informed him that I would not be involved in the MC world as a patch holder in the ARCOMc anymore. This was a decision I made after I realized who my true friends were. After being left alone to die in the battlefield; after all my brothers saw me lying in a pool of blood, lifeless, and without hope. A decision that I made when I learned that talk is cheap and actions are scarce. A decision I made, after I realized that the motto that I so strongly lived by, *Love, Loyalty and Respect,* to the Bandido Nation meant absolutely nothing to them when it came to a fallen comrade. A decision I made after I was sentenced to death without an inquisition, without a hearing or without a trial.

I could never again be a Bandido supporter. Not because I did not love or respect them, but because the Red and Gold brothers involved in my life chose to walk over an unjustly injured fellow soldier and never not offer any kind of support whether I was wrong or not. We might not have been in the same battalion or even the same state, but we were in the same branch, and I flew their colors for five years under the command of Bandido Murray. My orders came from him and I was accountable to him for all our actions. I represented the Red and Gold nation because I wore Bandido support colors on my Cut.

Monday, May 14, 2007

I was still asleep on the couch when I heard someone banging on my back porch door. Still in my pajamas I looked out the kitchen window to see who had awakened me from one of the few nights where I was able to catch some good sleep. It was Road Barron Vice President, Jim.

I opened the door, put my hand over my eyes to cover the bright sunshine forcing its way into my home, and greeted him with a warm hug. I was surprised to see that someone from the MC world breached the standing order not to talk to me. But then again, this was a Road Barron and they were not part of the ARCOMc. Therefore, in all legal aspects of protocol, he did not fall under the standing directive.

The first thing he said to me was, "What is going on? Is it true what they are saying? I just want you to tell me. I don't want this bullshit of he said, she said. I want to hear from you."

"Jim, it is not true. You have known me for years, and you know that I am not that type of person. I can assure you, every accusation fabricated by Tab is completely unsupported by proof and it is false," I said to him as I firmly looked him in the eyes and did not vary in speech or tone.

"That's all I wanted to hear," he said as hugged me and rushed off to work. I was impressed and touched by the fact that he'd come to my home to talk with me. In fact, he was the only patch holder who had shown true friendship other than San Jacinto High Roller, Lee and an Ozark Rider. It was ironic, that the first patch holders in my life four years earlier were Road Barrons, and the last patch holder to set foot in my home was a Road Barron.

It was about 11:30 pm that night when my friend, Pirate called me. He is not a patch holder but a friend of the MC community.

"I talked to Murray tonight and he told me something that you ought to know," said Pirate.

"What is it?" I asked him.

Pirate began to tell me that Bandido Murray told him that while he was in Texas at Bandido Gunner's funeral, a Bandido National Officer pulled him to the side and told him that there was a girl by the name of Tab running her mouth and talking to other Bandidos from out of state. He told Murray to clean up his mess.

"Do you think Murray wants me to know this?" I asked pacing back-and-forth on the back porch as I spoke with him on the phone.

"I'm sure he does. Why else would he tell me?" He replied with a serious attitude.

I thanked them for the information and told him I would keep in touch with him.

That same night Bandido Onion, out of Alabama called me. He personally wanted to know what had happened with me. I told him everything. When I finished telling him the facts he asked me if I was sitting down. "Yes, why?" I asked him with a panic tone.

"I am out in bad standing also," he said to me.

"What happened Onion? How can this happen to you? I asked in total amazement.

He explained everything that happened to him and how it occurred. All I could tell him was that at least now we were able to talk and be friends. He chuckled as he informed me that he would never again be involved in the Red and Gold world. He was also perplexed at the fact that the brothers he knew for many years, completely cut him off when he lost this patch. He made the statement. "It's like you become invisible…, like you never existed."

I sympathized with him, for I was still mourning the loss of my Red and Gold family or at least who I thought were my brothers. In all honesty, I did not miss the Highway Chicks (other than KB), but rather the Bandidos, and the support club members from Mississippi, Alabama and Louisiana. The brothers I missed the most were Mississippi Riders Trigger, Blinky and Pistol, Thunderhead Big Joe and Thunderhead Prospect Sam from Arkansas, Martyrs Lucky, Outsider Grizz, and Next of Kin Prospect, Toothpick from Arkansas, (the last two mentioned were my personal friends before they were patch holders but also chose to cut me off completely), and Bandido Jim from Louisiana.

I greatly missed not being able to speak with Hell's Lover Sonny and his crew. But most of all in my heart, I believe my greatest loss was the political comradeship of Sons of Silence President, Mitch. I had worked so hard to build an alliance of trust, and now in the twinkling of an eye, the rug had been pulled from under me.

Loneliness had become my companion, embedded deep in my heart and my soul. My Chaplain continued to call and pray with me over the phone. I was extremely grateful for his love and true Christian spirit. I moved my departing date one week ahead. I felt I had nothing left and it was a waste of my time sitting at home without a purpose. My children were my greatest support. They loved me regardless of status and were always there for me. My true friends were a great moral support and without Andy, Bubba, Sparkles, Wish, Micah and Stephanie staying with me, I would have probably used my 'get out of jail card' and clocked out.

I chose a fresh new start with the world ahead of me. I decided to take a long vacation to Florida and get away from the world I had submerged myself in for the past 5 years. I had the ocean to look forward. For a minute I had lost the vision of who I was, but now I wasn't flinching at the essence of my true self. I realized that if I had compromised who I truly was and my leadership values as well, it would have ended in a disaster. I was conscious that I operated on a more instinctive level than most of the people around me. I knew when something was amiss and had a sixth sense of a person's intent. I just had to break out of the vicious circle of being faithful to that, which harmed my soul.

14
Saying Good Bye to my MC Family

The day when I actually rented the U HAUL™ trailer and brought it home had finally arrived. I tried to be strong but could not hold back the tears when I thought of not being with my kids in the same state. It wasn't fair that I had lost so much in this chain of events and it was not rational that I was leaving my hometown, stripped of my glory while the perpetrators who caused my grief still had everything they wanted. At least it felt that way. Nevertheless, I had to be strong and move on to a higher plane with better things in store for me.

That last day of the three-week party that took place in my home, was a special going away dinner party, which started at my daughter's house and ended at mine. The night had almost ended, the dinner plates were stacked in the trash, the empty beer and liquor bottles on the table, and only the Home Crew remained until late at night.

The UHAUL™ trailer sat in my yard with my Road King inside it, boxes and furniture tightly packed around her. Bubba, Andy, and Wish finished packing the final loose items. It was quiet and sadness filled the empty house that had been my home for the past ten years. No one wanted to stay with me on that last night. They said they could not stand to see me drive off the next day. We all hugged and cried, said goodbye and made a pact to stay friends for life.

I watched as the cars left the driveway and turned onto the road. This time, it was just me, completely alone, with a taste of how the next year would be. It was hard to believe the home my late husband had brought for the kids and I would no longer be mine. I was sad, I was lonely, but needed to make this conscious move. I needed to say goodbye to my MC family and cut ties with what had been my life for the past five years. I needed to divorce my MC family and I was having a hard time doing so.

Early Sunday morning I got in my truck and left Arkansas with tears in my eyes. It was hard to leave my kids, my Home Crew, and my MC family, but I had to get away if only to finish writing this book. The route I took was the same road my club and I took every time we went to Jackson, Mississippi. Every turn and pit stop was a memory trigger. I saw the places where we had gotten our speeding tickets, where we stopped to eat, and all the landmarks along the way. The fondest of all memories was the Yield sign at the 65N crossroads near Lake Providence.

We were in Canton for the weekend at the Mississippi Riders Bike Build Off competition. It was the same weekend the Mississippi girls got their Probationary patches and our club's membership increased by four new members. This weekend also provided the unforgettable story of how Debbie T's jungle hammock busted and she came crashing down from the trees into the campground's soil. It was the best laugh we ever had!

As we were getting ready to return to Arkansas, Debbie T was convinced that she had found a faster route to get back home. I totally disagreed, for her road although shorter in distance, was curvy and had stoplights. My route, although further in distance was straight-through interstate. But in order to convince her that she was wrong and I was right we decided to have a race. I split the club into two teams, Debbie T's team and my team. The deal was that the first team to reach the Yield sign at 65N crossroads was to tie a red and gold bandana to it and continue to our usual pizza pit stop. The team that arrived first was to go to the pizza parlor and wait for the losing team to come and pay for lunch.

It was a fun-filled, exhilarating ride at 98 mph on Interstate 55 and then I-20 for me and Curve. My team made it first to the Yield sign. We tied the bandana and hauled ass to the lunch stop as we waited for Debbie T's team to come pay for our lunch and hear us brag.

That was only one of the many memories that surfaced as I drove my moving truck. I was reliving past club trips like a vivid 3-D storyboard video and it was sad. It was hard to say goodbye to yesterday.

Just because they took my patch did not mean that years of sisterhood and friendship would magically vanish. It would be a long time before these ties could be severed from my heart, and even then, there would not be any guarantee that I could do that. They threw me away but I could not do the same.

The day I crossed the Florida State line, things seemed to change emotionally for me. I wanted to leave the pain and sorrow back in Arkansas along with all the bad memories that had transpired in my life concerning the Highway Chicks and the Bandidos. As I traveled the highway along the ocean I felt a peaceful sense of relaxation. It was a fresh start for me in a venture that I knew was included in God's purpose.

It had been six weeks since the loss of my colors. I was still unsuccessful in the outcome of the reason behind my exile but I had I had chosen to move on and make my club life in Arkansas an experience from the past. I had been waiting for the right time frame to write a valediction message for the people I had shared my life with for the past six years. I wasn't sure if my words would carry anger or retaliation so I had to sit it out until I knew exactly what to write and how to say goodbye.

On Tuesday, May 29, 2007, I sat down and wrote a short, sincere heartfelt farewell email to those closest to me in the MC world.

"IF YOU ARE MY FRIEND, READ THIS... IF YOU ARE MY BROTHER, READ THIS. IF YOU CALLED YOURSELF MY BROTHER AT SOME TIME, READ THIS...*anyone else go do something useful with your life!*

- *Let it be known that I, Sadgirl, have never been disrespectful or disloyal to the Bandidos, the Red and Gold, or any support club.*

- *Let it be known that my vice president, TAB, wrongfully and without any substantiated proof, accused me of disloyalty to the Red and Gold nation, mainly because I was dating a Sons of Silence probate at the time, and you cannot help whom you fall in love with; and because I was writing a love story, soon to be published. She initiated a club revolt against my person and took my Colors.*
- *Let it be known that what she took were only pieces of fabric sewn by a lady in Little Rock. She was NOT able to take what is in my heart. She could not take God's love, and she was NOT able to take the love, loyalty and respect that I had sworn to the Red and Gold Nation. That will always be a part of my heart.*
- *Let it be known that I will not attempt to regain my status as a patch holder for it has been proved that the unfairness of my superiors was far beyond acceptance, when I saw that my fellow soldiers saw me lying helpless in the trenches of loneliness in the battlefield, and left me to die as they carefully tip-toed over me to save their own necks.*
- *Let it be known that in true Christian spirit I forgive Tab and anyone else who, by participation or omission, agreed with any accusation.*

I thoroughly enjoyed every good and bad moment with the Red and Gold Nation these past 6 years and unconditionally loved my boss, Bandido Murray, Bandido Jim, Bandido Stubbs, and Big Joe, along with my brothers from Arkansas, Mississippi, and Louisiana; Mitch and XXX (name withheld at patch holder's request). No regrets ever!

God bless each and every one of you as you venture further along in your life." Good bye

Sincerely, Sadgirl

I hit the send key and transmitted my farewell letter to hundreds of people from different MC clubs and several citizens who were my friends. This communication would terminate any inter-personal business affair that would be pending and bring closure to my life as a patch holder. At least that is what I hoped for. It was my heartfelt intention to let all who in some form or fashion, had affected my world as a patch holder.

I expected to receive vast amounts of festered hate mail from different people. However, as I began to open emails from different club members and several civilians, I saw that their words were encouraging and supportive. All except one. Here are just a few of the e mails I received in response to my farewell email.

From: Bandido Pervert 1%, *Houston, Texas*
Jun 1, 2007 5:18 AM

"Wow. That is crazy... I just don't know what to say. But sweetheart you said it best in your letter. You really did."

From: Bubba, *Martyrs MC, Secretary-Treasurer*
May 1, 2007 7:47 PM

"Can you give me the low down on what I just heard...Out in Bad Standing for LIFE? I haven't heard anything other than TAB is President... And this bulletin I just got on the Bad Standing.
   Would you fill a friend in?" LL&R

From: Tommy Smith, *Southern Knights MC, President*
Date: Tue, 29 May 2007 18:08:29 -0700
Re: A farewell Note

"Sorry to hear that. Sometimes our worlds take these complete crazy upheavals. Stay in touch." Tater

From: Tommy, *Tribe of Judah Motorcycle Ministry*
Tue, 29 May 2007 21:15:26 EDT
Re: A farewell Note

"Sadgirl, I am sorry this happened. I have always had respect for you and I wish you well. Let it be known that you have a friend with me and the TRIBE OF JUDAH MM. Please do not remove me from your email. I still have respect."

From: Taz, *Road Barrons MC, Memphis, Tennessee*
Tue, 29 May 2007 20:06:02 -0700 (PDT)
Re: A farewell Note

"I'll party with you anywhere, side by side. Respect those that giveth respect. My personal home is always open."

From: **Mel Brown,** *Patriot Guard, State Road Captain*
Tue, 29 May 2007 22:18:44 -0500

Re: A farewell Note
"Hi Girl, I'm going to miss you. Any of the clubs that didn't back you should hang their heads in shame. They formed their Coalition to back each other then didn't practice what they preach. Please stay in touch. Your loyal friend."
 Standing tall for defenders of America!

From: **Crazy Horse,** *Dream Riders Riding Association, Mississippi*
Wed, 30 May 2007 02:40:20 -0700 (PDT)

"I don't give a FUCK who you are in love with--You will ALWAYS have a place in Crazy Horses' heart. And I will always have a thing for you in a good kinda of way! HA! Please stay in touch because life is too short to lose the friends we have. I am in South Florida right now and trying to get something going down here, it's all about the kids.
 Love ya ALWAYS!!!!!"

From: Allen McCanliss, **Slow Hand,** *San Jacinto High Rollers MC, National Road Captain, Houston, Texas*
Date: Wed, 30 May 2007 06:07:48 -0500

"Good Morning Sadgirl... I hate to see it come down to this. I guess I'll never know the other side of this story as to why the chain of events happened to end your participation in the MC world. I wish you the best of luck in the future. I appreciate all that you have done to help get the Waldron Chapter started and will never forget it. You were a major part *of getting us approved. Even though you may or may not wear a patch in the future, you are still welcomed in my home. If ever in the area, give me a call. You have my number and e-mail, keep in touch. Take care and May God Bless!"*

From: **Leigh Ann Estes,** Highway and Hedges Motorcycle Ministry
Date: Wed, 30 May 2007 08:25:12 -0500

"Hello my sister! First and foremost, let me say that I love you and you have always been and continue to be in my prayers! I pray for you every day! I am convinced that the Lord is going to do mighty things through you. I understand what it is like to be turned on by people that you thought were your brothers and sisters. I too was turned on by a group of people that I loved very much and trusted. To make matters worse, they called themselves Christians and I had worked in the trenches with them side by side for six years in the prison ministry. They were like family! I hurt so bad over this that I did not think that I was going to make it through it. They revolted against Ewok and I just because of the change in a back patch! But I can tell you that God truly heals all wounds.

I still have problems sometimes but I now have peace in my heart because I know that God had to do something drastic to move ME out of the way, so that I could truly serve HIM! Now understand, I don't even begin to think that my situation is anywhere as difficult as yours, I am only telling you this because I understand how your heart feels.

I miss you so much! I find that I just don't have the drive to go the places that I once went anymore because I am afraid that if I allow myself to get close to anyone else there is a possibility that they will get stripped away from me. Your old world was a dangerous one. I say old world because you have a new world now! A fresh start and with God you will prevail. You are the strongest woman I have ever met and I have more respect for you than you ever will know!

Please stay safe my sister and don't lose touch! I am and always will be here for you! All you have to do is call. I will also be here awaiting your return. This friend, is your "desert" experience. God is going to prune you and train you up and you will emerge into the promise land! Your return will be a triumphant one because God is on your side. You will be stronger than ever!

Please let me know where the wind has blown you. Rest assured it will just be between us and hopefully we can still get together from time to time. We are still prayer partners! Be blessed my sister and stay strong! I love you!"

From: **Brick**, *Highway and Hedges Motorcycle Ministry*
Date: Wed, 30 May 2007 16:35:33 +0000 (UTC)

"Sadgirl, This is Brick, I just heard of this issue and my heart goes out to you. As my sister in the Lord, I respect you as that. I only wish we could have gotten to know each other. I am going to miss you. I always looked for you when I was at the Long Branch, or any event. The Lord has lead me to minister to the patched riders, but I am not supporting the pool tournament any longer. I will minister to people at events as God leads. I am not in rebellion over what has happened here. The Holy Spirit is directing me to other places.

Sadgirl, I want you to understand that I will stand in agreement with you on whatever direction you go. Please let me know what is going on, so I can focus my prayers in that area. I will be faithful to keep this door of communication open to you until the Lord comes. This is not a farewell note but a beginning of a friendship. Your Brother"

From: **Heavy Metal**, *Boozefighters 66, Romance, Arkansas (R.I.P.)*
Date: Wed, 30 May 2007 18:16:35 -0500

"I cannot speak for the rest of the club, but you would always be welcome to come to our events as far as I'm concerned. We are not territorial and all are welcome here. You have supported our functions well in the past. Good luck and keep on riding."

From: **Vietnam Bob**, *Vietnam Vets MC, West Tennessee Chapter*
Date: Thu, 31 May 2007 12:29:01 EDT

"I had heard something about this and wondered what had happen but knew if I waited long enough that the truth would surface. The times that

I met you, I saw nothing but respect for the Red and Gold and also for the Vietnam Vets M/C. Whatever happens you are always welcome in my camp."

From: **Woody,** Southern Cross MC, Tennessee, Business Manager
Date: Thu, 31 May 2007 15:31:36 -0500

"We will miss you."

From: Charlie Brown, **Quick Draw**, American Veterans MC, Scott County, Arkansas
Date: Fri, 1 Jun 2007 04:25:42 -0700 (PDT)

"Sad Girl, Wish you the best and please stay in touch. Drop me a line when your book comes out. I'm one of the few, of my brothers, that can read."

From: **Shep,** Sons of Silence, Arkansas
Date: Tue, 29 May 2007 21:57:53 -0700 (PDT)

"Welcome to the MC world. You worked so hard to have equal status as a 'patch holder.' Well congratulations, you did such a good job, that even I couldn't have contact with you. This has been a consequence of the world that you created. Please don't condemn those who had a share in and lived within your creation."

I did not expect Shepherd to respond to this email but he did. Out of hundreds of emails I received, his was the only one that wasn't sympathetic. It was the only one with a tone of anger, with a hint of hate.

I listed his email last in order due to my relationship with him as his girlfriend. There was a statement he made, however, that was not true. "...you did such a good job, that even I couldn't have contact with you."

I spoke on the phone with Sons of Silence, Brakeline on Saturday, May 26, and then again on Saturday, June 2 at 2:32 pm. Both times, he informed me that the Sons of Silence were allowed to speak to me any time they wanted. They had not participated in the "out in bad standing" order. They did advise Shepherd, according to Brakeline, that they "highly recommended him not speaking to me because of our relationship." But it was not a standing order.

The woman in me loved him beyond reasoning but I despised falling in love with him under a false pretense. I was a woman who had fallen in love with the wrong man. A man who seemed to be lost in his emotional world and I didn't know how not to love him. I also found it difficult to cut ties with the people whom I left behind in the MC world in Arkansas. The strange thing was that although I'd been 86'ed from that crowd, information of their affairs still came strong through emails and phone calls. People were upset that I disappeared and could not get an explanation from anyone. They were trying to find out what happened and why I wasn't there to explain. They didn't like Tab or her leadership but they said they had to respect it for Murray's sake.

The Descend From Glory

I managed to secure several informers that kept me up to date in the affairs of the HCWMC. I needed to know what was going on in order to finish this book. I needed to know how the club was holding up with their new self-imposed president, and wanted to know the sequence of events to the club's plummet.

One of my informers told me that the Highway Chicks had cancelled their HOG party at their clubhouse. The reason they gave was that the liquor license was in my name and it was no longer valid since I wasn't with them. In reality I never had a liquor license in my name anywhere in the United States. They had fabricated a lie to cancel the party and avoid being busted by the Alcohol Board of Liquor Control in Arkansas (ABC). I smiled for I knew exactly what was going on. I saw that the Highway Chicks were not the club they once were, and they were having difficulty maintaining that image. I was told that other patch holders seem to be losing respect for them and noticed how the atmosphere at the Monday night pool tournaments was not the same. There seemed to be a hostile environment. "Sadgirl, you were the peacekeeper among these clubs and you did it well," said a brother as he talked with me on the phone.

The Highway Chicks were slowly descending from glory each day and other clubs were beginning to see the reality of their affairs. It would be a matter of time before karma rolled around the corner to seek Tab and her accomplices out. They had lost the respect of many and the struggle to maintain what little they had left was obvious. They wanted everyone to see that nothing had changed since I left the club. But it had! They could not uphold the image of strength and solidarity because they didn't know how to.

Tab had even gone to the unethical lengths of slapping a full probationary patch on her girlfriend just to have a body. This was a major breech of protocol in the MC rules. This girl had never been a hang around, a prospect, or a supporter. She was Tab's girlfriend and not allowed to attend events with the HC in order to keep her personal life quiet. When my informer called and said that a girl appeared out of nowhere with a probationary patch on her back, I could not help but laugh and shake my head.

They were going downhill and doing it fast. The moral ethics of the club had deteriorated to a shadow of the splendor from the past. Although they were still pushing and attending as many Red and Gold events as they could, the downfall of the club was inevitable. Some factors that transpired that month and seem to stand out cannot go unmentioned. KB's bike was struck by lightning while parked at her home. Roadkill had turned her colors in and quit the club on July 13, and her boyfriend, Ozark Rider Swede, was put out in bad standings that same month. (Hum .... makes me wonder about karma). Debbie T quit the club again. She states,

Oct 7, 2007 8:35 PM

"I quite the club again and for the last time because I do not believe in living by other peoples rules. By wearing that patch, I allowed myself to be governed by a group of people that could care less about me. I'm not into being told when to shit and when to wipe my ass... that's not how I want to live my life.

When starting the club I was looking to create a sisterhood that would be untouched by any other. We would be of our own, make our own rules, have our own fun etc... BE REAL SISTERS. It never worked out that way. I put up with a lot of shit I didn't believe in hoping it would get better... it only got worse. I left the nest at age fourteen. I wasn't looking for a new daddy or momma at 38 years of age. I hope this helps explain my reasons for leaving a crazy life I'll never understand why others enjoy."

After Debbie T quit the club, I waited a few months before I contacted her. I wanted us to be friends as we always were, before the club existed. I had greatly missed her and the great times we had shared. Now that she wasn't in the HC, we could resume our friendship without the political bullshit that kept us apart.

The only new HC hang around decided to become a PBOL so she also quit the club. They were down to two members, one Prospect, and the new overnight Probationary member.

When the HC had their pancake breakfast on August 12, only one patch holder showed up. When they had their annual in September, only a few patches showed up. This was an evident sign of the loss of respect and support from the MC community in comparison to the hundreds of patch holders that attended our last annual when I was President.

I was informed that at their 2007 HC annual, Bandido Murray met with Tab for quite a while, and when the Thunderheads rolled in later during the evening, StreetDoc went straight to Tab and said that he needed to talk with her. Neither Tab nor the rest of the HC seemed to be happy campers after that. Their prospect Magic worked the door all day and displayed immense signs of sorrow. She could not understand why a stranger had showed up with a full probationary patch and she was still a prospect. She made the statement, "I don't know why there is nobody here."

The icing on the cake was when Tab slid on her bike and went down at a funeral in Mississippi, at a church in front of many bikers. How many more signs needed to be thrown at their face in order to realize that the HC were damaged from the inside out? They had lost the respect of many ARCOMc members and seemed to be swimming against the current but didn't know the techniques of an upstream swim.

Tab was afraid of my power and seemed to make it obvious. She was under the impression that Highway and Hedges would give me a patch and I could come back to Long Branch. She wanted to put me in a neutral, non-threatening organization where everyone could see that I was happy, subsequently allowing her to gain the respect she had stolen from me. I saw how ignorant and unprofessional her actions and pattern of thinking was. I knew that no matter how much she tried to make her president office a respected one, she would never attain it for she had obtained it illegally. She had stolen it from me under a false pretense and that would never validate the love, loyalty and respect that I earned for so many years.

No one said it better than Brakeline, "An *offer of support is more than just pride in wearing the same colors it is a **gift of a promise** to watch someone's back and **to have that rejected is a serious loss to the person or club who refused the honor**.*"

ABC once made a statement that carried a lot of truth to it. "We tried different things to keep us going… guys as hang around supporters, HC support members, associates… but there was always something missing that kept us from having sisterhood. The Webpage said HC is a sisterhood. I have to say that it is far from it. It is a few strangers who chose to ride a few miles together until they part."

I laughed quietly when I received a phone call saying that Shepherd told HC Prospect Magic, "When you patch out I will no longer be able to hug you." I was able to see that the HC had no respect, the one thing that they so fervently sought after. People shook Tab's hand, hell, they even hugged her, but behind closed doors the expressed comments about her were disrespectful. The women's MC that Debbie T and I had established in 2003 was at its lowest peak in numbers and strength. The club had no glory and appeared to be hanging by a thread.

Alone in the Wind

I was near the ocean hoping to find peace and serenity. I kept in daily contact with my friends who had nothing to do with the MC world, friends whom I'd known before I was a patch holder. I quietly talked to a handful of faithful friends from the MC world in Little Rock.

As I progressed in my life as an independent biker, I could not help but think about the way things would have turned out if I had stayed in the Club. Would the Bandidos have given us a Heart Patch eventually? (The round red and gold patch that support clubs wear directly over the heart on their cut that reads 'I support Bandidos MC Worldwide'). Would the Highway Chicks have been the first female MC club to wear the Heart Patch permanently? I could not help but wonder how far I could have taken the club. I guess that will always be an unsolved mystery for I decided not to pursue the MC world in the ARCOMc in light of the recent events.

I realized that what started out as a daring and illicit love affair between two patch holders from two different motorcycle clubs had ended in the termination of what had been my life for five years. It was like falling 30 stories from a high riser into the concrete ground. It happened so quickly and abruptly that before I realized what happened, I was lying flat on my back.

I was having trouble living my life as a non-patch holder and I was missing my brothers, nevertheless, I knew it was time to pick up the pieces and begin to mend the emotional damage that had been caused by my club and my brothers. I was a mess but I never stopped trusting God. I always prayed as I patiently waited for his will to explode in my life. I had to find new acquaintances and a different social life. I had to get used to riding my bike without my rags. I had difficulty adjusting to life as a non-patch holder and I didn't know how to make the transition, for I felt naked without my colors. I found it difficult to say goodbye to my MC family for it felt like my life had no purpose without Murray or the ARCOMc.

After two months, I finally got on my motorcycle and rode the highway beside the ocean in Florida. It was exhilarating and a great stress relief. I stopped at a local beach in Okaloosa Island and walked onto a fishing pier that went at least 1000 feet into the ocean. I watched the locals and tourists hook a variety of bait on their fishing poles and cast them deep into the ravishing blue-green waters of the ocean.

As I stood on the pier that was a least five stories high, I looked down at the swimmers who were enjoying themselves as they fought with the forceful waves coming from the open sea to the shoreline. I focused on a couple that seemed to be madly in love embrace each other while sitting in the sizzling sun that didn't seem to bother them. As I turned towards the north side of the pier, there was an oriental family with five small children guzzling hand fed noodles from their mother's hand, while their father attempted to catch the biggest fish of the week. They didn't seem to have a care in the world. Then there was the local drifter who just wandered up and down the pier hopelessly searching for someone's lost treasure.

I saw the 4x4 SUV's driven by the local sheriff on the deep white sand effortlessly patrolling the crowded shoreline of swimmers, fishermen, volleyball players, and couples in love that occasionally pulled out a can of cold beer from an ice chest. The lifeguards in their patrol chairs stood tall and proud as they watched beachgoers on their floats, sailboats, or just paddling around the dolphin populated waters of the beach.

Beyond the white sands of the coastline, I could see the variety of restaurants packed with hungry folks who were snagged into the establishments by the fresh aroma of boiling seafood. Most of them wore their swimsuits and flip flops as they sat in the covered outdoor patios watching the ocean as they enjoyed their modestly priced meals. One particular billboard caught my eye. "No shoes, No shirt, No Problem!" It rather reminded me of a tropical shack in a Caribbean paradise.

As I observed all these different people, I was able to see that for the past five years, I'd been trapped in a lifestyle that had significant value only to those directly involved in it. The people at this beach were normal everyday citizens who belonged to the world we shared and fished from the same ocean that we ate. They did not have one iota of concern with motorcycle clubs or their political opinions. They didn't care how many miles were put on a bike per year, and who supported what club definitely didn't seem to arouse an interest in their lives.

I had been living someone else's existence and building superficial relationships solely based on an emblem created by a community of motorcycle people. That didn't change the fact that the emotional ties still burned as a stronghold in my life or the fact that I loved my MC family. It didn't change the way I felt about things, just the perspective in which things were.

I took my cell phone out of my pocket and called Brakeline. He was perhaps the only patch holder in Arkansas who was secure enough with himself to defy the standing order and openly remain my brother and friend. It was 2 o'clock in the afternoon and I knew he'd be asleep, nevertheless, I left him a voice mail. *"Brakeline, you weren't joking when you said this is the fishing capital of the world. There are so many people fishing off the pier and it is such a different environment. I love it just as you said I would. The ocean is beautiful and the lifestyle is completely different."*

He sent me a message in an email on June 9, 2007 that ended in the following words, *"...Please keep in touch. Brotherhood (sisterhood) is in the heart and we have it. Love you girl."*

My mentor, my friend from the Sons of Silence Motorcycle Club in Arkansas, had not deserted me like everyone else had. He stood true to our friendship. He possessed a virtue that was obviously lacking in the Red and Gold world I knew: loyalty. I was proud to have this exceptional man in my life.

As I looked at all these different people, my perspective began to change. It was then that I saw a small piece of hope for me. My move to Florida was done entirely based on faith in the unknown. I had completely trusted the good Lord in believing that He'd take care of me and guide me in the direction that I needed to go. There was never any feeling or confirmation of my action. It was a blind leap of faith based on God's promise to me.

On that pier were small droplets of sand from the people's shoes and carry-on's. As I shuffled them back and forth with my foot, I isolated a grain of sand and focused on that one, almost microscopic, granule. In the eyes of the world, my sorrows were as big as this granule. I realized that I was letting this tiny affliction interfere with my life and rob me of all the happiness and joy God had intended for me as a human being. At that point, I took all my insecurities and resentments and threw them as far as I could into the sea as I observed the infinity of the ocean's fury. Afterwards, my life seemed so insignificant and my troubles practically invisible. I looked towards the horizon and realized that life as we know it was more than meets the eye.

I went home and cried. I cried because I had not focused on what I had, but on what I lost. I cried because I was finally able to see my problem as that tiny minute grain of sand. I cried because I realized that I had been created by God to bring glory to His Kingdom and I had deviated from that purpose. I cried because there were many times that I failed to attend my kid's special events just to go to an MC function of no significance. I remembered that it was the little foxes that spoiled the vine. With a world population of billions of people, I understood that only approximately 100 people or less knew of my distress.

That day I rode my bike into Destin, Florida. I felt like a free bird as I cut in and out of traffic in my cut off shorts and red bikini top. It was 95 degrees but the heat of the blacktop road made it feel like 130 degrees. It was a liberating ride and I rode hard. I rode alone in the wind and for the first time in months, I felt like there was life after the Bandidos and the MC life.

I was a biker on neutral grounds. I wasn't on either side of the fence, but in the valley that lies in the midst of nowhere. I was in the dark cold gorge where unwanted bikers are thrown away. I was at the place where patch holders gather from above, look down at these displaced bikers, and sinisterly laugh at them as they take glory in the injustice that has been committed against them.

I wasn't a patch holder. I wasn't in a motorcycle club. Those who for many years called themselves my brothers had disappeared out of my life, leaving no trace of the brotherhood that they spoke of for so long. But in spite of it all, in my heart will forever remain the memory of the love, loyalty, and respect I shared with the Red and Gold family and all the other bikers I met in my journey as a patch holder.

As for the betrayal from my MC family toward me, I can only express what I said in my farewell letter:

"… Let it be known that what she (Tab) took were only pieces of fabric sewn by a lady in Little Rock. She was NOT able to take what is in my heart. She could not take God's love, and she was NOT able to take the love, loyalty and respect that I had sworn to the Red and Gold Nation. That will always be a part of my heart…."

"…Let it be known that in true Christian spirit I forgive Tab and anyone else who by participation or omission agreed with any accusation. I thoroughly enjoyed every good and bad moment with the Red and Gold nation these past 6 years and unconditionally loved my boss, Bandido Murray…."

I believe that brotherhood (or sisterhood) should extend beyond a *patch*. Brotherhood should be given to the *person* wearing the patch. To whom that person is! It makes me think of the brothers that constantly fight as they are growing up. They get angry, call each other names, and sometimes do not talk for years – but they never stop being brothers for they are united by blood.

When an individual becomes a part of the MC world, new strong family ties are created for a lifetime. The bond of brotherhood (or sisterhood) makes us part of a collective organization called an MC, that is made up of individual personalities with unique qualities. True brotherhood (or sisterhood) should be indefinite, united not by a patch, but by love, loyalty, and respect.

As for me, I can say that my life in the MC world was NEVER about the patch I wore. It was about the *love, loyalty and respect* I had for the Patch Holder. It was about the love that I will forever have for the ARCOMc family.

In the end, all that will ever remain is LOVE.

"And now abide faith, hope, love, these three; but the greatest of these is love." *I Corinthians 13:13 NKJ*

15
Crash course on the MC Lifestyle

Being a part of the MC world has been the best experience of my life and I do not regret it. The wonderful people I met throughout the years brought everlasting memories of remarkable times. Looking back at all the parties, events, and riding stories, I can truly say it was the juncture of a lifetime.

In the five years that I lived in the motorcycle community, I discovered that there are three different categories of bikers. These are:
1. 1% Clubs
2. MC Clubs
3. Citizens

1% Clubs are comprised of 1%'ers (One Percenters).

The term 1%'er was first used by the American Motorcycle Association (AMA). Founded in 1924, The AMA has an unparalleled history of pursuing, protecting and promoting the interests of the world's largest and most dedicated group of motorcycle enthusiasts. The AMA focuses on rights, riding and racing through its government relations work, by sanctioning road and off-road riding activities and overseeing professional and amateur racing events. *(http://www.amadirectlink.com/whatis/index.asp)*

Recorded history states that on the July 4th weekend of 1946 in Hollister, California, the AMA sponsored the Annual Motorcycle Dirt Hill Climb Races. It was a safe, fun-filled event for the family to enjoy. People came from everywhere to see these exciting races. It was such a family oriented event that the town of Hollister only had a police force of seven.

On that specific year approximately 4000 bikers attended, including two specific motorcycle clubs: the "Pissed Off Bastards of Bloomington" (P.O.B.O.B.) and the "Market Street Commandoes". During one of the bar fights that got out of control and carried over to the street (like the saloon fights in the days of the Old West), one of the P.O.B.O.B. members was arrested and taken to jail. The heat of the moment combined with the effects of alcohol, caused an estimated 725 angry bikers to demand the release of this club member. Local authorities refused and the town was literally torn apart in what was labeled as a "riot".

Because the AMA sponsored this racing event, the press required an explanation from them. The AMA's response was defensive in their favor thus providing an acquittal of accountability. Their response was that 99% of motorcyclists were law-abiding citizens, and that only 1% of the motorcyclists that caused the riot that day were outlaws (criminals, bandits, or lawbreakers).

In the late 1950's, the AMA sponsored clean-cut rallies, and prizes were awarded for neat uniforms, prettiest and shiniest motorcycle. The ones that rejected this "square" image became rebels and rode contrary to the AMA standards. Therefore, instead of wearing a neat uniform for the club, they cut the sleeves out of their jackets, wore dirty Levi Jeans™, and cut their one-piece patch into three pieces as a form of protest. Instead of wearing the AMA patch, they fashioned their own patch into a diamond shaped patch with the 1% symbol, thus accepting the statement and label made by the AMA. Originally, any biker that wore a 1% diamond shaped patch made the declaration that they were the 1% or minority of outlaw motorcycle clubs and did not conform to the AMA standards.

The original AMA patch in 1925 was a three-sided diamond called a trilliant. The diamond designed by the "outlaw" motorcycle clubs is a four-sided polygon in which every side has the same length. It was the *Rhombus* created as a badge of honor.

All 1% clubs wear a diamond patch as well as an MC patch. These bikers labeled rebels adapted the offensive term given to them by the AMA and thus they became 1%'ers: Outlaw motorcycle clubs. The 1%'ers are not registered with the American Motorcycle Association (obviously). The diamond patch was perhaps not intended to be used as the universal symbol when it originated, nevertheless, has been adapted as such by all motorcyclists. Only those that earn the right to wear the diamond can do so after committing themselves to the lifestyle of the club.

All members are male and they must ride a Harley Davidson motorcycle. The majority of 1% clubs only allow the white race in their membership. 1%'ers are required to fulfill the gradual process of the lifelong stages of membership, which are Hang Arounds, Prospect, Probationary, and Associates. They must submit to extensive background checks by the club's officers, and thereby prove they are not law enforcement personnel or agents.

All 1%'ers must learn to ride in formation and learn all the rules of the road as required by the club. They must pledge their allegiance to the club, pay dues, fees, and fines when imposed. They must live by the club's laws at all times. They are the "big boys" of the MC community.

1% clubs maintain control and a strict criterion on MC clubs in the state or general area in which they reside. They are generally in charge of the State's MC protocol and unless a club violates a conduct code, they usually do not interfere with the club's activities. They are the only ones that can wear a STATE bottom rocker, and a diamond shaped patch with the symbol 1% on it. They have the power to authorize, terminate or decide the fate of an MC club, and sometimes riding associations. Many 1% clubs supervise the activities and color choice of local motorcycle clubs. They can enforce, discipline, or put an MC club on probation for violation of protocol. 1%'ers are extremely protective of one another and will recur to radical measures to bring honor to their club.

To be a 1%'er is a sub cultural lifestyle that becomes part of that person's existence. In sociology, anthropology and cultural studies, a **subculture** is a group of people with a culture (whether distinct or hidden) which differentiates them from the larger culture to which they belong. If a particular subculture is characterized by a systematic opposition to the dominant culture, it may be described as a counterculture. As Ken Gelder notes, subcultures are social, with their own shared conventions, values and rituals, but they can also seem 'immersed' or self-absorbed - another feature that distinguishes them from countercultures. He identifies six key ways in which subcultures can be understood: 1. Through their often negative relations to work (as 'idle', 'parasitic', at play or at leisure, etc.); 2. Through their negative or ambivalent relation to class (since subcultures are not 'class-conscious' and don't conform to traditional class definitions); 3. Through their association with territory (the 'street', the 'hood, the club, etc.), rather than property; 4. Through their movement out of the home and into non-domestic forms of belonging (i.e. social groups other than the family); 5. Through their stylistic ties to excess and exaggeration (with some exceptions); 6. Through their refusal of the banalities of ordinary life and mass-ification.

If the member has been in the club for most of his life, he will find it difficult to adjust to life without the club. Sort of like the inmate who has been in prison all his life and when he is released 30 years later, he cannot find his way around the free world.

Today's 1%'ers perspective is different. Their passion is riding a motorcycle and brotherhood. Although they still practice the old traditions of apparel and protocol, they have found that the criminal lifestyle in the 21st century is obsolete due to the advanced technology used by the federal government in crime solving techniques. Most criminal activities in 1% clubs are isolated incidents by individual members without the club's consent. A 1% Bandido President once told me, "There are more of them (referring to cops) then there are of us, so we stay out of trouble." 1%'ers, however, will defend their colors, turf, members and their associates without second guess to consequences.

"One percenters are serious bikers who ride every day. They work, have families, and have a reputation for riding hard and partying hard. The one percent patch does not imply criminal or outlaw. It implies dedication to their brotherhood and riding." *Reference: http //bikersmag.com/html/one_percent.html*

The following is an example of the laws and bylaws of a 1% Club. They are from the Devils Breed MC Honolulu, Hawaii. They retired the club after 30 years (1976-2006). They say, "We are all getting too old."

Submitted by Bulldog, Vice Prez Ret. DBMC 1%'er
http://www.rcvsmc.net/id6.html
(Motorcycle Club & Riding Club Education website).

1% Club Constitution, Laws and Bylaws, and General Rules
Revised DRAFT (8/00) Devils Breed Club Constitution.
Reference: http://www.rcvsmc.net/id6.html with permission from the website referenced above for "borrowing" the information.

Devils Breed M.C. is a motorcycle club and a non-profit organization. President, Vice President, Secretary, and Treasurer are all elected officers, along with two additional elected members, who are not club officers for the Executive Board. All others appointed by the President with a confidence vote from patch-holders in good standing is required.

PRESIDENT
The executive duties of the president are as follows:
1. To preside over meetings of both the Executive Board and the club as a whole.
2. To judge items not covered in the constitution or in the rules regulations.
3. Directorship gives the president authority to judge items not in the constitution.
4. To act as the personal representative of the club in the area of public relations; as a liaison between the DBMC and local-law enforcement agencies; and as a connecting link between

the DBMC and other outlaw motorcycle clubs.
5. To represent the club in any club business contacts and to supervise major economic transactions.
6. To assist DBMC officers in the interpretation of their club responsibilities, and to promote club life among members in general.

VICE-PRESIDENT

The executive duties of the vice president are to assume the responsibilities of the presidency when the president is unable to do so.

SECRETARY

The executive duties of the secretary are as follows:
1. To record and safeguard the minutes of the club meetings.
2. To maintain the Club Constitution, recording any additions, deletions, or modifications.
3. To handle any club correspondence.

TREASURER

The executive duties of the treasurer are as follows:
1. To monitor and record the club's income and expenditures.
2. To collect the dues and fines owing by members.

EXECUTIVE BOARD

The executive board consists of those members who were elected as officers of the club along with two additional elected members who are not club officers. The board holds scheduled meetings every two weeks. Emergency meetings can be called if a situation arises that demands immediate attention. The executive board is responsible for:
1. The monitoring of conflicts within the club.
2. The application of disciplinary procedures.
3. The evaluation of prospects and their progress.
4. The presentation of summarized assessments of the overall club situation to the membership (court).

ROAD CAPTAIN
The executive duties of the road captain are as follows:
1. To plan the travel routes and organize the basic itinerary of the club prior to going on a 'run' (tour).
2. To lead the club in formation while riding on tour.
3. To enforce club rules and procedures for group riding.
4. Designate a maintenance supervisor for all club vehicles.

SERGEANT AT ARMS
The executive duties of the sergeant at arms are as follows:
1. To maintain order at club meetings in particular, and club activities in general.
2. To ensure that members adhere to club rulings, policies, and expected models of conduct when dealing with other members or outsiders.
3. To defend club members, property, or territory from outside threats.

COURT
Court will consist of all patch holders that are eligible to vote.

ELECTIONS OF OFFICERS AND EXECUTIVE BOARD NON OFFICER MEMBERS
Officers of the club serve a twelve-month term of office, annual elections are held at the last regular meeting of the year, in December.
1. In order to be eligible for office, a patch holder has to have been an active member in good standing for a minimum of one year.
2. Patch holders who aspire towards a particular position will campaign informally for one month prior to the elections.
3. Electioneering is conducted on an interpersonal face to face basis.
4. Hopeful candidate will approach a member, inform them what he is willing to stand for office if nominated, ask for

member's opinion of his qualifications, and solicit the member's support.

Meetings
1. One organized meeting per month.
2. Majority rules.
3. If a vote is taken at a meeting and a member is not there, his vote is void.
4. Meetings will be closed except for prospective members and anyone there on business.
5. All meetings will be run on a parliamentary basis. Members will be evicted for unruly conduct.
6. Quorum for a meeting is sixty percent of membership and eighty percent for membership votes.
7. Everyone will attend the meeting on his bike if it is favorable weather, unless his bike is broken down or not running at the time. If the club calls a ride/meeting, all members will attend. If a member is working, sick, bike not running, he will be excused. However, if a Devils Breed repeatedly uses work as an excuse for not 'being there,' he will be 'talked to'.
8. Members must have colors with him when attending meetings.
9. Members must be of sound mine (straight) when attending meetings.
10. If a member attends a meeting and is fouled-up, he will be FINED.
11. There will be absolutely no booze or drugs consumed during meetings.
12. During a meeting there will be no talking among members until they get the floor through the president. A sergeant-at-arms, if not present, will be appointed and anyone not abiding by the above will be evicted.
13. Miss three (3) meetings in a row and you're out of the club.
14. Anyone missing meetings even if at work gets fined

$50.00 except for guys in hospital or jail or out of town for a period of time, including prospects.
15. Members must attend meetings to leave club and turn in his colors and everything that has the name Devils Breed on it (T-shirts, wrist bands, mugs, etc.).
16. If a member is thrown out of the club or quits without attending meetings, he loses his colors, motorcycle, and anything else that says Devils Breed on it, and probably an ass kicking.

Membership qualifications/ Prospects
1. Prospects must be at least 18 years old.
2. Prospects must have a Harley-Davidson motorcycle.
3. Prospects cannot do any drugs.
4. Prospects must show a sincere interest in club and bikes.
5. Prospects on the road with bike equipped for the road.
6. Prospect must be sponsored by one member who has known him at least one year (may be waived by vote).
7. Sponsor is responsible for prospect.
8. Sponsor can pull a prospect's rockers at his discretion.
9. Prospects must attend all meetings and club functions.
10. Prospects must do anything another member tells him to do, that a member has done or would be willing to do himself.
11. Prospect will stand behind club and members.
12. No stealing from prospects.
13. Prospect must ride his bike to meeting at time of being voted into club.
14. Prospect must pay that day $125.00 for his colors before receiving them. Prospect fee is $325.00: $200.00 is for annual dues, $100.00 is for the patch and $25.00 is for first month dues. The balance is due in 90 days. This amount is not refundable.
15. Prospect members must be voted in. Two 'no' votes equal a rejection. One 'no' vote must be explained.
16. Prospective member's prospecting period is at the discre-

tion of sponsor and the club. Directorship shall decide when vote is necessary.
17. Every patch holder on Island must vote for prospect to make center patch. Vote must be unanimous.
18. No prospect will be voted for center-patch with outstanding loan.
19. Only the sponsor or an officer may hand out a patch to a prospect. This will be done at a meeting with only patch holders present.

RULES AND REGULATIONS

The rules of the club will be strictly enforced. If anyone breaks them, executive board will deal them with. If these rules and regulations are broken, it could mean either immediate dismissal or suspension, whatever the executive board sees fit.

Breaking any of the following Rules will be reason for immediately kick-out from club and probably an Ass Kicking:
1. Failure to pay his dues according to the section dealing with the paying of dues.
2. No hype. No use of heroin in any form. Anyone using a needle for any reason other than having a doctor use it on you will be considered hype. (Automatic kick-out from club).
3. If any brother gets hooked on any drug that is dangerous to the club he will be helped first. Then he will be dealt by the executive board.
4. No narcotics burn. When making deals, persons get what they are promised or the deal is called off (Automatic kick-out from club).
5. If you're selling dope you don't do it as a club member, you don't wear your colors, you don't wear your club T-shirts (Automatic kick-out from club).
6. There will be no stealing among members. Anyone caught will get an ass kicking and be kicked out of the club (Automatic kick-out from club).
7. If a patch holder or prospect throws his colors or quits, colors are pulled (Automatic kick-out from club).

8. Members cannot belong to any other clubs.
9. If a group or individual attacks any member, the whole club shall stand behind him and fight if necessary. If, however, the member is drunk and aggressive and purposely starts an argument, the rest of the members will escort him away, or step between before trouble starts.
10. No member will disgrace the club by being yellow. (The above rules will be put forward to applicants. If they cannot abide by these rules and are not in favor of them, they will be denied membership to the club).
11. No member will destroy club property purposely.
12. No member will take the attitude that he doesn't have to help other members and other members don't have to help him
13. No member will go against anything the club has voted for and passed.
14. No member will get together on their own and plan something for themselves on club rides. It will be brought up to the whole club and the whole club will participate in anything that is decided upon.
15. The club will always stay together on rides, runs, parties, field meets etc. and will not fraternize with club's rival clubs. The only way a member will be permitted to leave the main group will be to notify the president or whoever is in charge. When the time comes that the majority feels it is time to leave, we will all leave together. Anyone staying behind for a good reason will do so at his own risk and can expect no help.
16. Members will have good attendance. Members must have a good reason for not attending meetings or rides, such as working, sickness, no transportation, and bike not running.

General Rules (SOP)

If anyone breaks general rules, executive board will deal with them and/or voted by the court.

1. No explosives of any kind will be thrown into the fire where there is one or more Devils Breed in the area.

FINE: Ass whipping and subject to the executive board.
2. Brother shall not fight each other with weapons; when any Devils Breed fights another Devils Breed, it is one on one, prospects same as members. FINE: $100.00 for breaking above rule or possible loss of patch.
3. If you don't help out the Club in its activities and you use the Club solely for your benefit, you will be warned. No second chance.
4. Do as you say or walk the line.
5. Devils Breed losing privilege of wearing colors will also lose privilege of voting and ruling over prospects.
6. The treasurer shall keep a clear record of all money paid in and out during the week and will balance it before every meeting; the books will be gone over once a week.
7. All Devils Breed fines will be paid within 30 days. Fines will be paid to the treasurer.
8. Members with extra parts will loan them to members. They must be replaced or paid for.
9. If you get busted and or go to jail, notify an officer or member so he can arrange for your bail.
10. Where we go on our rides will be voted upon by the entire membership.
11. Each patch holder/prospect is required to maintain a valid motor vehicle license, which includes the authorization to operate motorcycle.
12. Everyone must have an American bike. Consideration will be give to any member who is in between bikes but he must sincerely intend to get another bike in the near future.
13. If for some reason, such as a license suspension, a member can't ride on the road for a long period of time, or if he is without a bike for a short time, he will turn in his patch and upon getting back on the road, the patch will be returned.
14. If a member's bike is not running for a period of thirty days, unless he is in jail or hospital, his colors will be con-

fiscated. A member's bike must be running for at least one week (e.g., not fifteen minutes), to be exempt from the above rule. This period is subject to change at the discretion of the executive board. This is a MOTORCYCLE CLUB!
15. Confirmation vote is required for all new patch-holders at their 12-month point. Unanimous vote from all good standing members is required.
16. Absolutely no talking about Club business to persons outside the Club. No talking about Club business over any telephone.
17. If you are told you are too drunk to drive, you will turn over your keys to a brother. You and your scooter will be taken care of.
18. If the Road Captain or an Officer determines your bike is unsafe to ride, you are grounded until it is safe.
19. During funeral runs, no one will pack a passenger, patch must be seen.
20. The run for "Beer with Bob" and Jimbo is mandatory, no excuses.
21. All Club vehicles will be returned with all fluids full and in good condition. Maintenance will be done under the supervision of the maintenance supervisor; a patch holder designated by the Road Captain.
22. There shall be a wrecking crew consisting of the Sergeant at Arms, the Junior Patch, and whomever the Senior Patch may designate. The purpose of the wrecking crew is to check out bars, etc. prior to entry by President, Vice President, or Senior Patch.
23. Prospect will watch all bikes when members are at Club functions, in bars, and anywhere the senior member present deems necessary.
24. There will be a Club run on a Sunday once a month. Whoever picks the run route will lead the pack.

DUES/LOANS

1. Club dues will be paid each month, due by the first.
2. Two months overdue is the limit.
3. They are $25.00 per month and $200.00 yearly.
4. Dues will be $25.00 per month payable every meeting or every second meeting.
5. Annual Dues of $200.00 will be paid 1 October.
6. Upon failure of paying dues within two weeks, member shall be suspended and turn in his colors.
7. If within two months dues still aren't paid, the colors will be forfeited to pay them and member will no longer be considered a member. The only exception to this shall be if a member is in jail or if he is out of town for a period of time. If he is in jail, dues won't be expected, but if he is out of town dues will be paid when he returns.
8. All loans or debts will be secured by collateral. Members will agree upon payment. Two patch holders must be present in any personal loan transaction.

Respect
1. Respect is to be shown to all club members, officers, members, members', bikes, OL', ladies, house, job, etc. In other words, if it's not yours, 'Don't Mess with it.
2. Respect your colors.
3. No stealing from members.
4. No fighting among each other is allowed, any punches to be thrown will be done by the Sgt At Arms.

Colors
1. President gets colors from mother club in area when new member is voted in.
2. When a member leaves club, member turns over colors to president of chapter.
3. Respect your colors; don't let anyone take them from you except the president of the chapter.
4. No colors are worn in a cage, except during funerals and

loading or unloading a bike from a truck.
5. No hippie shit on the front.
6. Nothing will be worn on the back of your jacket except colors.
7. Colors must be worn at all times when riding or at Club functions. Only one of your brothers or your OL' lady can babysit your colors. Colors are not required to be worn to and from employment if not allowed by employer. If patch is lost or stolen, patch holder will be judged by court.
8. The only way a member of Devils Breed can retire and keep his patch is if local officers authorize him. Minimum time for retirement is 5 years.

OL' ladies
1. Don't fuck around with brother's OL' lady. (Probably an ass kicking and kick-out from club).
2. Property patches will be brought up before all patch holders for input. Majority vote from all eligible patch holders is required.
3. Members are responsible for their OL' ladies.
4. Members may have more than one (1) OL ' lady.
5. Members must state who his OL ' lady is.
6. Members may not discuss club business with their OL' lady.
7. No OL' ladies allowed at meetings.
8. OL' ladies are allowed unescorted at clubhouse only by prior arrangement by OL' man.
9. Property patch is worn optional on an OL ' lady. So if you see a chick you better ask before you leap.

Three examples of 1% CLUBS are Bandidos MC, Sons of Silence MC, Hell's Angels.

MC (Motorcycle Club) clubs are a group of loyal bikers that join as an organized alliance to ride their motorcycles. An MC club commands respect because of the level of commitment and self-discipline the members must exert. They have worked together as a unit to accomplish the solidarity of kinship and uniformity, which matures into what, is called "brotherhood". This camaraderie is shown in the love, loyalty, and respect they put forth to each other. Their strength is in numbers and allegiance to the club. The oldest known MC in the United States is the Yonkers MC, founded in 1903.

MC clubs have a structural organized government of president, vice president, treasurer, secretary, road captain, and sergeant-at-arms (sometimes called an enforcer). MC clubs wear a 3-piece patch and an MC cube. It is referred to as the club COLORS and it is what identifies the club. The patch consists of a top rocker, a center patch (logo) and a bottom rocker, usually with the name of the town, city or county. Some MC clubs have a slogan instead of a territorial rocker. An offset square cube with the "MC" letters meaning "motorcycle club" is on the back vest but can sometimes be incorporated into the patch design.

Many MC clubs conduct their affairs under the direct or indirect supervision of 1% clubs of the State they reside in. They have their own set of laws and bylaws that fall within the general MC protocols and requirements of motorcycle clubs. These clubs usually ride in formation and function as a collective unit (sort of like a military unit). Many MC clubs have clubhouses that are used for church, events, parties, and bunking quarters.

The six stages to becoming a full member in an MC are:

1. Hang around, friend or acquaintance.
2. Prospect.
3. Probationary or Probate.
4. Full Patch
5. Honorary or Associate.
6. Retired

This period varies for each individual club but generally the time required to complete all stages is approximately 1 ½ to 2 years.

A **hang around** is the first stage of a full membership. He is a guest of the club and aspires to one day be a member. (Herein after I will use the term *he* to refer to both male and female. (No sexual discrimination is intended).

A hang around does not wear colors, however he can wear club support gear with the appropriate color choice. Hang arounds will never be allowed at church nor will they have knowledge of the club's business. If the hang around decides that this lifestyle is not for him, he can walk away without any accountability to the club, as he is only a guest. If he decides he wants to purse the next stage of membership and receives the approval by the club's officers, then he must be invited to do so by a Patch.

A **Prospect** is the second stage to a full patch. This is the period of probability where the potential member must prove his trustworthiness and loyalty to the club. He is sponsored by a full member who also instructs and disciplines him in his new code of behavior. He is scrutinized by the club to ensure that he is not a member of any law enforcement agency and is worthy to someday become a full member. A Prospect is sponsored into the club by a patch. A 1% Prospect wears the STATE bottom rocker on his vest, while an MC Prospect wears either a bottom rocker or bar that reads PROSPECT. Prospects are servants to the club. The center logo (patch) is never worn, and many clubs consider it disrespectful to wear the club's name while they are in the Prospect period, being they have not earned the right to fly the club's name. They unquestionably perform specific tasks, janitorial/housecleaning clubhouse duties, and any other assignment ordered by a Patch. Prospects become full members after they have completed their trial period, have learned to conduct himself as a patch holder, and receives a vote from all or the majority of club members.

I am expanding more on the Prospect subject because it is a crucial step in the MC world. It is the time where a man (or a woman) decides if he or she is club material. SOS Brakeline sent the following general information to me when I was President of my club. I used it as an educational tool and guideline for my club. (The original is lost in the haze of motorcycle lore somewhere in cyber space).

Purpose of Prospecting.
It is a time in which:
- The man's attitude is conditioned so that he displays a

sense of responsibility and respect toward the patch holders of the club, without which he will not develop a sense of brotherhood.
- He is educated in basic MC protocol.
- He is given time to develop the habits that are basic to good security and good communications.
- To get the man into the habit of participating.
- To give his family time to adjust to the demands of the club.
- To experience and learn an essential degree of humility.
- To become accustomed to trusting the judgment, at times blindly, of those patch holders who will someday be his brothers.
- To break the man of habits that are self centered and self serving.

The list could go on but the point here is to demonstrate that prospecting has definite objectives and that a Prospect will go nowhere in the club if he is not aware of this and does not apply himself to those ends.

It's not possible to make a checklist of what is expected from a Prospect in all cases. There isn't any formula for success, but the key is ATTITUDE. Everything else can be learned in time, but a man's attitude comes from the heart.

The testing of a Prospect may come in many ways. It may be planned or spontaneous. In any event, when a Prospect is given a task, the patch holder is going to be looking for the man's attitude and the spirit in which he carries out the task. The Prospect should be alert and always attentive in looking for more to do. If he is ever in doubt of his priorities or he can't find something to do, he should ask.

The patch holders know which of the Prospects hustle and those are the Prospects that are spoken of with the greatest pride and respect. It is also the way by which confidence and trust are developed. These are the seeds of brotherhood.

Remember that you will be prospecting for the whole club and not just one individual or one individual chapter. The patch holders of one chapter are always held accountable for the actions of a patch holder of another chapter. It is therefore only right that the patch holders of all chapters have a hand in developing the Prospects on their way to becoming full patch holders.

Some Do's and Don'ts

- As a Prospect, strive to conduct yourself as a responsible patch holder at all times.
- Always display a positive attitude.
- Participate as much as you think is acceptable; then participate more.
- If you see a patch holder of your club that you have not met, take the initiative to introduce yourself. Always introduce yourself as "Prospect (your name) and name of your club."
- At all gatherings, make it a point to circulate when you have the time to do so and greet every patch holder that is there.
- Anticipate the brother's needs and offer to supply them. Don't wait to be told.
- Don't get over friendly with someone who is not a regular acquaintance of the club. If someone outside the club has questions, refer them to a patch holder.
- Never give out a patch holder's name, phone number, address, or any personal information outside the club.
- Never give out information about the club itself to outsiders. This includes, but is not limited to, where the club is based, how many members are in the club, etc.
- Always be security minded, look around and see what's going on around you in public places and report anything that seems suspicious.
- While in public places, always conduct yourself with your association with the club in mind. Remember that what you do, people will remember; good or bad.
- Never let a patch holder walk off alone in an unsecured area. If he is going to his car, his bike, or even just out

to get some fresh air, go with him. Watch his back at all times.
- If you are at an open function and pick up on some negative attitudes, especially from another club, quietly alert another patch holder immediately.
- Keep your eyes and ears open and feed any information that you may pick up on to a patch holder, especially information regarding another club.
- Remember that you are a Prospect 24 hours a day. Your association doesn't go on and off with your Colors.
- Remember that you are every patch holders Prospect, not just your sponsor's or just your chapter's.
- Never wear your colors out of your area without your sponsor's approval, and never out of state unless you are with a patch holder.
- If two or more patch holders are having a private conversation, don't approach them within earshot, especially if they are talking with a patch holder of another club. If you need to interrupt, put yourself in a place of visibility and wait to be acknowledged. If it is important that you interrupt, ask another patch holder to break in for you.
- Never use the term "outlaw club" when speaking to a member of another club.
- Never lie to a member of another club. If you are in a situation where you are asked about the club or its membership, it is acceptable to say, "That seems like club business and I really can't talk about it." If this doesn't put the subject to rest, offer to put him in touch with a patch holder for him to speak with.
- Never lie to members of your club.
- Always show respect to a patch holder of another club. Even though he's with another club, he's earned his patch; you haven't.
- Always carry a pen and paper, a watch and a calendar. Always carry anything else your club has instructed you to have with you at all times.

- Frequently ask the patch holders how you are doing and if there is anything you should be doing differently.
- Never ask when you may be getting your patch.
- Never call a patch holder "brother". He is not your brother.
- Never call another patch holder from another club "brother". He is not your brother, either.
- Remember, your patch is earned. It is not given to you.
- Never bring a personal friend or stranger into the presence of strangers without asking permission to do so first.
- At an open function, never turn your back to a patch holder of another club. This is not so much for safety reasons, but as show of respect.
- Always show respect and courtesy to patch holders of other clubs. Don't come across like you want to be best friends. Be professional in such encounters; keep it short, then move on.
- Keep away from women associating with other clubs.
- Never be quick to walk up to a patch holder of another club in a public setting, even if you know him well and the clubs are on friendly terms. If you want to greet them, walk up slowly and wait for him to indicate that he wants such a public display to take place. He may be on some club business and may not want to give the general public that the clubs are on such friendly terms. If he looks like he's going to ignore you, accept it and keep your distance. The best approach is always to wait for them to come to you, and let everyone else see that.
- Learn what your patch represents and the color combination. Be ready to answer to your club members when inquired.
- Know the number of days that you have been a Prospect.

Probationary or **Probate** is the third step to full membership. Not all clubs have this extra step. It comes after the prospect period and is an extended stage of testing the Prospect's trustworthiness and loyalty to the club. Usually it is 1% clubs that practice this custom. A Probationary can also be a member that has transferred from one chapter to another. An entire chapter can transfer and become a Probationary chapter.

Full member also called a Patch, or Patch holder, is a member that has completed all the required stages to become a full member in good standing. He has full voting rights and has earned the respect of the entire club. He wears his Colors anytime he is riding hisbike or conducting club business.

Retired members are members who have served a designated period of time (usually 10 years or more) in the club and can give up working for the club. Many clubs do not require owning or operating a motorcycle for this stage of membership as the member has already served his time. A retired member can keep his Colors and many times retains a position as advisor. It is a position of honor.

Some MC clubs have **HONORARY or ASSOCIATE** members. These are people who have proved their worth to the club. They do not wear colors and many of them do not have motorcycles. They can be professionals, clergy or simple individuals who bring value to the club. They are allowed to party and attend events but never to vote or sit in church. Although this is not a required step to full membership, it can count as hang around time if the individual ever decides to step up.

The different types of MC Clubs are

  A. Support Clubs
  B. Theme Clubs
  C. Independent Clubs
  D. Religious Clubs

The **SUPPORT CLUBS** are a harvester branch of a 1% club. They are under the direct command of their mother club and are accountable to them. They are just what their names say: a support, a backing, a defense club. They are the work force for the host club. They must pay dues as a club to the general president. They wear the colors of the mother club but have their own club name and center patch. Support clubs wear a diamond patch that read "13 Motorcycle" and support patches from the host club. They are inducted and trained by the host club and are well protected by them. They can use the mother's clubhouse to hold their meetings or events. A true support club makes their mother club proud and their conduct is admirable at club events.

Three examples of **support clubs** are
Desperados MC (Bandidos),
(http://www.desperadosmctx.com/)
Iron Horsemen MC, (Sons of Silence)
(http://www.ironhorsemen.net/)
Black Pistons MC (Outlaws MC)
(http://www.angelfire.com/fl5/blackpistons/index2.html)

THEME CLUBS fall into two groupings.
1. **Characteristic:** These have a common interest in direct relation to a distinctive trait.
2. **Motorcycle make and/or model:** These ride the same make of motorcycles.

CHARACTERISTIC THEME CLUBS are the ones that have a common interest, job or characteristic other than riding motorcycles. Some examples are military clubs (all military), law enforcement clubs (all law enforcement), firefighters clubs (all firefighters), gay and lesbian clubs (all gay and/or lesbian), ethnic clubs (Afro Americans, Puerto Ricans, Italians, etc…), political clubs (members are actively involved in government protesting and/or participation, clean and sober clubs (members do not use drugs or alcohol), female clubs (all women), over the hill clubs (people over 40 years of age), etc…. There are too many to list, but you get the picture. Theme clubs are becoming increasingly popular since it is easier to ingress in one of these. MC clubs emerge everyday in the United States and worldwide.

There are many web-wide based clubs without a home base. They operate their organization directly from a website. These are becoming increasing popular in the 21st century based on the fact that world internet users and population stats as of June 30, 2008 are up to 6,676120,288 internet users. That is a 305.5% of usage growth since 2000. (*Usage information comes from data published by Nielsen//NetRatings, by the International Telecommunications Union, by local NIC, and other reliable sources*). Web-based MC clubs follow the international design of patch design and do not interfere with local club politics. It is unusual for these clubs to have local meetings and or rides. This is because they are web based.

The newest trend in theme MC's are women bikers. More women are buying their own bikes and joining or starting up their own MC clubs. Many of them do it for fun and others do it because they want to be like the men. The biggest group of women bikers in the United States is the Women on Wheels (WOW). Many of the female MC clubs do charity rides for cancer, children, abused women, and anything of that nature. Various male bikers, especially the old school ones, do not approve or like women on motorcycles, but they cannot do anything about it. The 21st Century has evolved a new generation of bikers and women are included as part of the MC culture, just as women are doctors, lawyers, military officers and senators.

Three examples of **characteristic** theme clubs are
Vietnam Vets MC (all served in the Vietnam War),
Knights of Fire MC (all fire fighters),
Survivors MC (all clean and sober from drugs and alcohol).

MOTORCYCLE THEME CLUBS are the ones who ride the same bike. For example, everyone in the clubs rides Harley Davidson's, BMW's, trikes, or a specific type of motorcycle. They may or may not wear a 3 piece patch with an MC rocker. Some of them may only wear street performance gear while others may wear a one piece patch, a flag from the country of origination, or a registered trade logo.

Crotch rocket MC clubs are amazing to look at. The different classification of sport bikes are entry level, small capacity, super sport, super bike, hyper sport, and sport touring. The riders are large in numbers and have spectacular riding performance skills. They are fast and they are furious as the staging of tricks on bikes produce vast entertainment for all ages. They consist of both men and women and don't have the hang-ups that regular MC clubs have with colors. The majority of them range in ages 20 to 30 years and aren't afraid of the road. Many of the ol' ladies are beautiful young girls who dress sexy and have no shame in showing their goods.

Three examples of **motorcycle theme clubs** are

All American Indian MC – They all ride Indian motorcycles.
(http://www.allamericanindianmotorcycleclub.com/welcome.html)
Victory MC – They all ride Victory motorcycles.
(http://www.thevmc.com/start.html)
Vintage Japanese MC – They all ride vintage Japanese motorcycles.
(http://www.vjmc.org/index.htm)

INDEPENDENT CLUBS are MC clubs that function in the same organizational and structural manner as the support clubs, but do not support any particular 1% club. Some of them attend only MC events while others attend all US rallies and several MC functions that are open to the public. The only colors they wear are their club colors. They have their own meetings, events and functions. Some of them participate in promoting safe motorcycling and some clubs wear AMA or ABATE patches, country flags, or flash patches. Independent MC clubs are serious clubs for the dedicated biker.

Three examples of **independent clubs** are
Boozefighters MC *(http://www.bfmcnatl.com/)*
Top Hatters MC *(http://www.tophatters-mc.com/)*
Jokers MC *(http://www.jokersmcmichigan.net/)*

RELIGIOUS MC CLUBS

These clubs are an MC and they act like it. Everywhere I went I ran into the Christian motorcycle clubs. In the past five years they appear to have quadrupled. These are mostly baby boomers that either have found a sincere religious experience with the Lord Jesus Christ or have grown tired of the drugs and alcohol at parties. They have infiltrated national motorcycle rallies such as Sturgis, Daytona Bike Week, Laconia, etc., with their message and mission. Many of them set up booths and offer free water, coffee, and spiritual help. Their main goal is to preach the Gospel of Salvation and win lost bikers for Christ. Many of these religious clubs are wearing three-piece patches and a few of them wear support colors for 1% clubs. They have no shame in praying for someone and will do it in public at any given time.

Three examples of **religious clubs** are:
Servants for Christ MC
(http://www.diako.com/index.htmland)
Rugged Cross MC
(http://www.ruggedcrossmc.com/)
Soldiers for Jesus MC
(http://www.soldiersforjesusmc.com/index3.htm)

CITIZEN BIKERS.
      A. Riding Associations
      B. R.U.B.
      C. Weekend Warriors
      D. Displaced Bikers

The majority of bikers that I ran into are called citizens. This is the name the 1%'ers and MC patch holders have given the non-patch holders, or those that do not wear a 3-piece patch. The variation in this motorcycling community is very diverse, yet the commonality is the love of a motorcycle and the freedom it brings. Citizens can be independent solo riders or they can belong to part of a riding group or association. Remember that the one distinct feature about citizens is that they do not wear a 3-piece patch or an MC cube; however, they can wear flash patches or one-piece patches.

RIDING ASSOCIATIONS are those who wear a one-piece patch and have no correlation with MC Clubs. They are a club in the sense of the defined word, but their union is a fraternity. They do not wear an MC cube or a 3-piece patch. They have their meetings, events and most of them belong to a local ABATE, MRO, or AMA chapter. Some riding associations have an organizational structure, monthly meetings and dues, but they are not involved with the political rules of MC clubs. Many of these members look like billboards because they love to collect event pins and patches and put them on their vests. "The more pins and flash patches on the vest, the better the biker" is a popular slogan among many of these bikers.

Riding Associations are divided into 4 categories:
1. Social Riding Associations
2. Religious
3. Biker Rights
4. Advocate

Social Riding Associations are mainly for fun, get-together time. The majority of the associates do not want to be members of a traditional MC but enjoy the community of bikers as a group. They enjoy charity runs, poker runs, bar runs, national rallies, and anywhere they can have a good time. Some riding organizations act and ride like MC's but do not have the political hang ups of MC's. They tend to be a little more serious that the social ridings groups in the sense that their format is geared towards a strict organization. They are a "family group" and enjoy the road as much as everyone else.

Three examples of **Social Riding Associations** are
HOG (Harley Owners Group) *(http://www.harleydavidson.com/wcm/Content/Pages/HOG/HOG.jsp?locale=en_us)*
USA Highway Riders
(http://www.usahighwayriders.com/index2.asp)
The Iron Pegasus Touring Club based in the Iowa City.
(http://www.ironpegasus.org/)

Religious Associations are the religious ministries whose mission statement combines riding a motorcycle with spiritual ministry. In the United States the majority of the religious groups are Christian. Their back patch usually has a "MM" or "RC".

Three examples of **Religious Associations** are
CMA (Christian Motorcycle Association)
(http://www.cmausa.org/)
Tribe of Judah MM

(http://tribeofjudah.com/)
Highway and Hedges MM
(http://www.highwaysandhedgesministry.com/home.html)

Biker Rights Riding Groups or Associations are objective in their purpose of fighting, aiding, supporting and furthering the freedom and rights of all bikers. Most of them are involved in government politics and spend a lot of time lobbying for biker rights.

These motorcycle organizations exist to promote safe riding, offer safety-riding courses, lobby for biker rights, and raise charitable funds for nonprofit organizations. The majority of them are family oriented groups.

Three examples of **Biker Riding Groups or Associations** are
Riders for Justice (Colorado Biker rights)
http://www.ridersforjustice.com/
Modified Motorcycle Association of California (General biker rights)
(http://www.ridersforjustice.com/)
ABATE: American Bikers Aiming Towards Education (General biker freedom rights)
(http://www.arkansasabate.org/main5.htm)

Advocate Riding Associations campaign for a specific cause and are objective in their goal. They are similar to the Biker Rights Ridings Associations in the sense of fighting for a cause, but differ in the specific purpose of their cause. Some of them ride for a cure for cancer, and others lobby against child abuse, drunk driving, etc.

There examples of **Advocate Riding Associations** are
B.A.C.A. Bikers Against Child Abuse *(http://www.bacausa.com/ Internet/AboutBACA.aspx)*
B.A.D.D. Bikers Against Drunk Driving
(http://www.baddcentral.com/)
Dream Riders Riding Association. Campaigning for children's rights
(http://www.dreamriders.us/)

R.U.B. "Rich Urban Bikers".

They are the 'wavers' of the road. They have 101 ways on how to wave at another biker when passing him or her on the road. Most of them have brand new expensive bikes that seldom ride. They "trailer" to most events and many of them haul their bikes behind luxurious huge RV's. The first thing they do when they get to the hotel or campground is to unload their trophy bike and polish the already shinny chrome. I have seen countless times when RUBS wear full leather in 90-degree weather because chaps and leather jackets make them look like bikers. Many of them have white-collar jobs and live in fancy homes. Most RUBS do not like 1% or MC members and tend to stay away from them.

WEEKEND WARRIORS are people that buy a motorcycle and ride it only on the weekends when it is sunny. This could be due to lack of time because of a full time job or just because they only choose to ride on weekends. After the riding season is over, they sell or store the bike. If they can keep the bike for a year, it usually has less than 2000 miles on it and someone ends up buying it for a great price. Many patch holders call them "wanna-be's".

DISPLACED BIKERS are bikers who have belonged to either a 1% or an MC and are out of the club in either good or bad standing. These out-of-place bikers don't belong anywhere because they have a difficult time riding as regular citizens. They have the "club" mentality so they don't fit into a riding association. Many do adjust to *life after the club*. There are some, especially those that have been put out in bad standings, which cannot find their place in the motorcycle culture. They ride as lone rangers and many times without a purpose because they don't have a destination or rationale. Many displaced bikers end up selling their motorcycles.

I met hundreds of **OLD SCHOOL BIKERS** in their early sixties who still rode rat bikes, Panheads™, Shovelheads™, and Knuckleheads ™. Their saddlebags always had 2 quarts of cheap oil, a bottle of whiskey, a couple t-shirts and a pair of socks. Tied to the handlebars with bungee straps were a tool pouch, a Mexican blanket, and their 30-year-old leather jacket. Some of the motorcycles were assembled with parts from a dozen old bikes and many of the seats were made of cardboard. Their motel of choice was a car wash or a picnic table off an interstate rest area. They ride in the rain, sleet, snow and heat because they are old school and that is their only form of transportation. When they do have registration and insurance, it is kept a sandwich bag to keep it from getting wet. Their old lady's are hard-core biker bitches who are not afraid of the road and party as hard as their men. A large number of old school bikers come from the 1960's era and have the hippy mentality. Many of them look raggedy and smell funny, but are great people. They have a story to tell and it's worth listening to. Some of them are 1%'ers, others are MC patch holders, yet others are citizens. This is the typical stereotype of a biker by the general public and the media.

I met the **NEW BREED OF MC PATCH HOLDERS**. Those who had high-dollar dressers and the most expensive leathers money can buy. Their bikes are clean and many of them have the typical 'pretty boy' biker look. The colors on their back are so brand spanking new that they almost glow in the dark. Some of these bikers want to look and act like outlaws, but the reality is that they have no clue what an "outlaw" is. I personally know of one that rides around with a bandana covering his face because he does not want to be recognized by citizens. He is the sweetest guy anyone will ever meet, not capable of harming a fly, nevertheless, enjoys the image of a bad-ass biker.

They have great jobs and plenty of money to pay their monthly dues. These new breed MC bikers loan money to the broke ass brothers with broken down bikes, and many times pay for the group lunch on the road. They are not hard-core bikers but they love to ride and do not mind traveling hundreds of miles in one day. They love to be seen riding in a pack and enjoy the security of belonging to an MC club. Many of their old lady's hold good jobs and do not know what the biker lifestyle is but enjoy the parties and the social lifestyle.

I must not leave out the different riding pattern of the diversity of bikers.

RIDING PATTERNS (examples)
1. Event riders (public and private)
2. Rally riders
3. Long haul riders
4. Fun riders
5. Bar stool riders

The **EVENT** riders are predominantly 1% or MC club members that ride to private specific club sponsored events. They arrive in formation packs and leave in the same manner. For the most part there is an event fee to be paid at the gate and it covers the club's cost of music, food and beverages. Private events offer entertainment, food, beer, liquor, poker runs, 50/50 raffle tickets, bike games, exotic dancers, primitive camping whenever possible, or overnight stay at the clubhouse couch. Sometimes the party is open to the public and/or guests of the MC member. Women and ol' ladies are always welcomed.

RALLY riders are the bikers that live to ride to local and national rallies such as Sturgis, Bike week, etc. If one attends all of them, it's a year round party. These bikers also support poker runs, benefits, toy runs, and all events where there other bikers in large numbers. They develop "rally buddies" at these rallies the same way one acquires drinking buddies at a bar.

LONG HAUL riders are the bikers who ride cross-country and take scenic roads, back roads and anywhere they can get a tour of the country. While many bikers team up with a small pack to do this, it is predominantly couples who enjoy this kind of riding. It is a costly riding experience but worth the out-of-pocket expense. A good motto for these bikers is "The best part of any journey is the people we meet along the way."

FUN riders ride for fun. They don't have a destination, a party or an event. They just get on the bike and go to wherever the road takes them. Some of these riders do not return home for several days.

BAR STOOL riders ride from bar to bar. They can ride a bar stool better than their bike. Many of these are the idiots that get on their bike after they've been drinking and sometimes end up being scrapped off the road by EMT's. Loads of them are not bikers but wanna-be's who want to be seen by the locals as bikers. I feel for the chick that doesn't know any different and climbs of the back of this person's bike for a ride.

I cannot come to the end without mentioning the three riding methods of bikers.

RIDING METHODS
1. The packs (large and small)
2. The loners
3. The Couples

Pack riders are the ones who ride in large or small packs and seldom go on a ride by themselves. All 1% and MC members ride in packs whether large or small. Riding associations and religious clubs also ride in packs, but are more apt to ride by themselves if needed. The most common form of "pack" riding is in formation. Pack riding is very social and impressive.

Loners always ride by themselves even to attend rallies and events. The displaced biker finds him or herself riding the loner style. The loner rider seldom makes friends and prefers to ride the highway minding his or her business.

Couple riders are just that. A couple who doubles up or rides side by side and enjoy the road as they ride for fun. Occasionally, they might invite another couple to ride with them. They can travel cross-country on the bikes or with their bikes strapped to an RV, or they can take short Sunday leisure rides.

I must mention the riding styles of bikers.

RIDING STYLES
1. Place of honor.
2. Center line (left side)
3. Shoulder line (right side)
4. Hump riders (the middle of the lane)
5. Zig-Zag

Place of honor riders applies only to 1% or MC clubs. It is the inside or the left position where the president or club officer is protected by a rider directly next to him.

Centerline or left side-lane riders predominantly ride on the yellow dividing line on the road. The one that is closest to oncoming traffic.

Shoulder line riders ride on the right side closest to the lane on the shoulder (or the ditch).

Hump riders ride in the hump or crown of the middle of a lane. This is the place where it is most slippery and a very unsafe place to ride, especially when it is wet.

Zig Zag riders ride all over their lane and many times into the opposite lane. They are scary to ride beside and if you are following behind they make you dizzy.

The different variation of bikers I met in my five-year journey as a patch holder was mind-boggling. So many diverse people with a unique motorcycle enthusiasm lifestyle and culture, yet the common denominator was a motorcycle. How could there be room for narrow-mindedness, bigotry when the diversity was so ample? I learned that one group wasn't better than the other, just different.

I observed in my period as a patch holder that there is a commonality in the MC family. It is the love of riding a motorcycle and the desire to associate with each other. A desire that delights in the love, loyalty and respect that is offered by a person and received by another.

A good reference site that I found to educate and inform on the biker community is http*http://www.rcvsmc.net/*

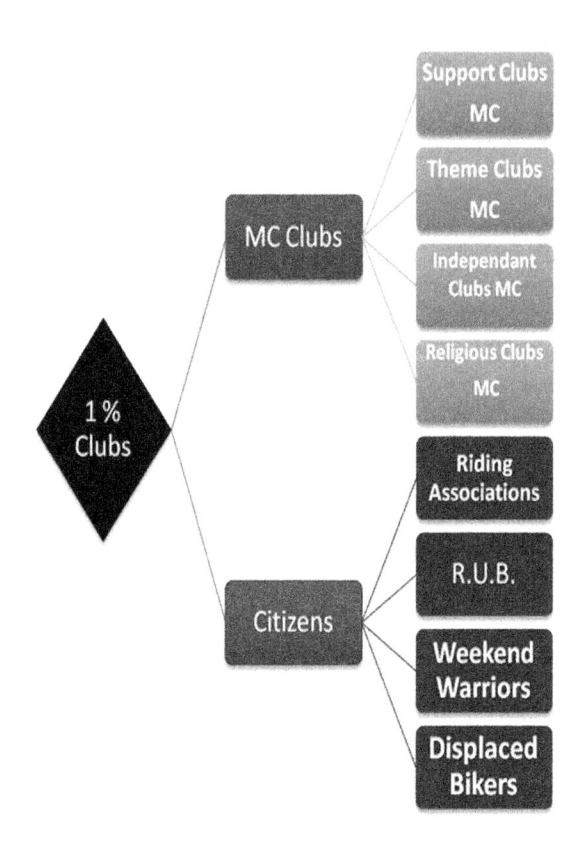

```
                    ┌─ Support Clubs MC
                    ├─ Theme Clubs MC
         ┌─ MC Clubs ┤
         │          ├─ Independant Clubs MC
         │          └─ Religious Clubs MC
1% Clubs ┤
         │          ┌─ Riding Associations
         │          ├─ R.U.B.
         └─ Citizens ┤
                    ├─ Weekend Warriors
                    └─ Displaced Bikers
```

Categorization of the Bilker Culture © SG

16
6 Steps to Starting an MC

Starting an MC in your town is not an act of God, rather an act of respect. There are thousands of MC clubs in the United States, and more are added daily to this growing list. At the end of this chapter I will include a list of web links that you can access and see for yourself.

Before I go into the steps for your new MC, it is important that I mention the ethical aspect to starting your own MC. The first thing to be aware of is that 1% clubs do not like new clubs popping up. This becomes a chore for them as they are at the top of the hierarchy and therefore strife to maintain jurisdiction over the MC clubs. This regulated influence is done for the safety of all bikers in the community. Let's say for instance, that a group of men refuse to join any branch of the United States Military for personal reasons. They decide to form their own branch of military service, design their own uniforms and purchase their own weapons. Suddenly, the news media reports that there is a new branch of the military called the "United Malicia Air Strength". Do you think that for one minute, the legal and established US Military is not going to immediately have them picked up, or worse shoot them? This new unauthorized group can pose a danger for both civilians and active military by using unknown weapons, unapproved tactics, etc. This is an extreme example for MC's but the point is that some type of regulation is needed.

1% and dominant MC clubs know the history of the biker community and are fully aware of any problems that might have occurred with MC's. They are aware of previous and current colors and patches, and know which ones are to be avoided. Let's say you chose a name for your club that is a good strong one, but you did not consult with the proper channels before you created and put on the patch. Two months down the road when you are riding in the wind enjoying yourself, someone pulls you over and tells you to take that patch off. You ask why and they inform you that a club with the same name killed one of their members. Oops....

Yes we all have the right to wear whatever we want because we live in a wonderful democracy, but there are consequences to our actions. What would happen if you walked into a courtroom in session in a swimsuit? Or if you wore a KKK robe into Harlem, New York? Of course we have the freedom to wear and do whatever we want; nevertheless, the consequences must always follow our actions.

I highly recommend that you talk to the 1% club in your state or the dominant MC club if there isn't a 1% club. It is the politically correct thing to do and it will save you a lot of heartache and embarrassment in the future.

Step 1: MOTIVE AND INTENT

The first thing you must do when starting an MC club in your town is to be sure that is what you really want to do. You must examine your motives and intentions and they must be sincere. You do not want to start a club because you have a beef with someone and you want to outdo them or just show them that you can. That would be the wrong motive for starting a club, in addition you would be involving other people in a personal situation that you have and it would not be fair to them. Ask yourself, "Why do I want to start an MC? What is the attitude in my heart towards the bikers in my own backyard?"

Step 2: SURVEY

The second thing you must do is to survey the existing clubs in your immediate area. Why would you want to start an MC club in a town with a population of 600 when there are already 3 MC clubs in the vicinity? Have you considered joining an existing MC club, and if so, have you ruled out all options for not joining? Have you taken into account any Riding Associations that may be needing members?

Step 3: COMMITMENT

Thirdly and most importantly is commitment. This is the reason why it is important that your motive and intent be sincere. If it is not, all the time and money invested would be a waste and you will be a failure in this department. A commitment is a promise of loyalty that you faithfully give to the project you have embarked on. You must be able to answer the question, "Will I be committed to this club at all times? Will I have the time needed to cultivate it? "

Will you be available to rescue your members in the event they get stranded, or get in an altercation with another club? Do you have bail money for your members? Better yet, are you committed to spending your hard-earned money bailing your club member out of jail if need so? Will you have the time and money to attend other MC events? Are you willing to give up family time to go on a run? If you answered "no" to ANY of the above questions, then you are not ready to be a president for a motorcycle club. Remember that if you cannot give 100% of your time, it is better to consider joining an existing club.

Before you go to step four, make sure you have done your homework and understand the MC culture and protocol. I suggest you go online to different MC web sites and study their clubs activities. Compare different clubs and see how well educated you are in the MC modus operandi. Learn the membership requirements of a motorcycle club and learn who the "boys in charge" are.

If you still insist on starting your own MC, the following step must be enforced if you want to start off on the right foot.

Step 4: RESPECT

Ask permission of the 1% club in charge of the state you are in. Although this is not mandatory, I highly recommend that you follow this protocol, for ultimately they are the ones who generally run the business of the MC clubs. If there is not a 1% club in your state, then go to the dominant MC club and ask them.

This is done out of respect for those who have earned the right to wear colors. If you show the proper respect, you will be given the same. Be prepared to bring a color design of your patch, laws and by-laws, club guidelines, and any prospective members you might have. Be prepared to answer questions and you need to be honest. If you don't have an answer to a question, let him know but never lie. He will understand that you are a newbie.

Be prepared to answer the following questions:
1. Why do you want to start an MC?
2. What kind of MC do you want to start?
   It is a traditional one, religious, social? Is it a military, biker rights, cop clubs? Is it an RA?
3. How many possible members do you have? Who are they and have they been in an MC previously?
4. Is it an all male club or is it coed?
5. Do you have a mission statement?
6. Are you willing to submit to the protocol and perimeters that the 1% or dominant club establishes for you?
7. How will you react if you are denied?

If you are denied permission you have two choices. Choice 1: You can ask for a probationary MC or you can ask for a Riding Association (RA) authorization. Try and negotiate a compromise with the man in charge if this is what you really want. They may approve you but with a different patch design or a one-piece patch. Maybe they will allow the name but change the color choice. Maybe they will tell you not to wear the MC until a probation period has transpired. In the end it is up to the 1% or dominant club. If they say NO, even to the compromise, then it is over, period! (Perhaps you can return in a year and re-up your request). Choice 2: The other choice is to say "fuck it" and proceed with your plan. You may have the Constitutional freedom to do this, however, the 1% clubs will make your club miserable to the point where no one will want to be part of your club. It is an unspoken ethical code of conduct of the MC world. If you want to be a part of this world then you must learn to play the rules of the game.

Personally, I suggest that you ask permission and do the right thing. You want to keep your members safe and enjoy the road for many years to come.

Step 5: ACCOUNTABILITY

Be accountable. If you are given permission to start an MC in your town, and your patch is approved, you will probably be responsible to the club that gave you permission to fly. Make sure you stick to the agreement made between you and the 1% club (or the dominant MC) and do not make any changes unless you consult with them first. For instance, you don't want to put a 13 Motorcycle Diamond patch on just because everyone else has one, and end up getting it ripped off because your club has not been authorized to wear this kind of patch. The 1% club will not interfere in your personal club business unless you infringe on their turf or Colors. Save yourself the embarrassment of getting pulled over and told to take a patch off.

Step 6: ASSOCIATE/SOCIALIZE

Be friendly. A friendly MC supports local events, charity runs, poker runs, ABATE political biker rights, and many others. Don't be labeled a "Welfare Rider." We all have to get along and support each other. Remember that the commonality among bikers is the love of riding a motorcycle. The road is large enough for everyone to share.

In a nutshell these are some very important words to remember, Motive, Intent, Survey, Commitment, Respect, Accountability, Associate.

Motorcycle Club Links

1. http://www.motorcycleclubsindex.com/

2. http://bikersmag.com/html/motorcycle_clubs.html

3. http://home.earthlink.net/~rcvsmc-edu/id19.html

4. http://www.bikersites.com/motorcycle/Community/Organizations/Clubs/Clubs.cfm?catStart=1

5. http://www.dmoz.org/Recreation/Motorcycles/Associations_and_Clubs/

6. http://bikersden.com/dnn/Default.aspx?base

7. http://www.arn1e.co.uk/clubtext.htm
8. http://www.motorcycleclublist.com/
9. http://en.wikipedia.org/wiki/List_of_motorcycle_clubs
10. http://www.cycletrailerrental.com/clubs.html
11. http://www.motorcyclepit.com/clubs.php
12. http://priestess.us/html/womens_mc.html (Women clubs only)

17
Original Laws and Bylaws of Highway Chicks Biker Club

Central Arkansas, September 2002
Club Founders are Debbie T and Sadgirl
Laws and Bylaws complied and composed by Sadgirl
Submitted to Bandido Murray by Sadgirl at Long Branch Saloon,

Little Rock, Arkansas, 2:32 pm
For approval of new club formation.
Approved by Bandido Murray 1%
September 21, 2002

ARTICLE # 1

A. This organization shall be known as HIGHWAY CHICKS BIKER CLUB, a motorcycle-riding club for female biker enthusiasts.

B. It will not discriminate against any race, religion, creed, nationality, or other basis, and will not violate laws emulating public policy.

ARTICLE # 2

The officers of HIGHWAY CHICKS BIKER CLUB shall be: President, Vice-President, Secretary/Treasurer, Road Captain, and Sergeant of Arms.

ARTICLE # 3
President and Vice President

The duties of the President shall be:
   A. To preside at all meetings.
   B. To have general supervision of the affairs of HIGHWAY CHICKS, and run the organization under the guidelines set down by the Executive Board.
   C. To appoint any person or committees to special tasks.
   D. To personally represent the organization on proper occasions, lobbying and business contracts.
   E. To assist all other officers of the organization and handle problems in general, that may arise.
   F. To promote interest in the part of each member in HIGHWAY CHICKS life and its activities.
   G. To sign or approve all checks with the Treasurer.
   H. To vote only when necessary to break a tie.
   I. Manage office for HIGHWAY CHICKS.
   J. Required to own and/or operate a motorcycle and ride to at least seven events per year (exception: medical reasons).
   K. In the event the President cannot fulfill these duties, the Vice President will automatically assume full responsibility in carry out the Office of President.

ARTICLE # 4
Secretary/Treasurer

The duties of the State Secretary/Treasurer shall be:
   A. To keep and review all organization records.
   B. To perform all duties pertaining to this office under the supervision and direction of the Executive Director.

C. To be responsible for Accounts Payable and Receivable.
D. To be responsible for the transfer of monies between accounts.
E. To be responsible for any investments made in with HIGHWAY CHICKS funds.
   1. Changes to investments must have full Board approval.
F. To be responsible for all insurance policies regarding HIGHWAY CHICKS events.

ARTICLE # 5
Road Captain and Sergeant. Of Arms

The duties of the Road Captain/Sgt. Of Arms shall be:
A. To have general control over activities including events, rides, and public relations with other clubs.
B. To sit on the Executive Board of HIGHWAY CHICKS.
C. To arouse interest in HIGHWAY CHICKS on a Regional level.
D. To answer to the Executive Director in regards to any problems that may arise.
E. Attend State functions and help where needed.
F. Required to own and/or operate a motorcycle and ride to at least seven events per year (exception: medical reasons).
G. To plan and prepare the ROAD CHIKCS annual calendar of events/

ARTICLE # 6
Executive Board

The duties of the Executive Board shall be:
A. The Executive Board is comprised of the Board of Officers of the HIGHWAY CHICKS.
B. To set guidelines and have general control over HIGHWAY CHICKS affairs.
C. To investigate any written complaint registered against a

member or officer.
D. To make final decisions concerning conduct problems.
E. The Executive Board will meet a minimum of six times per year.

The Advisory Committee:
A. The Committee shall consist of four members and the Executive Director.
B. The Executive Board will elect three members, and one appointed by the Executive Director.
C. If one member resigns or is suspended, the Executive Director will appoint a temporary replacement until the next Board meeting. The Executive Director cannot appoint more than one temporary committee member.
D. Terms will consist of two years, although a member can be voted in again after his first term.
   1. Two members of the original committee will serve two years, with the other two serving three years.
E. The Executive Board must be advised of any decisions made by the Committee within ten working days.
F. The Executive Director will vote only in the event of a tie.
G. The Committee will meet once every month or as needed.
H. Non-Director members of the Committee will be reimbursed for travel expenses under the same guidelines as used for Directors.

The duties of the Advisory Committee shall be:
A. Review the financial statements monthly and report on these to the Board.
B. Review the projected budget for the year, and report on this to the Board.
C. Review and recommend changes to the Board concerning HIGHWAY CHICKS properties, goals, and programs; research new programs.
D. Review and recommend applicants for positions of Executive Board.

ARTICLE # 7
Constitution Changes

This constitution is subject to change if thoroughly discussed by the Executive Board at a meeting where a quorum is present and after its third reading. Must be done by a majority vote.

ARTICLE # 8
Annual Fees and Membership

A. All event income goes to HIGHWAY CHICKS general fund for operating costs. Income will be forwarded to the Treasurer then disbursed as designated by the Club.
B. HIGHWAY CHICKS ANNUAL MEMBERSHIP FEE. Full-New $15.00, Full-Renewal $15.00, Couple-New with same address $25.00, Couple-Renewal with same address $25.00
C. All reasonable expenses, phone, travel, office, should be reimbursed to member as voted on. If money is available and receipts are turned in. These expenses must be approved by the Club or Officers before incurred.
D. Monthly dues of $10.00 must be paid by all full-time and associate members. These dues will be turned in at the monthly meeting. The Treasurer will collect the money and hand over a receipt to the member. The money will be deposited in the general fund of the Club.

ARTICLE # 9
Identification and Patch

A. HIGHWAY CHICKS is a biker club. Back patches will be worn at all HIGHWAY CHICKS functions and rides. A member who does not wear a patch to a function will not be allowed to participate.
B. HIGHWAY CHICKS back patch is a 3-piece patch designed strictly for fashion purposes, without an "MC" cube. The patch will also be known as the Club "colors".
C. As the club grows and expands, additional city location iden-

tification patches may be added to the existing design.
- D. HIGHWAY CHICKS Biker Club is a motorcycle enthusiasts riding club. It is not a 1% or outlaw club.
- E. Membership cards, T-shirts, stickers and other HIGHWAY CHICKS products are encouraged as HIGHWAY CHICKS Identification as approved by the Club.
- F. We encourage club membership in HIGHWAY CHICKS, **but HIGHWAY CHICKS will remain as an independent organization.**

ARTICLE # 10
Highway Chicks Functions

- A. All HIGHWAY CHICKS functions must be sanctioned in order to use the HIGHWAY CHICKS name in advertising.
- B. Functions must be sanctioned to use HIGHWAY CHICKS money in promoting and hold the event.
- C. Charity events do not need to be sanctioned but must be voted on and approved by the Club.
- D. No alcohol or alcoholic beverages will be sold or provided by HIGHWAY CHICKS or its members unless properly and legally licensed and insured.
- E. HIGHWAY CHICKS will support other biker clubs by attending their events, rides, rallies or functions as voted on by the Club. All attending members must wear their back patches at all supporting functions.
- F. No HIGHWAY CHICKS member will be allowed to ride in any event if they are intoxicated with drugs or alcohol. Any member caught riding their motorcycle or trike under the influence of drugs and alcohol will be put on probation and fined a minimum of $25.00 per offense. After the third offense, the Executive Board or Officers will expel the member from the Club, and asked to turn in their patch.

ARTICLE # 11
Withdrawal From Office

A. Any member withdrawing from his or her office for any reason cannot resume said office until re-elected at regular election time the year after.
B. Upon any member, giving up his or her office another member may be appointed by a majority vote to fill said office for current term.

ARTICLE # 12
Resignation or Suspension of an Officer

A. If an officer resigns for any reason, he or she must sign resignation form and immediately turn over all HIGHWAY CHICKS property and paperwork.
B. If an officer resigns an office to accept an appointment to another office. He or she must sign an agreement same as if elected.
    1. Executive Director can appoint someone to assume position, in the event there are no assistants in place.
C. Any Officer not performing their job, at anytime within the 3-month period after assuming office may be removed from office by the executive director or the Officers of the Club.

Rules for Suspending Officers from Their Positions

A. After a thorough investigation of an Officer, the Executive Director can suspend an officer of any events or activities of concern for thirty (30) days.
B. If suspension is needed to be permanent, a letter must be submitted to the Executive Board requesting suspension within five (5) working days from date of suspension.
C. The officer under suspension must request an appeal in writing within five (5) days to the Executive Board from date of notification by registered letter.

1. If no appeal is requested the suspension becomes permanent.

2. If an appeal is requested, a hearing will be scheduled within ten (10) days from date he received registered letter to investigate and make a ruling on the matter.

D. Executive Director can suspend an officer in the event that the job is not being fulfilled properly.
E. A member may be expelled, or have their membership suspended, for conduct unbecoming a member of HIGHWAY CHICKS; a warning letter must be sent to the member by the Officers before any suspension or expulsion proceeding occur.

18
Highway Chicks Motorcycle Club Updated Laws, Bylaws and Guidelines

Updated March 18, 2006

(Reprinted exactly as the original updated one, without grammar or format corrections)

1. Highway Chicks Motorcycle Club (hereinafter referred to as HC) was established in the town of Hot Springs, Arkansas on September 21, 2002. Probation period lasted one year under the leadership of President L. Murray from the Bandidos. After the probation period was over, we were officially established as a legal motorcycle club by Murray, at Long Branch Saloon on September 30, 2003
2. HC is a motorcycle club. Colors will be worn at all functions and rides. A member who does not wear her colors to a function will not be allowed to participate. A fine may be imposed.
3. Hang arounds must wear support shirts.
4. HC patch is a 3-piece patch with a women's MC cube and a Garland County bottom rocker. The patch will also be known as the Club "colors".
5. Club Colors belong to the Club and not to any individual

member. If a member resigns or is expelled, the colors must be surrendered to the Club (or will be taken by force).

6. If a member passes away being a HC, the colors will be buried or burned with the body.
7. HC is not a 1% club but supports 1% clubs and outlaw clubs.
8. We encourage club membership in HC, but membership is by invitation only.
9. HC is a member of the Arkansas Coalition of Motorcycle Clubs.
10. A person who wears a "property patch" from another motorcycle club cannot be a member of the HC.
11. HC do not wear property patches from other clubs. To do so is a violation of our laws and bylaws.
12. All members of HC are not allowed to belong to other clubs or organizations.
13. HC members much wear "Red and Gold" support colors on a designated place on their vests. The patch "Support the Fat Mexican" and "Love, Loyalty, Respect, Por Vida" will be worn by all members.
14. There are 5 types of membership:

   a. Full patch holder. This person has a motorcycle 750 or over and has fulfilled the probation period. All Officers must be patch holders.

   b. Prospect. This person wears a probation bar without the club colors and has a motorcycle over 750. A prospect has no voting rights. Probation period depends on the Club's decision, but is no less than 6 months. This time is for you to prove your trustworthiness loyalty and ability to follow instructions. Prospects never, ever drink alcohol at a club function. Prospects will be addressed as "prospects" by HC with MC patch holders until she patches out. All prospects will serve the Club to the fullest of her ability without question. A Prospect is a servant. Hang around time must be completed before

Prospect patch can be awarded.

c. Hang around. Hang around time is to be determined by the President. Time will be no less than three (3) months. This time is for you to prove your trustworthiness, loyalty, and ability to follow instructions.

d. HC supporter of Property Members. These members can be either male or female; they wear a support shirt or a HC supporter, small patch in front of their vest. They have no voting rights but can attend club meetings when invited to do so by an Officer as long as they are with a full patch holder. Supporters attend all functions and participate in the work load with specific tasks. A supporter or property is a servant.

e. Charter Members of Retired. The Charter Members are the original founding members of the HC. They can wear Full Colors and attend club meeting when invited to do so. Charter members must wear "Charter Member" small patch in front of their vests. If they are retired from the Club, they must wear a "retired" patch in front of their vest. They must also wear the "Red and Gold Support the Fat Mexican" patch in the designated part of the vest. Charter members are only females and can be retired or active.

15. All membership in HC has the club's support and protection as we are a family and all the laws of brotherhood apply.
16. All HC functions must be sanctions in order to use the HC name in a ride.
17. Functions must be sanctioned to use HC money in promoting and holding the event.
18. HC hosting a Club event will not be allowed to drink.
19. HC will support other biker clubs by attending their events, rides, rallies or functions as approved by the Club. All attending members must wear their colors at all supporting

functions.
20. No HC members will be allowed to ride in any event if they are intoxicated with drugs or alcohol. Any member caught riding their motorcycle or trike under the influence of drugs and alcohol, will be put on probation and fined a minimum of $25 per offense. After the third offense, the Club President, Vice President or Sergeant at Arms will pull her colors.
21. Mandatory rides are obligatory and a $50 fine will be imposed if member does not attend.
22. All HC will conduct themselves as patch holders when attending an event. That means there will be no drunkenness, no sexual soliciting or implication, and no misconduct in any manner that will reflect on HC badly.
23. All HC members (Associates, Prospects and Patch holders) must pay joining fees and monthly dues.
24. All members in HC must wear an Arkansas Coalition pin and/or patch.
25. A member may be expelled, or membership suspended for conduct unbecoming a member of HC. A warning letter must be sent to the member by the Officers before any suspension or expulsion proceeding occur. Ultimately, it is the decision of the President to suspend, cancel or expel membership in the Club.
26. HC is sanctioned by the Bandidos MC and the Arkansas Coalition of Motorcycle Clubs.
27. HC members must wear colors at all times when on a motorcycle. This means even if you are going to the gas station of to get a gallon of milk.
28. Each member will own at least a 750 cc motorcycle.
29. No more than thirty (30) days down time per year. After thirty (30) days a $500 fine will be paid to the Mother Chapter.
30. You may not wear your patch behind a patch holder of another club. You may wear your patch behind your own sister, no other exceptions.
31. You may not wear your colors inside of a cage.
32. Road Captain will inspect bikes on a regular basis. This in-

cludes shakedown rides.
33. Any patch holder that commits suicide will not be allowed to have a HC funeral.
34. Must be twenty-one (21) years of age to be considered for membership.
35. If you borrow another patch holder's property (bike, tools, etc.), you are responsible for the return of the property. It will be returned in as good or better condition as when you borrowed it.
36. Prospects must be sponsored into the Club. Prospects will not be at any bike event with other patch holders without their sponsor or a patch holder from their home chapter. Prospects may not consume alcohol in public.

DON'T (S)

Things that will cost your patch:

1. Don't lie.
2. Don't steal. This includes property/significant others.
3. Needle use will not be tolerated. Neither will smoking of any chemicals. This includes coke, speed. If it doesn't grow, don't smoke it!
4. Don't sleep in your colors.
5. Don't take your patch off to fuck somebody.
6. If your colors aren't welcomed, you are not welcomed.
7. Don't ride your motorcycle without your colors.

DO (S) *(Written by Sadgirl on Guideline Section)*

1. Show loyalty, trustworthiness, devotion and dependability to:
   a. The Club
   b. One another.
   c. Your profession.

2. Show accountability, answerability, responsibility and liability with:
    a. Communication.
    b. Information.
    c. Submission.
3. Show dedication, devotion, commitment and allegiance with:
    a. Singleness of purpose.
    b. Uniformity.
    c. Events.
4. Show support, holdup, sustain and keep up:
    a. Physically.
    b. Financially.
    c. Socially.
5. Display your representation, mark, icon or character in:
    a. Conduct.
    b. Appearance.
    c. Product.

New Chapters

Requirement for a Chapter:

1. Five (5) member minimum – one (1) charter member.
2. Hold weekly meetings.
3. Keep pictures (including tattoos) and information on all members.
4. $20 per month, per member, sent to Mother Chapter by the first of each month.
5. Patches visible by 150 feet.

6. Mother Chapter can grant a "lifer" patch on a person-to-person basis.
7. One (1) property patch per member.
8. Property may not be in public with patch without Patch holder in view.
9. One (1) member, preferably an Officer, must attend at least one (1) meeting with Mother Chapter per month.

Financial Updated Changes as of March 18, 2006
(Unanimously approved by the Highway Chicks Officers)

Joining fees for Prospects and Patch holders	$50
Monthly dues for Prospects and Patch holders	$100
Fee for colors	$75 and up
Transfer	$50
New Charter	$1000

OFFICERS

PRESIDENT:
Keeps the club in order

Makes all decisions not covered in the by-laws

VICE PRESIDENT
Takes on President's duties, is President is unable to carry them out.

Performs other duties as assigned by President.

TREASURER

In charge of club treasury.

Disperses club funds as approved by President.

Responsible for ordering club attire.

SECRETARY

Keeps minutes of all meetings, as well as files.

SGT AT ARMS

Makes sure the President's orders are carried out.

Collect all fines imposed by President.

In charge of order and security at meetings or any function.

ROAD CAPTAIN

In charge of all club runs approved by the President. Inspects all motorcycles to make sure they are legal and road approved.

19
Highway Chicks Statistics 2002-2007

Highway Chicks Membership from 2002 – 2007

Club Founders
Sadgirl
Debbie T
Original Charter Members
Debbie T
Sadgirl
Vickie
Linda
Rebecca
Cheri C
Patch Holders
ABC
Tab
Curve
KB
Roadkill
Magic
Prospects
Puddles
Rattles

Supporters
Bonnie
Glitter Girl
Too Short
Felisha
Phat Girl
Barbara D
Full Time
Carma
Half Time
Moon Raye
Rocky (R.I.P)
Connie
Sparkles

Short Fuse	Toni
Probationary	Robbie
Tuesday	Moe
Mars	Half Breed
Tweety	G String
Honorary Officer	Wizard
Punkin	Polish

The First's ....
Highway Chicks WMC Accomplishments

September 2002 – April 2007

We were the FIRST motorcycle club in Arkansas to accomplish the following endeavors.

1. We were the first Arkansas female Club with a 3-piece patch and a territorial bottom rocker.
2. We were the first female club in the ARCOMc.
3. We were the first club to wear a County bottom rocker in Arkansas.
4. We were the first club to create the MC Officer's Dinner.
5. We were the first club to attend out of state COC meetings on a monthly basis.
6. We were the first female Club to wear the Bandido Support Heart Patch that reads, "I Support Bandidos MC Worldwide".
7. We were the first female legal Bandido Support Club in the world.
8. We were the first female Club to attend a Bandido National Event.
9. We were the first female Club to ride with the Louisiana Bandidos.

10. We were the first club to create the ARCOMc calendar (Sadgirl).
11. We were the first club to create the ARCOMc logo (Sadgirl).
12. We were the first female Club to host an ARCOMc pool tournament.
13. We were the first female Club to have male MC Prospects ride the tail of the pack.
14. We were the first club in Arkansas to have members living out of State that weren't Nomads.
15. We were the first female Club in Arkansas to wear the 13 Motorcycle Diamond Patch.
16. We were the first club that designed the *Love, Loyalty, Respect por Vida* Patch.
17. We were the first Red and Gold support club to have a clubhouse in Hot Springs.
18. We were the first Red and Gold Support Club with the largest clubhouse in the State of Arkansas.
19. We were the first club to have the largest number of people attend a clubhouse event. Three hundred fifty people in one day (Sadgirl's benefit in March 2005).
20. We were the first club to bring 23 different MC Presidents and Officers under one roof for a meet and greet party (MC Officer's Dinner. February 2007).
21. We were the first Red and Gold Support Club that bridged the Red and Gold MC Clubs from Louisiana, Mississippi, and Alabama into Arkansas and vice-versa.
22. We had the first female patch holder (Sadgirl) ride beside Bandido Murray 1% up front.
23. We were the first female MC club that had a patch holder (Sadgirl) hold an Officers position (Secretary) in the ARCOMc, and sit at the President's table.
24. We were the first female MC club that had a patch holder (Sadgirl) sit at the Outsiders MC church.
25. We were the first club (Sadgirl) to put a MM in the

ARCOMc pool tournament rotation.
26. We were the first club to open the doors for Highway and Hedges Motorcycle Ministry.
27. We were the first club to have a baby dedication at Long Branch Saloon.
28. We were the first club to have a Prospect married to another Prospect from another club. *Highway Chick Prospect KB and former Silent Few Prospect Doobie.*
29. We were the first club to have a Patch married to another Patch from another club. *Former Highway Chick Curve and former Silent Few Half Breed.*
30. We were the first club to have a Patch shacked up with another Prospect from another club. *Former Highway Chick Roadkill and former Silent Few Prospect G String.*
31. We were the first club to have our President date a 1%'er from another club. *(Former) Highway Chick President, Sadgirl and Former Sons of Silence 1% Shep.*

Unforgettable Moments of the Highway Chicks WMC 2002-2007

1. The day Sadgirl and Debbie T first talked with Murray in 2002.
2. Suicide night.
3. The iceberg Margarita.
4. Our first Heat Patch.
5. Our second Heart Patch.
6. When KB broke the bed.
7. Debbie T's crashing jungle hammock.
8. The pajama party with TSF at our clubhouse.
9. The bug in the eye (twice).
10. When ABC dumped her bike with Tab on it at the Gray Ghost clubhouse entrance.
11. Curve's suicide ride to Alabama.
12. Mudflap's balls of steel.

13. The great race to the "Yield" sign.
14. Partying with Bandido Jed.
15. The ride to Daytona.
16. Taking Flash with us to Daytona.
17. Full Time and Half Time.
18. The Big Bubba Belly Contest.
19. The guys riding behind us.
20. The blue Jell-O Shots.
21. Debbie T's potato feet.
22. The flying nasal spray that hit KB.
23. PBOL Dummy's stories.
24. Short Fuse's erratic riding style.
25. Cheri C's ducks in her bra.
26. The party at Puddle's house with the Next of Kin Prospects.
27. Rattles and the effect of Crown Royal.
28. Bonnie's trip to Pluto.
29. Glitter Girl's ceremony at Lucky's.
30. Felisha and Baby Huey.
31. The day Sadgirl met Sonny.
32. Full Time riding bitch with Debbie T.
33. Our first wet t-shirt contest.
34. Moon Raye's massages.
35. Robbie's dedication to the clubhouse.
36. Our private drinking overnight parties.
37. Too Short's drama.
38. The camel in the road.
39. Barbara Dee's "I drank too much" nights.
40. The day Tab rode to a funeral in a skirt.
41. The pile-up pictures.
42. The pancakes that taste like clutch.
43. The Lemon Drops that taste like furniture polish.
44. Curve's flying cell phone while riding.
45. When Bandido Dwayne tried to catch Debbie T falling from the jungle hammock.
46. The hurricane at the campground in Mississippi with the Mississippi Riders.

47. The dead ostrich in the road.
48. When KB won a vibrator as a door prize at Boozefighters 66.
49. The friendship of Sadgirl and KB.
50. Big Rick.
51. Our pit stops at Mira, Louisiana.
52. Blinky and Trigger.
53. The Jonesboro runs.
54. The karaoke nights with Robbie.
55. The Hell Lover's parties.
56. Our lipstick pit stops.
57. Flying helmets as we rode.
58. The Swamp Rider's yummy fish fry.

20
Glossary
1% and MC Terminology

The following word definitions are the most commonly used terminology in the 1% and MC world. I have omitted motorcycle parts and any general biker lingo. The ones listed here are specific only to the 1% and MC culture and by no means are the thousands of slogans that would need a book of its own to list.

They are included as part of this book in an effort to help the reader that is not associated or familiar with the MC world to understand the lingo used.

1%. This term derived from the American Motorcyclist Association (AMA) sometime in the 1960'. They used it in reference to the small percentage of outlaw motorcycle clubs. The Hells Angels tailored the 1% symbol into a red and white diamond shaped fabric patch and became the first elite 1% club. Today, a 1%'er is identified by the diamond shaped patch that he wears on the left shoulder near the heart or on the back on his cut.

1% Club. An exclusive league of men who ride Harley Davidson Motorcycles in a pack, and are a culture with their own set of laws and ethical code of behavior.

1% Support Club. A branch of a 1% club. They are just what their name says: a support, a backing, a defense club. They are the work force for the 1% club. Many times, they must pay dues as a club to the Mother Chapter. They wear the colors of the mother club and serve as a harvester club for new patch holders for the 1% club. Many support clubs wear a diamond patch that reads "13 Motorcycle" and support patches from the host club. They are under the direct command of their mother club and are accountable to them. They are inducted and trained by the host club and are well protected by them. They can use their clubhouse to hold meetings or events. A true support club makes their mother club proud and their conduct is admirable at club events.

8 Ball (Eight ball). Patch worn on colors, earned by committing homosexual sodomy with witnesses present.

22. Patch representing that the member has been in prison.

69. Patch worn on a member's colors, or tattoo, symbolizing that the wearer has committed cunnilingus or fellatio with witnesses present.

99%. The term used by AMA in 1946 when asked by the press in reference to the Hollister incident. It refers to the percentage of law abiding bikers.

666. Satan's mark.

A.B.A.T.E. *Originally...* A Brotherhood Against Totalitarian Enactments. *Then...* A Brotherhood for Awareness Through Education. *Finally...* American Bikers Aiming Towards Education. ABATE is an organization comprised of men and women.

A.M.A. American Motorcycle Association.

ARCOMc. Arkansas Coalition of Motorcycle Clubs.

Absorbed. When a larger club overtakes a smaller club into their club.

A Patch (Patch Holder). A member of a motorcycle club that has completed all the required stages to become a full member in good standing.

A Sit-Down. A meeting to resolve conflicts.

Annual. A yearly celebration of the club's anniversary.

Associate. A person who is a friend or acquaintance of a club. He does not have to own a motorcycle and he does not wear colors. He/she adds value to the club.

BAMBI. Born Again Middle Age Biker Idiot.

B.O.L.T. Bikers Of Lesser Tolerance. The focus is primarily legislative action, through direct contact with legislative representatives, or through the judicial system where direct challenge to unjust laws will garner legislative attention.

B.O.T.B. Bitch On The Back.

B.T.B.F. Bikers Together Bikers Forever.

Bandido MC Heart Patch. The round Red and Gold patch that Bandido support clubs wear on the left side of their Colors directly above the heart. It reads "I Support Bandidos MC Worldwide."

Bar. A straight rectangle fabric patch that goes on the member's vest.

Billboard. A biker whose vest is covered in an assortment of patches.

Bike Show. An organized event where motorcycles are entered into an exhibition to compete for 1st, 2nd, and 3rd prize. There are different categories for diverse types of motorcycles.

Biker. A person who rides a motorcycle as a lifestyle. He or she may or may not fit the typical stereotype of what a biker should look like.

Birthday Party. See Annual.

Bitch Pad. The back seat of a motorcycle.

Black Wings. Earned when the wearer performs cunnilingus on a Black woman in front of witnesses.

Brain Bucket. A helmet.

Bottom Rocker. A u-shaped fabric form in the club colors that identify the geographic location or identity of the club. Some clubs use a straight bar instead of a u-shape. It is part of the patch.

Bottom Rocker Pulled. When the bottom (emblem) rocker is taken away from the member's vest because he committed a club violation. Sometimes a member is put on probation until he can once again prove himself to the club and earn it back. If a bottom rocker is pulled from a full member, he is bumped down to Prospect.

Broken Wings. A patch meaning the rider has been in a crash.

Brother. One who shares a common ancestry, allegiance, character, or purpose with another or others. This is how a club member refers to another member of his club that has patched out. It involves entrusting his life into the other club member's hands, knowing that he will defend and protect him, even if it cost the other's member's (his brother) own life.

Brotherhood. A term used by 1%'ers and MC clubs to communicate each other's association. It is a unified kinship of goodwill and trust imparted unto one another.

Bummer. A motorcycle wreck.

Burnout. Spinning the rear wheel while holding the front brake. Many places have contests to time how long it takes for the tire to blow out.

Bunk House. The clubhouse's designated, secured sleeping quarters.

Business. The principal topics of the club that comprise the club's affairs. These include but are not limited to colors, territory, patches, membership, laws and bylaws, church meetings, and club activities.

C.O.C. Coalition of Clubs.

Cage. A vehicle (car, truck or van).

Caged it. Drove the vehicle.

Cager. The vehicle driver.

Car Wash. The "hotel" of the old school biker when it was raining, sleeting or snowing.

Center Patch or Center Piece. The logo or symbol that identifies the club's objective. It is located in the middle of the back club colors (on the vest) between the top and bottom rocker. It is part of the patch.

Chapter. Localized groups of an MC club.

Church. Clubhouse or club meeting.

Citizen. A non-patch holder. One that is not a member of a 1% or MC club.

Clubhouse. The building where the club meets for meetings or parties.

Colors. The Patch. Refers to the specific emblem with specialized colors that identifies the club. Colors contain the club's name, the club's crest (insignia or symbol), the club's chapter geographic location (if applicable), and an MC cube. 1% clubs wear a diamond. Club Colors is the club's pennant.

Compound. The secured, designated camping area for a specific club at a private event.

Cross. An emblem worn by 1%ers either as an earring, patch or sometimes a pin attached to the colors.

Crotch Rocket. A slang term for some types of sport bikes, mainly super sport and super bikes. The name is derived from the way the rider sits on the bike and from the speed and acceleration of which these bikes are capable. A sport bike's foot pegs and shifter are located farther back than a conventional or 'cruiser' motorcycles; this puts the rider in a position that is more streamlined and aerodynamic and places the rider's crotch (the region of the human body between the legs where they join the torso, overlapping the groin) in very close contact with the seat.

Cue Patch. The separate descriptive patch that identifies the club. For instance MC, WMC, RA, etc). It is not counted as part of a three-piece patch.

Cunt Control. A female who is designated to keep the other ol' ladies in line.

Cut. A term derived from the early stages of motorcycle clubs, where the custom of cutting the sleeves (and sometimes the collar) of a leather or denim jacket began. When reference is made to a "Cut" it refers to the Colors.

D.I.L.L.I.G.A.F. Do I Look Like I Give A Fuck.

D.F.F.L. Dope Forever Forever Loaded.

D.O.T. Department of Transportation.

Displaced Biker. Bikers who have belonged to either a 1% or an MC and are out of the club in either good or bad standing. Displaced bikers don't belong anywhere and many cannot ride as a citizen. They have the "club" mentality so they don't fit into a riding association either. Many do adjust to *life after the club*; however, there are some, especially those that have been put out in bad standings, which cannot find their place in the motorcycle culture. They ride their motorcycle without a purpose and many of them end up not riding at all.

Duty Bag. A bag a Prospect carries that has all the necessary things a patch holder might need.

Drop the Bike. When a rides falls sideways on the motorcycle either riding or sitting still on the bike.

Dump the Bike. See Drop the Bike.

Enforcer. A club officer that makes sure the president's orders are carried out. The Enforcer collects all fines imposed by the club president and is in charge of order and security at meetings or any function.

Formation. A group of motorcycles riding in an arranged configuration.

F.T.P. Fuck The Police

F.T.W. Fuck The World or Forever Two Wheels.

F.U.B.A.R. Fucked Up Beyond All Recognition.

F.U.B.A.H.O.R. Fucked Up Beyond All Hope Of Recovery.

Fall Back. When a group of motorcycle riders are riding in formation and one of the riders asks another to drop behind or hang back.

Flash Patch. Generic patches sold at motorcycle rallies or on the internet.

Flying. Riding the motorcycle wearing the club colors.

Flying Low. Speeding.

Full Patch. A colleague (also called a Patch or Patch holder) that has completed all the required stages to become a full member in good standing. He has full voting rights and has earned the respect of the entire club.

GBNF. Gone But Never Forgotten.

Grey Beard. An old biker.

H.O.G. A riding group formed by Harley Davidson owners called "Harley Owners Group."

Hang Around. A person who aspires to belong to the club but in order to do so, he must spend time with the club at rides and events. A "hang-around" does not wear colors; however, he can wear the club support gear he is associating with. It is the first stage of a full membership.

HOG. What some citizens call their Harley Davidson. 1%'ers and MC members will never refer to their bike as a HOG. It is disrespectful.

Honorary Member. See Associate.

Incognito. When a club member is not wearing his colors. He is undercover or pretending to be somebody else.

Independent. See Citizen.

LL&R. Love, Loyalty and Respect.

LLR& T. Love, Loyalty Respect and Trust.

Laid it Down or Over. To put down the bike in its side due to an accident or a mishap.

Lid. See Brain Bucket.

MC. Motorcycle Club

MM. Motorcycle Ministry.

MC Cube. A square (most common shape, but can sometimes be incorporated into the patch) fabric with the letters "MC", meaning Motorcycle Club. It is located in the club's patch design.

MSF. Motorcycle Safety Foundation.

MRO. Motorcycle Rights Organization.

Ma & Pa Club. Social riding organizations that act and ride like MC's but are not.

Mama. A woman who is the property of the club and must comply sexually any time, as many times as she is expected to. This was a common practice back in the 1960's.

Mother Chapter. The original parent first chapter that birthed the newer club.

Nomad. Club member wearing a full patch but the bottom rocker reads "Nomad". He is a wanderer or a traveler for the club and may attend church and pays dues to different chapters. In some clubs, a Nomad is also an enforcer. It is a position of respect.

National. An organized nationwide gathering of local chapters.

Not Flying. A patch holder who is riding his motorcycle and not wearing his colors.

Ol' Lady. The club member's wife or girlfriend.

O.M.G.'s. Outlaw Motorcycle Gangs.

Old School Biker. A motorcycle rider who adheres to the original traditions of motorcycle clubs or culture that originated in the sixties. The general public stereotypes old school bikers with the physical appearance of long scraggly hair, worn leathers, a party animal, and rides a rat bike with fluid leaks.

One Piece Patch. Refers to the specific single part emblem with specialized colors that identifies a riding association or organization. Colors contain the club's name and the club's crest (insignia or symbol).

Originals. A member's first set of Colors which are never to be cleaned.

Out in Bad Standing. When a 1%'er or an MC member is expelled from the club in a dishonorable status. A person that is "Out in Bad Standing" cannot return to the club or join another club unless his former club clears his name.

Out in Good Standing. A person who leaves the club in an honorable status. He can return to the club or join another one.

Outlaw Biker. A 1%'er, a 1% support club biker, or a hard core biker that associates with either, and adheres to their own set of rules. This term is used by the FBI to refer to certain bikers and/or biker clubs.

P.P.D.S.P.E.M.F.O.B.B.T. "Pill Popping Dope Smoking Pussy Eating Mother Fucking Outlaw Brothers Bikers Together". Could be on tattoos, colors, or business cards.

Patch Holder (A Patch). See Full Patch.

Patch. See Patch holder, and Full Patch.

Patched-out. A Prospect who is promoted to full patch holder.

Patch Collector. See Billboard.

Pig. Law enforcement civic or federal.

Pin Head. A biker whose vest in covered in an assortment of pins.

Place of Honor. Applies only to 1% or MC clubs. At the front of the pack, it is the inside or the left position in a riding formation where the president or club officer is protected by a rider directly next to him on his right side.

Politics. The government (administration, management and regime) that rules the club's structure.

Poker Run. An organized run where there are five stops. The biker collects a playing card from each stop. The person manning the poker stop marks down the card the player got. At the last stop, the player has a complete poker hand. The biker with the best hand at the end of an allotted period wins a prize (usually cash). Sometimes there is a prize for the worst hand also.

Probationary or Probate. Not all clubs have this extra step. It comes after the prospect period and is an extended stage of testing the prospect's trustworthiness and loyalty to the Club. A Probationary can also be a member that has transferred from one chapter to another. He has the necessary knowledge of MC for he has served as a prospect.

Prospect. The second stage to a full patch. This is the period of probability where the potential member must prove his trustworthiness and loyalty to the club. A Prospect is sponsored into the club by a patch. The Prospect must first be a hang-around with the club.

Protocol. The Code of behavior by which the club is governed and abides on a daily basis.

Property Of. Refers to the patch holder's ol' lady.

Property Belt. Refers to the specific emblem in club colors, which the patch holder's ol' lady wears on her belt. The Property belt will say "Property of" and the name of the patch holder. She wears this so everyone else knows that she is taken by a club member.

Property Patch. Refers to the specific emblem in club colors that the patch holder's ol' lady wears on her vest. The Property Patch will say "Property of" and the name of the patch holder. She wears this so everyone else knows that she is taken by a club member.

Pull a Train. For a girl to have sexual inter course with each member in the group, any way he would like it, one after another.

Pussy Pad. See Bitch Pad.

Putt. To go on a motorcycle ride.

R/A. Riding Association. R/A's are the riding groups who wear a one-piece patch and have no correlation with MC Clubs. Some riding associations have an organizational structure, monthly meetings and dues, but they are not involved with MC political rules.

R/C. Riding Club *or* Religious Club.

RUB. Rich Urban Biker. A term usually used by real bikers to describe the weekend wannabe rich boys who buys a nice, chromed out bike 'cause they can. They do not know how to work on a bike and the only things in their tool pouch are a cell phone, a credit card, a GPS tracking device, and a map with all the repair shops across the US.

Rags. See Colors.

Rat. Someone who walks off with club private information and disperses it to law enforcement or rival clubs. An informant that may or may not be paid. A "snitch" is the lowest form of dishonor a club member or anyone can bring upon a club.

Rat Bike. An older bike that looks like it's made of scrap metal and different bike parts. It is ugly, dirty and peculiar.

Red and Gold. These are Bandido Colors. The term 'Red and Gold' is used to refer to either the Bandidos or a Bandido Support Club.

Red Cross. Earned by committing homosexual fellatio with witnesses present.

Riding Bitch. A derogatory term for riding on the back seat of the motorcycle.

Riding Buddy. A friend that accompanies another biker on a ride regularly.

Riding Dirty. Riding while carrying drugs.

Riding Double. A term for riding on the back seat of the motorcycle.

Road Name or Handle. The nickname a person has or earns. It is not his birth name.

Run. A club sanctioned ride for a day, or a period of time, to a certain location for a party, camping, or special event.

Sergeant at Arms. See Enforcer.

(X)FF(X). A patch that is worn by MC members to denote their lifetime loyalty to the club. (X) stands for the name of the club.

SFFS. Saved Forever Forever Saved or Set Free From Sin.

SFFS (in Arkansas). Sons Forever Forever Sons.

SYL(X). Support Your Local (X) stands for the name of the club.

Saddle Up. Get ready to get on the motorcycle and leave.

Sanctioned. A club that has been approved by the 1%'ers to co-exist as a motorcycle club.

Scoot. Motorcycle

Sheep. See Mama.

Sisterhood. A term used by women in MC clubs to communicate each other's association. It is a unity of goodwill and trust imparted unto one another.

Skid Lid. See Brain Bucket.

Slab. Interstate.

Sled. See Scoot.

Snitch. See Rat.

State Rocker. The bottom rocker with the name of the state that the club resides in. This is for 1% clubs only. Some law enforcement clubs have recently adapted this tradition.

Static. Harassment from law enforcement authorities or other members of motorcycle clubs.

Stripe. A small rectangle patch usually worn on the front of a vest.

Supporter. A person who is not a member of the club but follows them and is a benefactor of the club.

T.W.O . Two Wheels Only.

Tail or Tail Gunner. The last motorcycle in a group of riders.

Tar Snake. An uneven, slippery patch in a road crack

The Big Four. A term designated by the Federal Bureau of Investigation (FBI) and Criminal Intelligence Service Canada to refer to the four Outlaw Motorcycle Gangs (OMG's) which are the Bandidos, the Hell's Angels, the Outlaws, and the Pagans (listed in alphabetical order).

The Pack. A group of motorcycles riding in together.

Three Piece Patch. A club's specific emblem with specialized colors that identifies the club that is comprised of three individual pieces. It includes the top rocker, the center patch, and the bottom rocker. It also includes the MC cube but is not counted as a fourth piece.

Thirteen "13" Motorcycle. A fabric patch in a diamond shape, worn by 1%'ers and support clubs. The original and most common meaning is that '13' stands for the thirteenth letter of the alphabet 'M' and it stands for "Motorcycle." In the last few years, it also adapted 'marijuana' and 'meth' as a representation. It is said that whoever wore the patch either used or sold the product. Most clubs that wear this patch wear it traditionally and in no way are involved with using or trafficking the products.

Trailer Queen. A motorcycle that spends more time on a trailer being hauled to events than on the road being ridden.

Trailered. When a bike is hauled to a rally on a trailer.

Top Rocker An inverted u-shaped fabric form in the club's colors that has the club's name. It is part of the patch.

Toy Run. An organized parade of motorcycles where each rider brings a new unwrapped toy for a child. At the end of the parade, the toy is dropped off and a civic organization distributes them to needy families.

Trophy Bike. A bike that is immaculately clean and shinny because it is hardly ever ridden.

Turf. The territory that 1% and MC clubs claim. There has been much bloodshed between rival clubs because of turf.

Turn in Colors. To quit the club and surrender all the club's patches and property.

Turn Out. When all members come together in the case of an initiation for a new member, or for a girl to pull a train for the first time.

Upside Down Patches. Worn to protest.

W.H.O.R.E. We Haul Our Bikes Everywhere.

WMC. Women's Motorcycle Club.

Wanna-be. A person who may look like a biker and talk like one, but does not own one. Also refers to motorcycle owners who seldom ride their bikes.

War. To declare 'War' on a rival club is to engage in a group battle that may include killings, setting fires to clubhouses, and any form of physical violence that may end in prison time for the club members involved.

War Horse. Well-ridden, road-worn bike.

War Wagon. A vehicle used to transport the club's armory during a ride when trouble or war is expected from other clubs.

Wash Out. A club member who is a disappointment and a failure from another club.

Weekend Warrior. People that buy a motorcycle and ride it only on the weekends when it is sunny. After the riding season is over, they sell or store the bike. If they can keep the bike for a year, it usually has 2000 miles or so on it and someone ends up buying it for a great price.

Welfare Rider. Bikers who ride but never contribute to the struggle against biker rights.

Went Down. A crash (accident) while riding a motorcycle.

White Cross. Earned when a person digs open a grave, removes an article from the deceased with witnesses present, and wears it on his colors.

White Power Fist. Patch worn on Colors, which denotes the belief of white supremacy.

Wings. An emblem worn by 1%ers, as a pin or patch. All wing earning must be witnessed.

Wrench. A bike mechanic.

Yard Dog. The patch holder in charge of the clubhouse security.

50/50 Raffle Tickets. A game of chance where a person buys a ticket and keeps it until the winning number is called. All the money from the ticket sales is thrown into a pot. At the end, who ever has the winning ticket wins half the money collected from ticket sales. The other half goes to the sponsor.

Photos & Memories

Highway Chick President Sadgirl in 2007

Highway Chicks WMC in 2006

Original HC Charter Members. From left to right upper: Vickie (R.I.P.), Rebecca, Linda, bottom: Sadgirl, Cheri C, Debbie T

Highway Chicks WMC club founders, Sadgirl, Debbie T

Original Highway Chick Patches on 1st Anniversary. From left to right: Felisha, Sadgirl, Debbie T ABC, Crissy

Sadgirl with Arkansas State President, Bandido Murray in 2003

Bandido Murray with Highway Chicks Sadgirl, Debbie T, and ABC in 2003

HC WMC at its greatest membership peak in 2003.
The male supporters increased our membership dramatically.

Some of the different Patches that attended our 1st MC Officers Dinner at the HC clubhouse

Sadgirl with Sons of Silence Brakeline

Sadgirl with Bandido Chaplain One Wire

HC WMC President Sadgirl presenting Probationary bottom rockers to the Mississippi Crew girls.

Sadgirl and Tab with Bandido Nomad Stubbs

Sadgirl leading Highway Chicks WMC Patches, Prospects and Probationary members

Bandido Mississipi State President Dwayne with Highway Chicks WMC

Debbie T with Bandido BW 1% (Arkansas)

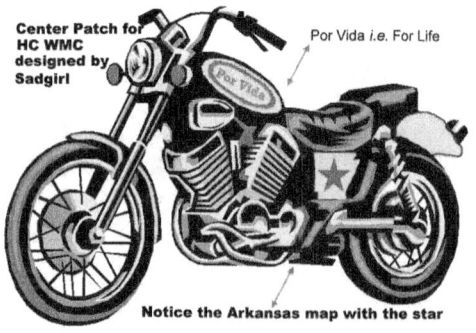

Center Patch for HC designed by Sadgirl

Highway Chick Prospect KB and Silent Few Prospect Doobie

Sadgirl with Highway Chicks at a pit stop in Alabama

Sadgirl at 2006 Bandido Turkey Run in Corpus Christi with Bandido Jim

| 311

Highway Chicks second Bandido Heart Patch

Sadgirl with President Bandido Jim 1% & the Louisiana Bandidos in Houston, TX

Prospect KB with Highway Chicks WMC

Sadgirl with Swamp Rider Jimbo

Designed by Sadgirl in 2006

Sadgirl accepts an award from Military Vets National President, Dog Bone at HC 4th Annual

Mississippi Riders Blinky, Pistol, Trigger at HC clubhouse

Party at HC clubhouse

Highway Chick Debbie T and Sadgirl with Silent Few Half Breed

Sadgirl with PBOL Dummy

Mississippi Coalition of Club members. Sadgirl is number nine from left to right

Sadgirl with Montgomery Pistoleros MC at HC clubhouse

HC President Sadgirl with Red and Gold club brothers from Louisiana and Oklahoma at the Gray Ghost MC clubhouse

HC helmet pit stop in Louisiana

From left to right: Shepherd, Highway and Hedges MM Senior Punkin, Sadgirl

Texas Hells Lovers at HC clubhouse

Left: HC 2nd Set of Colors,
1st had a straight bottom rocker titled Hot Springs.
Right: HC Final Colors created and designed by Sadgirl

Sadgirl at HC clubhouse with Red and Gold brothers

ARKANSAS

Coalition of Motorcycle Clubs

ARCOMc logo designed by Sadgirl

From left to right: Gray Ghost MudKat, KB, Sadgirl, GG President John Frank at Bandido gathering in Houma, Louisiana

Highway Chicks riding behind Louisiana Bandidos in Corpus Christi

Sadgirl with Alabama Pistoleros at Pistolero Yankee's (GBNF) funeral

Louisiana Bandidos at HC clubhouse

The last photo with Sadgirl as Highway Chick President, PBOL Dummy, the Highway Chicks and Bandido Murray in 2007

CPSIA information can be obtained
at www.ICGtesting.com
Printed in the USA
BVOW08s1841220217
476914BV00001B/28/P